CULTURE, PLACE, AND NATURE

STUDIES IN ANTHROPOLOGY AND ENVIRONMENT

K. Sivaramakrishnan, Series Editor

CULTURE, PLACE, AND NATURE*

Centered in anthropology, the Culture, Place, and Nature series encompasses new interdisciplinary social science research on environmental issues, focusing on the intersection of culture, ecology, and politics in global, national, and local contexts. Contributors to the series view environmental knowledge and issues from the multiple and often conflicting perspectives of various cultural systems.

Forest Guardians, Forest Destroyers

THE POLITICS OF ENVIRONMENTAL KNOWLEDGE IN NORTHERN THAILAND

Tim Forsyth and Andrew Walker

A McLellan Book

UNIVERSITY OF WASHINGTON PRESS

SEATTLE AND LONDON

For Diane

FOREST GUARDIANS, FOREST DESTROYERS IS PUBLISHED WITH THE ASSISTANCE OF A
GRANT FROM THE McLELLAN ENDOWED SERIES FUND, ESTABLISHED THROUGH THE
GENEROSITY OF MARTHA McCLEARY McLELLAN AND MARY McLELLAN WILLIAMS.

© 2008 by the University of Washington Press
Printed in the United States of America
Designed by Pamela Canell
12 11 10 09 08 5 4 3 2 1

University of Washington Press
P.O. Box 50096, Seattle, WA 98145 U.S.A.
www.washington.edu/uwpress

Library of Congress Cataloging-in-Publication Data
Forsyth, Tim.
Forest guardians, forest destroyers : the politics of environmental knowledge
in northern Thailand / Tim Forsyth and Andrew Walker.
p. cm. — (Culture, place, and nature)
Includes bibliographical references and index.
ISBN 978-0-295-98792-7 (hardback : alk. paper)
1. Forest management—Thailand.   2. Forests and forestry—Economic aspects—
Thailand.   3. Forest ecology—Thailand.   I. Walker, Andrew, 1961–   II. Title.
SD235.T5F68 2008   333.7509593—dc22   2007039025

The paper used in this publication is acid-free and 90 percent recycled from at least
50 percent post-consumer waste. It meets the minimum requirements of American
National Standard for Information Sciences—Permanence of Paper for Printed Library
Materials, ANSI Z39.48–1984. ♾♻

CONTENTS

FOREWORD

ANTHROPOLOGISTS—AND AREA SPECIALISTS—never tire of pointing out the inadequacies of stereotypes through which public understandings of regional cultures or problems of social change in specific
locations are formed. Such critiques may have started out as the assertion of particular exceptions to ready rules of cultural reckoning and social
analysis—"That's not the way it is/was in my village,"—but they have
not remained as mere challenges from the worm's eye perspective or native
point of view. In the last two decades environmental anthropologists and
anthropologists of development have thoroughly examined the relations
of power in which all conservation and development activities are conducted. Scholars have analyzed the cultural processes and political
actions through which powerful modes of representation take shape,
endure, and have serious consequences for the lives of poor people
enmeshed in the making of assertive nation-states and in the formation
and circulation of global discourses of economic development or environmental conservation.

This new scholarship, starting in the early 1990s, has generated fruit-
ful collaboration among anthropologists, geographers, sociologists, cultural critics, and the occasional historian and has redirected scholarly
attention from apparently self-evident cultures and societies designated
by names of countries or peoples. Not only as anthropologists of environment or development, but participating in a broader movement inter-
rogating the relationship of culture to place, these scholars have embarked
on the more difficult task of providing a nuanced cultural analysis of the
multilevel social conflicts and connections in which these collective iden-
tities and entities come to attain a recognizable shape and stability.

The forceful and evocative work in this volume by Tim Forsyth and Andrew Walker participates in these newer scholarly trajectories, but it also has a larger ambition. Informed by debates in the sociology of knowledge and science, *Forest Guardians, Forest Destroyers* proposes alternate approaches to the study of environmental problems and policies, with a view to both generating new theory and new practical possibilities. With admirable clarity and attention to apposite detail, Forsyth and Walker show how environmental politics and environmental knowledge are simultaneously constructed as fields of human conflict and enterprise. Their mastery of literature and data is impressive, yet lightly worn, and their argument rolls off the tongue smoothly in spirited prose. Moving between social classification and ecological processes, they discuss vividly issues such as the interrelationship of rainfall and deforestation, and the public misunderstandings of forest hydrology that inform policy and popular debate.

One of the attractions of this work is the way it travels across scales of analysis. The large-scale treatment of national and international discourse on forests, hill tribes, floods, and so on, is combined with fine-grained case studies at the village and watershed level that actually provide substance to the critique initiated more broadly. Forsyth and Walker question livelihood stereotypes associated with specific tribes. They also effectively challenge ideas about forest hydrology as process and as historically recorded outcomes. These threads of skepticism are woven together in the study of village-level changes in agriculture, water use, and labor process. In similar fashion the authors discuss soil erosion, chemicals in agriculture, and biodiversity, presenting and challenging prevalent crisis narratives. A sobering insight of this study is that the people blamed (usually poor, upland tribal communities) are themselves most at risk from the problems they have supposedly created for others.

It is rare for authors to combine deep area knowledge (in this case a lifetime of working in northern Thailand), sophisticated grasp and application of many theoretical perspectives, and prose that is compelling without being strident. When such a combination occurs, as in this book, the reader is instructed, kept absorbed, and left with much to ponder.

K. SIVARAMAKRISHNAN
Yale University
September 2007

ACKNOWLEDGMENTS

THERE ARE MANY PEOPLE TO THANK in a project that has covered as much ground as this book. Research and writing in Thailand, Canberra, and London has benefited from many forms of assistance. Particular thanks are extended to Nicholas Farrelly for enthusiastic and relentless assistance in tracking down elusive material and providing penetrating commentary on it; Pascal Perez and Alan Ziegler for providing invaluable advice and guidance on biophysical and agronomic matters; Michelle Scoccimarro for playing a key part in the research in Mae Chaem that is referred to regularly in this book; Rungnapa Kasemrat and Supranee Davis for invaluable assistance in recent phases of fieldwork in Thailand; Nicolas Becu for providing useful historical data on Buak Jan; Kay Dancey and Hannah Gason for preparing the maps and diagrams; and Runako Samata for providing the photos for figures 3.2, 7.1, and 8.1. Others who have assisted with this project over the years include Don Alford, Sawasdee Boonchee, Eloise Brown, Ian Calder, Claude Dietrich, Jane Hanks, Jack Ives, Penporn Janekarnkij, Samantha Jones, Nootsuporn Krisdatarn, Peter Kundstadter, Ben Maathuis, Nina Pangahas, Chakrit Potchanasin, Varaporn Punyawadee, Sairung Saopan, Karn Trisophan, Francis Turkelboom, and John Walker. The World Agroforestry Centre (ICRAF) in Chiang Mai assisted with the preparation and provision of the GIS data referred to in chapter 5. Staff at the Regional Community Forestry Training Center and the *Bangkok Post* library also provided valuable information.

Important thanks must also be extended to the government agencies in Thailand that have facilitated various aspects of our research: the

National Research Council, the Royal Project Foundation, and the Land Development Department. And particular thanks to the many farmers in the region who have endured our questions while being generous hosts and great companions.

Three readers from the University of Washington Press provided encouraging and critical feedback on the initial manuscript. Particular thanks to Peter Vandergeest (who chose not to be anonymous) for pressing us to clarify important aspects of our argument.

At various stages financial support has been provided by the Australian Centre for International Agricultural Research, the Wenner-Gren Foundation for Anthropological Research, and the Economic and Social Research Council of the United Kingdom.

Very special thanks to Diane Podlich, Mali Walker, and Joshua Walker for their great patience.

This book draws on some previously published material. Parts of chapter 2 are based on a 2004 article in *Asia Pacific Viewpoint* 45 (3). The section in chapter 3 on the Karen draws heavily on a 2001 paper in *Asian Ethnicity* 2 (2). Chapter 5 is a revised version of a 2003 paper in *Development and Change* 34 (5). And parts of chapter 6 draw upon a paper in *Geoforum* 27 (3).

Forest Guardians,
Forest Destroyers

1 *Environmental Crisis and the Crisis of Knowledge*

THESE DAYS, MANY PEOPLE ASSUME that developing countries are undergoing some kind of environmental crisis. Thailand is no exception. James Fahn—who spent a decade writing for the environmental section of a Thai newspaper[1]—portrays this pessimism in his book, *A Land on Fire*, where he describes how Thailand seems to "consume itself through its breakneck pursuit of progress" (Fahn 2003:10). Writing of the "environmental catastrophe that is Thailand today," he argues that "virtually every resource the country owns has been squandered with too little thought for the future." Population growth and inconsiderate economic development have left the nation's forests devastated, "their amazingly rich biodiversity became endangered before it could even be fully recorded." Commercial agriculture with "wanton use of pesticides has poisoned the countryside." Long stretches of the beloved coastline have been converted to shrimp farms and "the seas have been plundered of their fish" (Fahn 2003:5).

Forest Guardians, Forest Destroyers challenges this deeply pessimistic viewpoint. The aim is not to greenwash—to suggest that environmental problems do not exist or that environmental policy is unnecessary. Instead, the chapters that follow present a deeper political analysis of how and why—and with whose influence—environmental problems are defined the way they are. Along with a growing number of analysts from diverse backgrounds, this book questions the accuracy of "environmentalism as usual" and proposes that many popular descriptions of environmental degradation actually impede appropriate environmental management and sustainable development. The aim is to replace these

3

simplistic ideas with a more biophysically nuanced and politically representative understanding of environmental change.

The geographic focus for this book is the highlands of northern Thailand.[2] Current discussions of environmental degradation in this region are influenced by misleading and simplistic explanations, which may fail to address the causes of environmental problems and which may lead to policies that unnecessarily restrict the livelihoods of many residents of this region. Again, it is not the intention of this book to argue that environmental problems do not exist in northern Thailand or that urgent action is unnecessary in certain locations. The argument is that environmental knowledge—or the principles that are used to explain biophysical problems and to guide regulatory responses to them—has occupied a curiously unexamined role in politics to date. Analyzing the politics of environmental knowledge, and opening it to broader and more inclusive discussion, will help make environmental understanding more effective and will contribute to better solutions for the challenge of sustainable development in Thailand.

POLITICIZING ENVIRONMENTAL KNOWLEDGE IN NORTHERN THAILAND

For many readers, "northern Thailand" inspires images of teak forests, Buddhist temples, lush green rice fields, and remote hillside villages inhabited by colorful "hill tribes." The region has grown rapidly in popularity as a tourist destination, and for many visitors from both inside and outside Thailand it is a place of astounding beauty, environmental wonder and cultural diversity. So, why focus on this bucolic region?

The Political Significance of Northern Thailand

Northern Thailand is, without doubt, the most researched zone in mainland Southeast Asia. Research has been conducted in fields as diverse as anthropology, geography, economics, development studies, epidemiology, hydrology, and ecology. Physical scientists have often been inspired by the region's striking mountainous terrain, its complex geology, its world-renowned forests, and its agricultural and hydrological resources. And social scientists have been attracted by the breathtaking diversity of ethnic groups and the mosaic of cultures juxtaposed in a complex landscape of valley bottoms, hill slopes, and mountain ridges. The ethnic minorities in the hill zones of northern Thailand are often considered to be very different from their lowland neighbors, and they have held an enduring fascination for researchers, development workers, missionaries, and NGO activists. Northern Thailand is also an important frontier area. In physical terms, the region's mountains form a rugged edge of the plains of central Thailand, and the northern provinces were only fully integrated into the Bangkok-based administration in the twentieth century. More importantly still, the region is the southern gateway to the mountainous and inaccessible terrain that links Southeast Asia to China via the remote northern borderlands of Burma and Laos. Until the 1990s, northern Thailand was the closest Western travelers could get to neighboring communist countries without special permission, thus making it a popular research location for people wanting proximity to these countries.

In political terms, northern Thailand occupies an important and unusual niche. During the Vietnam War, and in the decade that followed, northern Thailand was seen as a strategic base from which to resist the incursion of communism from China, Vietnam, and Laos. Thailand was seen to be the "last domino" in Southeast Asia, and this influenced research and politics in the region in various ways. In the 1970s and 1980s, the mountainous terrain and porous borders of northern Thailand provided refuge for communist insurgents, with a number of districts declared "pink zones," where sometimes violent confrontations occurred between insurgent forces and government troops. Given the international prominence of these security concerns, Thailand (and especially its northern and northeastern regions) became the recipient of various aid and development programs seeking to win over the "hearts and minds" of impoverished villagers. Enormous amounts of development aid and infrastructure investment were poured into previously remote districts. At times this was combined with some heavy-handed military action against suspected communist sympathizers in the uplands (Hearn 1974). The Thai government even allowed a group of Chinese Nationalist soldiers—who had fled from the forces of Mao Zedong—to settle on the Thai-Burmese border in Chiang Rai province and act as an anticommunist force from the 1960s to the 1980s (McCoy 1972:352; Bo Yang 1987).

Another concern has been the control of opium and its derivative, heroin. Northern Thailand is part of the infamous "Golden Triangle," and its cool highland slopes were an important site of opium cultivation in the 1970s and 1980s. Writing in 1972, McCoy (1972:358) estimated

that the picturesque poppy fields of Thailand's northern mountains supplied the raw material for 70 percent of international opium production.
Highly mobile caravans of mules and packhorses made their way along
the region's mountain trails, which linked remote upland villages with
opium traders in the lowland centers. No doubt, sections of the Thai military and police played a key role in the trade, but under sustained international pressure decisions were made at the highest government levels
to bring it to an end (McCoy 1972:316; Renard 2001). Many of the early
government and nongovernment interventions in the northern uplands
were motivated by the objective of eliminating opium cultivation.

These geopolitical concerns intimately influenced, and were entangled
with, knowledge collection in the region. For example, in the early 1970s,
American and Australian anthropologists working in the region were
accused of working for the CIA or associated agencies, with overt military and counterinsurgency objectives (Wolf and Jorgensen 1970; Wakin
1992; Hinton 2002). These claims were exaggerated, but they led to some
restrictions on research activities and a five-year embargo on publishing
any results coming from Chiang Mai's Tribal Research Institute (Wakin
1992). More generally, there is little doubt that a substantial proportion
of research and development intervention in the region has been influenced
by the view that the upland populations are, in certain important ways,
problematic.

The illicit imagery of communist refuge, permeable borders, and rampant narcotic trade has become a significant component in popular imag-
inings of the northern uplands. And persistent ethnic conflict in the
neighboring upland regions of Burma and Laos has added force to these
anxieties. Characterization of the upland population as unruly and
problematic easily carries over into discussions of environmental management. In fact, the political intrigues of northern Thailand influence
the very language and contexts within which environmental change has
been described. To take just one lighthearted example: Many agricultural
plots in northern Thailand are covered with a characteristic short red
grass during the early dry season. The grass—*Rhynchelytrum repens*—
is called "grader grass" in Australia because of its tendency to grow quickly
on recently cleared soil, and it has been associated with certain types of
shifting cultivation in the uplands of northern Thailand. Yet, in some
highland regions of Thailand, this grass is called "communist grass"—
because, apparently, "it came when the communists came" (Forsyth
1992:135).

The Environmental Significance of Northern Thailand

It is therefore difficult to discuss knowledge about environmental change in northern Thailand without referring to the region's complex and contested political past. Current debates about environment and development in the region are still influenced by knowledge produced during earlier times, and these debates still reflect concerns about national security and the negative impacts of illicit activities. Four themes are dominant:

Water supply and watershed functions. The northern uplands are the headwaters of Thailand's primary river system—the Chao Phraya—that waters the central plain and that has nurtured the national capital, Bangkok, since its founding on the swampy river banks in 1782. It is no surprise, then, that accounts of environmental processes in the uplands often open with justifying statements about the key role of the region in national environmental health. This eco-interdependence finds potent expression in two important hydroelectric and irrigation dams, the Bhumiphol and the Sirikit—named after Thailand's much revered king and queen—that interrupt the flow of the northern rivers on their southward path toward Bangkok. These two dams provide the bulk of the central region's irrigation water and electricity supply, bringing the environmental realities of their northern catchments into the heartland of Thai concerns. And there are now profound anxieties about the sustainability of northern Thailand's contribution to the nation's hydrological health. Declining water levels behind the Bhumiphol Dam—inflows are estimated to have declined by almost 20 percent over the past thirty years, with further declines expected (Molle et al. 2000)—have prompted concerns that the mountainous uplands are no longer delivering the environmental bounty expected of them. Most commonly, the finger of blame is pointed at upland deforestation. As upland catchments are degraded by forest destruction, the reliable flow of water to central Thailand's rice farms, factories, and cities is put at risk.

Forest protection and biodiversity. As well as being regarded as key water sources, northern Thailand's upland forests are also considered important for "wilderness," the protection of biodiversity, and, where allowed, selective logging and plantations. The Thai Royal Forest Department was founded in 1896 primarily to oversee the extraction of teak logs from Thailand's northern forests, but in recent years its role has changed to forest protection. In 1989, a national logging ban was passed in response to national concerns about forest loss. Since then ambitious national targets have been set for "conservation forest," and national parks and wildlife conservation areas have proliferated—many of them in the northern uplands—in order to protect newly recognized wilderness values. Most recently, forest conservation has come to be seen as a primary strategy for preserving Thailand's internationally recognized abundant biodiversity. Once again, northern Thailand has been a focus of concern. As Fahn (2003:112) writes—reflecting widespread sentiment about the international importance of the extraordinary natural diversity in the uplands—"there are more species found on one mountain in northern Thailand than in some entire countries."

Agricultural mismanagement. The agricultural activities of upland farmers—who are stereotypically associated with "shifting cultivation" or "slash-and-burn" farming—are often targeted as a primary cause of upland degradation. Slash-and-burn agriculture is a popular name for forms of cultivation that involve cutting down forest (or forest regrowth) and then burning the forest biomass to add nutrients to the soil. Over the decades numerous observers in northern Thailand (and elsewhere) have claimed that this "primitive" technique is a primary cause of forest loss. This supposedly inefficient and haphazard form of upland agriculture has also been blamed for soil erosion on mountain slopes—which adds to farming problems in the uplands, creates sedimentation in the lowlands, and reduces the water-holding properties of soil.

More recently, upland development projects have been criticized for supporting supposedly damaging forms of agriculture. In particular, crop-substitution initiatives—aiming to replace highlanders' production of opium by giving them alternative cash crops such as cabbages, potatoes, or strawberries—have been blamed for accelerating erosion and encouraging further deforestation in pursuit of commercial gain. New forms of commercial agriculture are also regularly linked to the excessive use of agrochemicals (fertilizer, pesticide, and herbicide), which are alleged to contaminate water supplies and damage fragile upland soils.

Ethnic conflict. Environmental concerns in the uplands are enhanced by well-publicized outbreaks of intercommunity conflict. Lowland farmers frequently blame the forest clearing and increasingly commercial agriculture of their upstream neighbors for water shortages, siltation of irrigation systems, and chemical contamination of water supplies. These conflicts often take on an ethnic dimension because many upland farmers are members of ethnic minorities (the so-called hill tribes) while lowland farmers are predominantly northern Thai. These disputes are characterized by an increasing level of violence as lowland farmers, some-times backed by state officials, take matters into their own hands and attempt to forcibly evict upland farmers. Conflicts are compounded by widely held ethnic stereotypes that portray some groups of upland farm-ers as environmentally destructive, others as environmentally benign. The "environment" has become a new ideological battleground in the north.

The Politics of Environmental Knowledge in Northern Thailand

Anxiety about these issues has generated an enormous amount of pub-lic debate about the appropriate direction for environmental management in northern Thailand. For many observers, this debate can be divided simply between two groups. On the one hand, there are "nature-oriented" conservationists who seek to protect upland areas in order to preserve forests and to maintain lowland supplies of water. For conservationists, conflict is undesirable but perhaps inevitable if nature is to be adequately protected. They argue for an array of regulatory measures that restrict human impacts on the vulnerable natural environment. Often, "scientific" findings are harnessed to underline the fragility of upland ecosystems and the negative impacts of human activities upon them. Idiosyncratic forms of Buddhist ecology are sometimes used to broaden the appeal of this message. This conservationist position is perhaps most notoriously rep-resented by the Royal Forest Department. In 1998, the department's direc-tor general "ruled out the principle of coexistence between man and nature in tackling the problems of people living in the forest." He justified the expulsion of upland residents from conservation areas on the basis that "the forest exists for hundreds of years but you are just born. . . . You can live in the forest if you live like barbarians. But now your life is civ-ilized and we have no more forest left, so you have to go" (Plodprasop Suraswadi quoted in Chakrit 1998; see also Brenner et al. 1999:25).

On the other hand there are the "people-oriented" development prac-titioners and NGO activists who want to protect upland lifestyles. This viewpoint places priority on local governance and democratization as counterpoints to conservationist concerns, which people-oriented advo-cates portray as insensitive to the needs of poor farmers and too akin to a heavy-handed state. These proponents regularly argue that longstand-ing traditions of local resource management can form a basis for the effec-tive management of natural resources in the uplands, provided they are given appropriate state recognition and protection from the persistent inroads of commercialization. Indeed, it is often asserted that the northern uplands have high environmental value precisely because of the low impact, nature-friendly farming systems practiced by many of those resident there. For example, one upland development worker, Tuenjai Deetes, said, "the rain catchment forests will also be more effectively protected if the authorities do not promote mono cash cropping or intensive chemical use in the highlands, and instead support natural farming which helps restore the natural balance" (quoted in Sanitsuda 1993).[3] In this alternative vision of the uplands, the emphasis is on the value of farmers' traditional knowledge rather than on regulations to exclude upland farmers.

How is this book positioned in this ongoing debate? Put simply, it criticizes both positions. The chapters that follow present diverse evidence to question common conservationist beliefs that (for example) upland deforestation causes lowland water shortages. But the book also questions counterarguments such as the claim that "traditional" upland agriculture can provide a basis for socially and environmentally sustainable livelihoods. Both positions reflect particular social and political influences on the production of environmental knowledge. These different forms of knowledge have important political implications that are not reducible to a simple "state" versus "local" dichotomy. Instead, this book proposes that a critical assessment of this political context can move the environmental debate beyond this simple standoff between apparently opposing positions. In fact, when competing viewpoints are explored in detail it becomes evident that in some important respects they are based upon very similar, yet highly contestable, understandings about the underlying environmental processes in the uplands. These widely shared understandings—or, as discussed below, "narratives"— are what this book seeks to assess critically and make more transparent. This approach will allow a more nuanced understanding of environmental change in northern Thailand and a greater chance to develop policy options that are more meaningful to land users in the region.

EVALUATING ENVIRONMENTAL KNOWLEDGE

The basic argument presented in this book is that environmental debates about northern Thailand fail to acknowledge the social and political factors that underlie how environmental knowledge is made and used. This lack of attention results in misplaced social and environmental policies and the suppression of genuinely open debate about upland development. A number of issues relating to both "scientific" and "local" knowledge warrant detailed attention.

Environmental Science Is Not Politically Neutral

One consistent issue that emerges throughout this book is that many popular beliefs about environmental change in northern Thailand are challenged by research inside and outside of Thailand. The usual processes of "scientific progress"—where ongoing scientific studies are supposed to challenge and reform current beliefs—have not operated in Thailand. But is this the result of scientific practice itself? Or is it a matter of how scientific knowledge is used? In fact, it is both.

Scientific knowledge is usually defined as a form of understanding that is based on a system of rules and practices that make it more legitimate and trustworthy than other knowledge claims (Hess 1997). Adhering to these rules and practices is usually associated with other desirable properties, such as accuracy (or "realism") in representing how biophysical processes work; a universalism or transferability of explanations from place to place (at least until such explanations can be shown to be inapplicable); and social neutrality, or a lack of bias. Usually, this approach is called a "positivist" approach to science, and the rules are often called the "scientific method." Its aims are to seek generalizable cause-and-effect statements based on established methods of sampling and inference.[4]

Certainly, accuracy, universalism, transferability, and neutrality are desirable properties in explaining environmental change. But many social scientists have argued that these properties may not be as achievable when using positivist science as many would hope. First, much positivist science does not take into account the linguistic and semantic influences on how environmental change is described and measured. Positivist science may provide powerful and uncontroversial insights when the objects and criteria under research are clearly defined and universally applied, such as for the breaking point of steel of a certain chemical composition. But these definitions may not be as clear-cut for environmental problems, where single words are often used to define inherently variable things. Hamilton and Pearce (1988:75) comment,

> The generic term "deforestation" is used so ambiguously that it is virtually meaningless as a description of land-use change. . . . It is our contention that

the use of the term "deforestation" must be discontinued if scientists, forest land managers, government planners and environmentalists are to have meaningful dialogue on the various human activities that affect forests and the biophysical consequences of those actions.

Second, there is little consideration in positivist science of how research is organized around culturally specific notions of "problems." Much scientific knowledge, unsurprisingly, has been generated in order to address a social problem or need. But how, and by whom, are social needs and problems defined? The identification of environmental changes as problematic may vary according to different social norms. Moreover, different land users may experience the same environmental changes in different ways according to their different economic activities or physical location. (Put simply, upland farmers are likely to have very different environmental perspectives than lowland farmers.) However, when one specific definition of a problem is used, this influences the generation of knowledge and reduces the attention given to alternative evaluations that may produce different knowledge. Social scientists have called this process "problem closure" in order to show that scientific knowledge and the definition of problems are deeply connected (Hajer 1995:22). Listening to alternative social needs or definitions of problems might therefore produce alternative forms of knowledge.

Third, the generation of scientific knowledge is also closely connected to the definition of expertise and the ability to participate in scientific discussion. Positivist science, by definition, requires training in the scientific method and a willingness to present arguments for peer review. But how far does gaining expertise also imply social exclusion? For example, one defender of the scientific method claimed that scientific knowledge must be endorsed by "a social system composed of persons who have received a specialized training, hold strong communication links amongst them, and initiate or continue a tradition of inquiry (not just of belief)" (Bunge 1991:246). Yet, against this, various social scientists have argued that defining scientific expertise too closely may result in barriers to public debate and the (knowing or unknowing) adoption of one specific problem closure (see Jasanoff et al. 1995; Wynne 1996). Different scientific networks or disciplines may also consider knowledge as legitimate that other networks and disciplines may not (Collingridge and Reeve 1986).

Furthermore, some have argued that the political closure of expertise may result in the "stabilization" of certain scientific statements, which means that they are discussed as though certain, even though they might appear uncertain if a wider group of people were consulted (Callon 1986; Funtowicz and Ravetz 1993). These dilemmas may be multiplied when expertise is transferred internationally, or across cultures, and where scientific knowledge is used for political activism and lobbying, such as through the emergence of what have been called "international epistemic communities" and "advocacy coalitions."[5]

These criticisms should not be taken as suggesting that environmental science can never be used constructively, or that there is no point seeking knowledge that is accurate and transferable. Indeed, this book regularly draws on positivist research to indicate how current environmental policy often ignores complex empirical findings, preferring to draw on simplified statements of cause and effect.

But as a result of these concerns, some social scientists have argued that knowledge based upon positivist science alone may not be as objective and transferable as claimed because of the implicit assumptions about problem closure and the linguistic definitions of objects under study. Moreover, "scientific progress" may not occur merely by conducting and publishing scientific research. Rather, expert institutions, social norms, cultural orientations, and policy frameworks may determine how and when different research is accepted as legitimate and authoritative.

Scientific knowledge may therefore be used to enhance preexisting means of establishing authority, rather than being authoritative in its own right. And policymakers or activists may use the word "scientific" to legitimize knowledge claims that are not necessarily accurate or objective, or which have not been constructed using the scientific method. These concerns may be even more salient in rapidly developing countries such as Thailand, where social and environmental changes are rapid, but formally recognized environmental knowledge is usually generated by a limited number of organizations, including the state and international development organizations.

"Local Knowledge": Not Always Easily Identifiable or Locally Determined

Partly as a result of these sorts of concerns about scientific knowledge, many have turned to "local knowledge" as a more open and democratic alternative. Since the early 1990s, many policymakers and lobbyists (such as those at the 1992 Rio Earth Summit) have urged greater use of so-called local knowledge in environmental policymaking. Such local knowledge was claimed to be more representative of farmers' and forest-users' experience of ecosystems, and consequently offered the potential to improve environmental policy by placing policies more in touch with people "closer to nature" who have intimate and long-term experience of environmental processes. In turn, this often means that local knowledge is associated with values of traditionalism, community, and local democracy. In Thailand, these various values have come together in a strong campaign by NGOs and activist academics that asserts that *phumpanyaa tongtin* (perhaps best translated as "local wisdom") can form the basis for sustainable local management of natural resources. The Thai constitution of 1997 specifically emphasized the role of local communities in natural resource management.

Of course, environmental policy in touch with local people and their knowledge of environmental change is a desirable outcome. This is one of the main arguments made in this book. But, as with scientific knowledge, the claims made about local knowledge need to be scrutinized. "Local" knowledge cannot be seen as a simple antidote to "scientific" knowledge.

First, anthropologists have questioned what local knowledge really means. Few localities are composed of homogenous social groupings that share common approaches to knowledge or environmental management (Geertz 1985; Pottier et al. 2003). Remote villages or even regions may have high proportions of populations from specific ethnic groups or cultural traditions, but there is still considerable diversity in terms of wealth, gender, rank, or other forms of social differentiation. Moreover, villages or regions may not have stable populations, but might incorporate significant levels of local, regional, and even international mobility. It is therefore difficult to assume that what is labeled local knowledge is necessarily representative of all people in selected areas. This argument has been made about some approaches to so-called community-based natural resource management, which critics have suggested places too much emphasis on optimistic notions of local inclusiveness and on the possibility of "communities" existing outside the influences of state and market (A. Walker 2001a; Agrawal and Gibson 1999).

Second, the concept of "local" can position people in ways that may not be favorable or desirable. What emerges in many discussions of local knowledge is a political geography where some people or regions are seen to be local (and hence less powerful), while other groups or regions are not. This is particularly important in locations such as northern Thailand, where substantial parts of the uplands are peopled by ethnic minorities that conform to the popular imagery of "exotic" and "remote" tribal populations (E. Cohen 1989) and where many villages are located at the upper extremity of national territory, and hence seen to be on the periphery. Clearly, ethnic minorities in northern Thailand have forms of knowledge that can be linked to their specific histories and circumstances. But some social scientists have argued that defining this knowledge as "local" or "traditional" may not actually empower these people but instead reinforce preexisting power structures that shape how they are seen by outsiders (Agrawal 1995; A. Walker 2001b; Jasanoff and Long-Martello 2004).

Third, as with scientific knowledge, much of what is presented as local knowledge is a response to particular perceptions of social problems. In northern Thailand, much of the writing about *phumpanyaa tongtin* (local wisdom) is shaped by concerns about the local impacts of state regulation and commercialization. As a result there is a strong sense in which the packaging and promotion of local knowledge, especially by NGOs and activist academics, selectively emphasizes those aspects that are oriented to subsistence agriculture and traditional engagement with natural resources (A. Walker 2001b). By contrast, very little is written about *phumpanyaa* in relation to, for example, commercial agriculture, chemical use, or strategies for dealing with state officials. Once again, the prior definition of a social problem ("problem closure") shapes the way that knowledge is considered salient and then communicated according to contemporary political trends.

Environmental Knowledge and Visions of Social Order:
Coproduced and Mutually Enforcing

So, environmental knowledge is not produced in "neutral" scientific or local contexts. The position adopted in this book is that the production of environmental knowledge both reflects and reinforces social structures. This does not simply refer to the specific organizations or scientists who conduct research, but the enduring and often-invisible ways society allocates roles and values to the environment and to different social groups.

Positivist environmental science may reflect these social influences in a number of ways: the influence of problem closure; the way in which research is conducted by, or consults with, different social groups; and the ways in which research findings are presented or seen as legitimate. Research based on accessing local environmental knowledge may also carry social implications in terms of how localism is defined, by whom, and for what political objectives.

These linkages between social influences and knowledge production have not always been fully acknowledged by political analyses of environment in developing countries. For example, much previous work in the field of political ecology has adopted an approach to environmental and social change inspired by a positivist view of ecology, often combined with neo-Marxist analyses of resource struggles (for example, Bryant and Bailey 1997). As a result, much previous work has linked environmental degradation to the impacts of global capitalism; environmental processes are discussed in terms of unproblematized assumptions about biophysical cause and effect; and political actors are often described in terms of the democratic potential of civil society and NGOs in opposition to the socially and environmentally destructive alliances of investors and centralizing governments.

In Thailand, this approach is well illustrated by Fahn (2003). Despite his environmental pessimism, he describes how a "vibrant" civil society unifies Thai society against the impact of capitalist modernization and the activities of politicians heavily involved in logging, such as General Chavalit Yongchaiyudh, an ex-commander in chief of the Thai army and prime minister from 1996 to 1997. Optimistically, Fahn (2003:324) writes, "the green urge is universal and transcends national and cultural boundaries: that is a powerful sign of hope." Other political ecologists working in the region have also argued that empowerment of local networks and institutions in Thailand can provide a bulwark against the socially and ecologically disruptive intrusion of the external forces of both state and capital (for example, Hirsch 1993, 1997a; Pinkaew 2001).

But increasingly, social scientists are beginning to acknowledge that environmental knowledge, ecological processes, and social actors cannot be approached in such predetermined ways. Clearly, economic growth and capitalism can degrade environments and cause social marginalization. But reducing degradation to simplified causes resulting from economic change overlooks the biophysical complexity of environmental processes and the diverse ways that people identify or interact with them. Similarly, dividing social actors or "levels" (such as state and community) into known positions of positive or negative influence on environmental policy overlooks the strong divisions that can exist within civil society (and within "communities"), and the complex and dynamic relationship between state and society (Peluso 1993; Sivaramakrishnan 1999; Scott 1998; Sturgeon 2005).

Conventional approaches to political ecology have provided valuable insights into the power relations concerning some aspects of environmental change. But the political ecology vision is often constrained by a two-dimensional vision of social order based on state versus community, or capitalism versus traditional economy, and this has resulted in explanations of environment and society that have oversimplified complex experiences and processes. There is a need to develop ways of understanding environmental politics that acknowledge, more openly, how conceptions of environmental causality and society are linked and gather the appearance of certainty, and to use this analysis to build more informed and inclusive approaches to environmental management and policy.

What might this new form of environmental understanding look like? And what are the implications for explanations of environmental change? These questions are increasingly discussed in terms of "environmental narratives."

ENVIRONMENTAL NARRATIVES AND THE POLITICS OF STATEMAKING

Environmental narratives are simplified explanations of environmental cause and effect that emerge in contexts where environmental knowledge and social order are mutually dependent. In literary analysis, a "narrative" refers to a storyline that gives meaning and structure to a sequence of events, often arranging them in terms of beginning, middle, and end, sometimes with predefined functions for specific types of actor. In environmental studies, the term "narrative" has been used to describe succinct summaries of environmental cause and effect that are seen as factual within popular debates or policy networks, but which are essentially based on highly selective participation in problem definition and knowledge production. As a result, environmental narratives frequently impose meanings that are acceptable to their creators or users, but which may contain unwelcome implications for other social actors and high levels of simplification of complex and uncertain physical processes. As Hajer (1995:64–65) writes: "Storylines [or narratives] are devices through which actors are positioned, and through which specific ideas of 'blame' and 'responsibility' and 'urgency' and 'responsible behaviour' are attributed."

Environmental narratives therefore have four important characteristics:

- Narratives "stabilize" complex and uncertain processes of environmental change into relatively simple and transferable summaries that frequently do not reflect the physical complexity of environmental change or the range of social experiences of such processes. Nor are these stabilized summaries necessarily consistent with the results of current empirical research conducted by biophysical scientists.
- They reflect, and reinforce, different social orders by being based on particular valuations or experiences of environmental change; particular notions of expertise; and particular sets of ideas about which social groups should carry the burdens of blame and responsibility.
- Consequently, narratives serve an important political function by giving apparent scientific legitimacy to environmental policies that are actually based on forms of knowledge that are more uncertain and contested than commonly thought.
- And, at the same time, environmental narratives help to produce stabilized social categories by allocating particular roles (or subjectivity) to social actors in the simplified stories of environmental change. In other words, environmental knowledge and social order are coproduced.

Many of the commonly heard explanations for environmental problems in northern Thailand, such as "deforestation causes water shortages," "upland cultivation causes erosion," and "commercialized cash cropping is environmentally destructive," are environmental narratives. These narratives frequently pay little regard to environmental research conducted in Thailand or elsewhere. Yet they serve important political functions by enabling the Thai state to increase its control over resources and people, and by providing many of the ground rules within which environmental debate takes place and diverse social actors negotiate with the state. As Scott (1998) has shown, one of the key techniques of modern government is to introduce simplifying regimes of social classification and spatial organization that render localities legible in the eyes of the state. Environmental narratives that condense and selectively summarize complex processes play an important role in this simplifying process.

Importantly, these narratives are buttressed by selectively chosen elements of both scientific and local knowledge, even though day-to-day political conflicts present these different forms of knowledge as polar opposites. Rather than concentrating solely on short-term political conflicts, narrative analysis can help focus attention on the underlying assumptions that frame the debate and draw attention to the way they reduce political debate to "choices" or "alternatives" that are restrictive. As this book argues, in northern Thailand this narrative framing is evident in the common tendency for environmental debate to bifurcate into two positions: that upland farmers are either forest destroyers or forest guardians. Both sides share the underlying preoccupation with upland forest preservation, a preoccupation that is often based on simplified narratives of environmental crisis rather than a realistic appraisal of the role of forests (and other landscape elements) in upland ecosystems.

Previous Approaches to Narrative Analysis

Research on environmental narratives is not new. "Examples of Environmental Narratives" (pp. 20–21) summarizes some prominent research about such narratives in developing countries concerning deforestation, desertification, and so-called Himalayan Environmental Degradation. To date, such narrative analysis has demonstrated how narratives have presented inaccurate representations of environmental cause and effect and have stabilized complex processes of change in order to legitimize certain policies. This is a very important line of analysis that this book seeks to contribute to. But some critics of narrative analysis have suggested that environmental analysis should go further than this, saying it should focus less on deconstructing narratives and should instead suggest more practical means for explaining environmental change and for building effective governance.

There have been two main approaches to studying environmental narratives. The first influential approach is Cultural Theory (Thompson et al. 1990; Roe 1991),[6] which argues that narratives are inherently linked to different worldviews resulting from how far social groups are willing to follow rules or act communally.[7] Four main cultural groups are identified: egalitarians, individualists, hierarchists, and fatalists. These are associated, in turn, with worldviews of environmental fragility; environmental resilience; the possibility of managing change; and a fatalistic attitude to change. These positions can, somewhat simply, be transposed to the respective political positions of NGOs, businesses, states, and people powerless to influence policy, such as poor villagers. Cultural

EXAMPLES OF ENVIRONMENTAL NARRATIVES

Himalayan Environmental Degradation
In the 1970s, conservationists began to fear that the Middle Hills of
Nepal were under immense degrading pressure from soil erosion and
deforestation resulting from population growth (Eckholm 1976). An environmental narrative emerged of a vicious cycle of population growth leading to deforestation and cultivation of oversteep slopes, which would then
create landslides and yet more land clearing. This narrative was quickly
challenged from various perspectives. First, the available information
about deforestation did not suggest one general pattern, but great variety
and uncertainty: one survey of various estimates of deforestation between
1965 and 1981 revealed a variation in rates by a factor of 67, even after
excluding some apparent typing errors. Second, much concern about environmental degradation overlooked the role of nonanthropogenic biophysical processes connected to tectonic uplift and intense monsoon
rainfall, which may outweigh human influence. Third, many degrading
processes such as landslips were experienced as unproblematic by farmers who either anticipated them, or even used them to assist in paddy
construction.

Critics of the environmental narrative do not suggest that there are
no environmental problems in Nepal, or that farming does not contribute
in some way. But they challenge the simplistic reduction of degradation to
the one narrative and instead seek more meaningful and diverse ways of
addressing environmental change. A further question is why—in the face
of so much contradictory information—the narrative of Himalayan degradation is still adopted by some government departments and aid agencies (Thompson et al. 1986; Ives 2004; Ives and Messerli 1989).

Deforestation and Desiccation in Africa
For centuries, various observers have adopted a narrative of population
growth, overcultivation, and agricultural mismanagement, leading to
deforestation, desertification, and declining soil fertility in many parts of
Africa. Such views have been promoted by colonial scientists, government
agencies, and some international NGOs, who have supported land-use
and population restrictions as a way to avoid a downward spiral of envi-

ronmental collapse (Brown 2001). These views have been challenged by researchers who have instead highlighted nonanthropogenic causes of change and the political and social influences on the explanation of environmental change. The concept of "desertification," for example, provides an image of humans despoiling a fragile dryland ecosystem, and some early accounts of change blamed humans for the expansion of deserts. But research has shown the influence of intermittent wet and dry periods that control sand dune advance, and that long-term nonanthropogenic climate change is the ultimate cause of the distribution of deserts.

In some locations, analysts have argued that public perceptions of drought may be based on too-few data: for example in the Sahel, the common perception of drought since the 1970s is giving way to a belief that current levels of precipitation are the norm (Hulme 2001:24). In other regions, other problems are related to the notion of desiccation. In the West African state of Guinea, many experts have claimed that deforestation by agriculturalists has resulted in the expansion of savanna into areas once covered by dense, closed forest, indicated by relics of small forest "islands." Research, however, has suggested that forest islands may instead result from the actions of local villagers who created them to supply forest products and to assist defense. This work also coincides with ecological work that shows the dynamism of the savanna-forest boundary regardless of human action in recent centuries, suggesting that common estimates of human-induced deforestation are highly exaggerated (Fairhead and Leach 1996, 1998).

The implication of these studies is not that environmental problems do not exist in Africa, but that many common narratives present simplistic environmental explanations of highly uncertain biophysical changes and support policies that unnecessarily restrict poor people's livelihoods. Observers are now suggesting that environmental problems in Africa no longer be framed as supposed damage to mythical states of ecological equilibrium, but instead in terms of risk to health and livelihoods from phenomena such as drought. These views inevitably require greater levels of consultation with poor people in defining both environmental problems and policy responses (Saberwal 1997; Thomas and Middleton 1994; Bassett and Zuéli 2001).

Theory argues that most environmental debate makes the mistake of trying to assess which worldview is more accurate, when the key point is to acknowledge that all coexist simultaneously. This was illustrated famously in the book, *Uncertainty on a Himalayan Scale* (Thompson et al. 1986), which showed that different activists and organizations have highly varied estimates about rates of erosion and deforestation, though all attempt to claim certainty. But Cultural Theory has been criticized for simplifying social divisions into a limited number of categories and for looking mainly at worldviews, rather than addressing difficult questions of environmental causality (O'Riordan and Jordan 1999). The common accusation from environmental scientists is that Cultural Theory is too relativist, and hence cannot contribute to scientific progress. (Relativism, in its most extreme form, is to see all knowledge claims as equally valid, although in practice it is often used to show that the social context of an observer affects how they see.)

The second main approach has involved a more poststructuralist emphasis on analyzing narratives in historic and linguistic settings. According to Hajer (1995), for example, narratives are "storylines" or environmental discourses that have evolved as the result of historic problem closure and related research and debate.[8] Words such as "deforestation" or "shifting cultivation" therefore do not simply imply some clear-cut universally defined process of biophysical change, but carry implicit notions of cause, effect, and social responsibility that reflect who helped shape them in the past. Similarly, theorists such as Latour (1993) have argued that such apparently natural concepts as erosion or pollution should be seen as "hybrid" mixtures of physical experiences and human values. Environmental narratives have therefore also been discussed as a form of "governmentality," or the achievement of political ends by locating decisions in apparently neutral science and expert institutions that remove discussion from the public domain. It has often been claimed that state forest departments perform this role by generating statistical summaries of forest functions and implementing so-called scientific forestry with a focus on log extraction, rather than generating multiple views of forest use based on wider public consultation (Sivaramakrishnan 1999; Agrawal 2005:59; Forsyth 2005).

Moreover, narratives are increasingly not seen as the result of a limited number of actors (such as the state, environmental NGOs, or international development agencies) but as arising out of complex coalitions that build discourse over time. Recognizing these synergies between different actors also involves acknowledging that the actors themselves sometimes cannot be neatly separated. According to Hajer (1995:65), political actors with different short-term objectives may form "discourse coalitions" when they agree upon environmental narratives in order to achieve their aims. These coalitions may sometimes be intentional as actors seek to gain visibility and cultivate connections with each other. But more frequently actors may be more subtly drawn into reinforcing discourses because discourses—by definition—control what is sayable or not within political debate; they provide the "assumptions, judgments, and contentions that provide the basic terms for analysis, debates, agreements and disagreements" (Dryzek 1997:8). For example, middle-class conservationists and the state in Thailand may disagree over questions of the management of national parks, but both of their arguments may reinforce the view that upland farmers are degrading the upland environment. And, hill farmers, with the support of NGO allies, may gain political capital and establish legitimacy by presenting themselves as environmentally benign, but in doing so reproduce prevailing assumptions about causes of environmental degradation and the appropriateness (or otherwise) of different forms of upland agriculture.

Advancing Debates about Narratives

But the analysis of environmental narratives has raised some important concerns. First, some observers are concerned that narrative analysis—by pointing out that much environmental rhetoric is misplaced—may legitimize the dismissal of environmental problems. Certainly, there is a need to question why claims about environmental crisis are made and whose interests they serve. "Crisis narratives," Roe (1991:1066) argues, "are the primary means whereby development experts and the institutions for which they work claim rights to stewardship over land and resources they do not own." But "greenwash"—or the uncritical dismissal of environmental concern—is as much an environmental narrative as exaggerated claims about crisis. The objective of narrative analysis is, rather, to indicate how political interests and social processes have reduced environmental complexity to simplified statements that do not necessarily assist environmental management, and which often have unfortunate social and political impacts.

Second, others have suggested that narrative analysis only serves to deconstruct environmental understandings, rather than contributing to scientific progress. Indeed, much narrative work has emphasized the contingency of truth claims, rather than clarifying "truth." According to Latour (1993), seeking to "purify" hybrid objects into known natural and social properties is simply to pretend to find reality. Yet, at the same time, narrative analysis has also provided strong empirical and theoretical challenges to many mainstream explanations of environmental change. For example, visions of environmental collapse in the Himalayas, or agriculturally induced desertification in Africa, have been profoundly challenged by narrative analysis, which has shown that these iconic images of ecological crisis are based on selective framings of problems and selective information. But do these studies result in a new form of "falsification," in which simplified narratives can be dismissed as being misleading and unproven? Or does engaging in narrative analysis only demonstrate the social contingency of truth claims, and hence the difficulty of achieving overall scientific progress? There seems to be an ambiguity in whether narrative analysis should contribute to more accurate, and locally grounded, forms of explanation or whether it should merely help to show how societies claim certainty about complex environmental problems. In short, the contribution of critical narrative analysis to scientific progress is still unclear. These issues are partly reflected in a tendency for research on environmental narratives to demonstrate either the simplification of environmental explanations within certain contexts (Thompson et al. 1986) or to demonstrate how narratives are a further tool in how states shape localities and citizens (Agrawal 2005).

And, third, what is the best way to approach the governance of environmental knowledge in order to avoid the problems that narratives pose? Narratives result from the subtle and often unseen coproduction of environmental knowledge and visions of social order. Orthodox scientific progress—based on the influence of published research—is often not sufficient to counter their persistent influence. And sometimes, the definition of local knowledge as an antidote to environmental narratives may reflect—and even reinforce—central narrative assumptions. Indeed, some authors have used the terms "actor networks" and "governmentality" to indicate how social norms may influence the gathering of knowledge, the identification of local knowledge, and the transferring of these assumptions to new locations and contexts where different values may be more appropriate (Callon 1986; Murdoch and Clark 1994; Jasanoff and Long-Martello 2004). Under these circumstances, how is it possible to challenge narratives by emphasizing local knowledge if it is not clear how far such knowledge is constituted outside of existing networks of power? Similarly, how might it be possible to reform environmental narratives without imposing new narratives, simply inverting old ones, or reproducing prevailing assumptions?

This book challenges common presentations of environmental crisis in northern Thailand. The intention is not to deny the existence of environmental problems, but to argue that common explanations that link upland agriculture with environmental degradation are overly simplistic and do not provide a sound basis for addressing the challenges of upland resource management. Moreover, the tendency for the debate about environmental degradation to regularly revert to distinctions between "forest guardians" and "forest destroyers" is unproductive and socially unjust. It is necessary to understand the political factors that generate such simplified statements in order to develop more sophisticated and nuanced understandings of environmental change.

The chapters that follow engage with the question of scientific progress by critically considering the ways in which scientific knowledge can be applied constructively within narrative analysis. Empirical studies of environmental change are used in this book in two main ways. First, these studies can demonstrate that there is a wide range of research from both positivist and nonpositivist perspectives that provides alternative findings to those proposed by narratives and does not support their simplified visions of reality. (In some cases, such as the impacts of land use on chemical pollution and biodiversity loss, there are surprisingly few empirically strong studies.) As a consequence, these studies show that policy networks, despite their regular appeals to "science," have not really adopted orthodox approaches to scientific progress, and that narratives make claims about environmental certainty that cannot always be demonstrated. Second, some of the main studies considered in this book demonstrate the value of scientific research that is attuned to locally specific definitions of problems and competing orientations to environmental change. They highlight the need to acknowledge local problem closure and offer an alternative to positivist forms of inference by indicating how processes are organized into cause and effect by particular viewpoints. Generalization is not abandoned but it is approached critically, via a process of triangulating multiple explanations and diverse accounts of environmental change.

And in relation to the governance of narratives, this book argues that the production of environmental knowledge and the politics of statemaking need to be considered together. It concentrates most on highlighting how the politics of statemaking inherently creates visions of environmental crisis and associated classifications of social groups. In particular, the book focuses on the narrative presentation of some groups as environmental victims, others as heroes, and others again as ecological villains. The aim is to show how simplified narratives have underpinned normative visions of both environment and society. Making the governing force of narratives transparent opens the way for challenges to inappropriate and repressive forms of regulation, creates the potential for genuinely alternative accounts of social and environmental change, and provides a basis for more accurate and socially inclusive forms of environmental governance to emerge. This process of narrative disruption involves drawing on diverse forms of knowledge; it involves critically reflecting on the variety and uncertainty in the accounts of actors such as farmers, NGOs, and scientists. It also involves considering the means by which each seek legitimacy and authority in the debate.

2 *Mountains, Rivers, and Regulated Forests*

MOUNTAINS AND VALLEYS DOMINATE the upper northern provinces of Thailand and this basic geography resonates in many aspects of the region's social organization, economics, and culture. The earliest Thai settlements (or *muang*) were located in intermontane valleys at Chiang Saen, Chiang Rai, and Chiang Mai where irrigation systems supported abundant rice production on the flat riverside plains. The cultivated appeal of these lowland *muang* was clearly evident to early European travelers in the region:

> Imagine a number of lovely villages clustering among their coconut and areca palms, in a beautiful wide valley surrounded by forests and hills, the glistening yellow paddy-stalks bright in the afternoon sun, with the black backs of the buffalo moving lazily about; the homely red of the little oxen, and the moving islands the elephants make whisking the paddy in their trunks; with the village sounds drifting down the quiet air—the distant drum at the monastery, whose grey roof stands above the other houses, or the far-off "poot-poot" of the "poot-bird" in the jungle . . . and you have an idea of the lovely scene which spread before us that evening as we emerged from the hills. (Smyth 1895:17)

Smyth's bucolic description taps into a potent thread in northern Thai cultural orientation. These lowland settlements, both in their small and large forms, were the meritorious centers of chiefly power, religious devotion, and economic accumulation. As a number of writers have demonstrated, in the sociospatial symbolism of northern Thailand the lowland

27

muang represents civilization, cultural development, and agricultural sophistication: "the Northern Thai place a definite moral and aesthetic value on human settlements, in contrast to uninhabited country. All beauty lies in human settlements" (Davis 1984:82; see also Turton 2000 and Stott 1991). Not surprisingly these lowland settlements are culturally valued as the natural and appropriate home of the "Thai" people who live there, thus generating one of the most popular forms of ethnic self-labeling among the Thai of the north—*khon muang* (people of the *muang*).

This description of the lowland plains of northern Thailand contrasts strikingly with the traditional cultural vision of the hills. The hills were the wild and forested spaces of sparse settlement where malevolent spirits roamed uncontrolled and where European travelers such as Smyth (1898:109, 171–72) cursed the "rough forest country" and "singularly stupid . . . spirit-worshippers" who lived there. In northern Thai culture the lowland *muang* was spatially and symbolically distinct from the upland *pa*, a word formally translated as "forest" but which continues to carry with it the older connotations of wildness, cultural paucity, and a lack of domestication. In the word couplings that Thai speakers enjoy so much, *pa* is readily paired with *thuen* (*pa thuen*), a word that signals illicitness or illegality as in illegally cut timber (*maay thuen*), illegally distilled whiskey (*lao thuen*), or even an illegally slaughtered pig (*muu thuen*) (Stott 1991:144). The *pa* is a dangerous place, best approached with caution. This sense that the upland forested zone lies outside the civilizing control of the lowland *muang* is an important theme that runs through much of the discussion in this book.

Of course, for many in the modern world, the traditional values accorded to the upland *pa* have shifted. For some, the forest has come to represent a desirable contrast with the rampant commercialization and crass modernity of the lowland cities. The forested uplands can now be a place of peace, solitude, and refuge. For many, the wild *pa* has been transformed into *thamachat*, the modern Thai word for "nature" that carries a sense of abundance and pristine order without the disturbance of human influence (P. Cohen 1984b). The uplands are also the site of natural resources (*sapyakorn thamachat*) that are now officially recognized as being crucial to the welfare and prosperity of the lowland *muang*. And for some others the cultural savagery of the residents of the uplands has been transformed into cultural diversity, indigenous ecological knowledge, and self-sufficient values that, perhaps, indicate a way forward for a nation in crisis. These, then, are the different visions of the forested uplands that have emerged as part of recent Thai experiences of modernity. The distinction between *muang* and *pa* remains, but the wildness of the *pa* has taken on much more desirable connotations.

So, while on the ground the old dichotomy between settled river valleys and wild mountains has been disrupted by demography, many of the ideological dimensions of the lowland-upland contrast continue to inform popular approaches to protection of the forested uplands and widely held perceptions about the appropriateness of different upland lifestyles. Extending the power of the lowland *muang* into the upland forest has been a key aspect of statemaking in modern Thailand, and various forms of scientific knowledge have been marshaled in support of this bureaucratic effort. In Scott's (1998) terms, the Thai state has used a range of simplifying strategies to make the uplands more legible and governable. However, this extension of state power has not proceeded unopposed and there have been persistent efforts to promote more community-based approaches to the management of upland resources, often drawing on alternative knowledge traditions. But, despite many differences, both official and alternative approaches to environmental management in the uplands place primary emphasis on forest conservation. A "discourse coalition"[1] has emerged in which diverse political positions are underpinned by a common preoccupation with the desirable wild(er)ness of the *pa*.   *discourse coalition*

LOCATING THE UPLANDS IN NORTHERN THAILAND

The uplands of northern Thailand have been described as the eastern extremity of the Himalayan mountain chain (Ives 2004:20). Four main mountain ranges sweep down from the north creating a series of upland ridges that divide northern Thailand between its Burmese and Lao borders (see figure 2.1). These mountainous uplands reach their highest peak (2,565 meters) at Doi Inthanon, which is located only 87 kilometers to the southwest of Chiang Mai (304 meters). The influence of these mountain ranges on the region's landscape is striking—around 60 percent of the northern region has an elevation above 500 meters, with almost 20 percent of the region located above 1,000 meters (Donner 1978:667). Of course, by Himalayan standards, Thailand's mountains are small-fry and in Thailand the snowfalls and glacier flows that dominate the mountaintops in India and Nepal are completely absent.

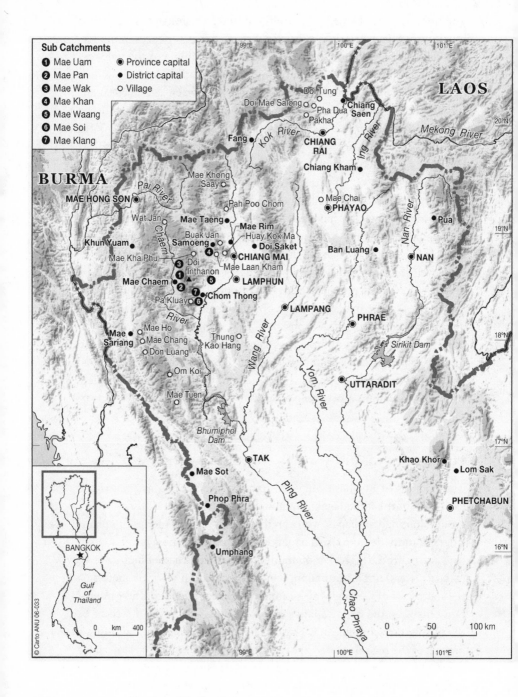

FIG. 2.1 *Northern Thailand*

Rainfall rather than snowmelt feeds the major river system that flows southward from Thailand's mountain ridges. The most important river in Thailand is the Chao Phraya, which cuts its way through the heart of Thailand to enter the Gulf of Siam just downstream from Bangkok (Van Beek 1995). This river is fed by four main tributaries that run through the intermontane valleys of the north.[2] The Ping River is the largest of these northern tributaries, with a catchment area of over 26,000 square kilometers. The lowland valley of the Ping River is the economic and administrative heart of northern Thailand. The region's largest city, Chiang Mai, is located on its western bank roughly at the center of a large crescent of lowland plain upon which irrigated agriculture is gradually retreating in the face of urban expansion and industrialization. Some 100 kilometers downstream from Chiang Mai, the Ping River feeds into the Bhumiphol Dam—named after Thailand's king—the second-largest irrigation and hydroelectricity facility in Thailand. The Wang River flows roughly 100 kilometers to the east of the Ping, with the provincial center of Lampang on its middle reaches. A similar distance farther east again is the Yom River, on which there have long been controversial plans to construct the "Dancing Tiger Rapids" dam to the north of the provincial capital of Phrae. And farthest to the east, running parallel to the mountainous border with Laos, is the Nan River, the second-largest of these four river systems but the least settled and the most forested. The Nan River flows into the Sirikit Dam—the largest earthen dam in Thailand—named after the queen and further underlining with royal symbolism the national significance of these northern river systems. As one account (Adeel et al. 2002:3) of central Thailand's Chao Phraya basin emphasizes: "During the dry season, water availability entirely depends on the water stored in the Bhumiphol and Sirikit reservoirs at the end of the rainy season. . . . Water stored in the Bhumiphol and Sirikit dams allows irrigation of approximately half of the delta region."

In this region of mountains and rivers, how can the "uplands" be defined? To start with, areas clearly outside the uplands can be excluded. These are the large alluvial plains of the major river systems, "lowland" areas that are estimated to make up about 10 percent of the total area of northern Thailand (Schmidt-Vogt 1999:28). Given their historical status as the centers of settlement, administration, and commerce, it comes as no surprise that all the current provincial capitals in the north are located in these lowland areas. Their elevation is typically around 300 to 400 meters above sea level. Next are the low foothills that surround

FIG. 2.2 (top and facing page) *Upland landscapes in northern Thailand*

the plains, which are often closely incorporated in the lowland agricultural and settlement systems and do not warrant the term "uplands." Beyond these foothills lies the upland zone that is the focus of this book. In terms of elevation, these uplands lie at about 500 meters and above, and they account for 60 percent of all land in northern Thailand. The uplands include diverse landscapes: high mountain peaks and ridges; upland plateaus; mountain slopes (typically dissected by numerous small streams); and small intermontane valleys with irrigated rice terraces. The transition from mountain peak to narrow valley bottom can be abrupt and dramatic. For example, the small Mae Uam River, which is considered in detail in chapter 5, has its source near the peak of Doi Inthanon at about 2,400 meters. Little more than 10 kilometers downstream it flows into the Chaem River, one of the Ping River's main tributaries, at an elevation of only 480 meters. In such upland landscapes there are clearly close linkages between upstream and downstream environmental processes (figure 2.2 pictures a variety of upland landscapes).

Upland Climate and Hydrology

The key feature of the northern Thai climate is the seasonal pattern of rainfall. The wet season typically commences about May and lasts—

though sometimes punctuated by a relatively dryer spell—until October. The dry season proper usually commences in about November, and from December to March there is minimal rainfall. Monthly rainfall totals of zero commonly occur during this dry period. Donner (1978:675) provides a brief account of this broad rainfall pattern in northern Thailand, highlighting the strong monsoonal and maritime influence:

> The Pacific-born typhoon storms blowing in the north-western direction reach the region every year in June, bringing heavy rainfall and resulting in a sharp rise of the rivers. On their way back from the north, these typhoons bring some rain again in August and the heaviest rains of the year in September before they disappear in a southern direction. This regime is superimposed on the south-west monsoon blowing from mid-May to mid-September and supplying fairly regular rainfalls every year.

Temperatures also vary throughout the year, though not as markedly as rainfall. The hottest month is usually April, when maximum daily temperatures in Chiang Mai may reach around 36 degrees Celsius (with minimums of about 22 degrees). The cool season is December to January, when maximum temperatures in Chiang Mai are around 28 degrees, although average minimum temperatures are a much more brisk 15 degrees, sending early morning marketgoers scurrying for jackets and woolen hats.

An important, but often neglected, issue is the effect of elevation on climate. Given that almost all administrative centers in northern Thailand are located in intermontane valleys, the bulk of the climatic data collected reflects relatively low-elevation conditions. This gives only a partial picture. While the broad seasonal patterns in lower-elevation and higher-elevation locations are similar; elevation does have a very significant impact on both rainfall and temperature. This is clearly reflected in figure 2.3, which compares data from the city of Chiang Mai (304 meters) with data from a research station in the uplands (1,402 meters). The data demonstrate that rainfall is 85 percent higher and that maximum temperatures are regularly almost 10 degrees Celsius lower at the higher-elevation site.

Hydrological issues are crucially important in a region where irrigated agriculture is a vital part of the economy and often a livelihood imperative. As would be expected from the rainfall data, streamflow in the region's rivers—and their small mountain tributaries—is strongly sea-

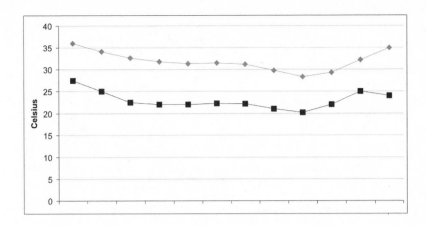

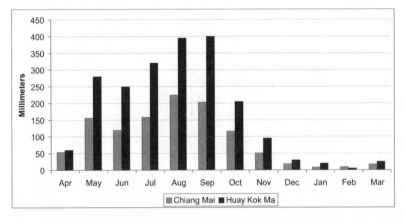

SOURCES: Elliott et al. (2003) and Northern Meteorological Centre (2004)

FIG. 2.3 *Maximum temperature and rainfall in Chiang Mai and Huay Kok Ma*

sonal. Data from the Chaem River catchment, to the west of Chiang Mai, illustrates a pattern that is found throughout the region: river discharge is lowest in April (at the end of the dry season), but then grows steadily from May to August, typically peaking in September and declining again between October and March. In figure 2.4 this pattern is observable in both the main stream of the Chaem River and a small tributary, even though they have very different absolute sizes and discharges.

Finally, there is considerable year-to-year volatility in upland rainfall and streamflow, creating great uncertainty and risk for the region's farmers (Enters 1995:95; Alford 1992:267). Some simple illustrations high-

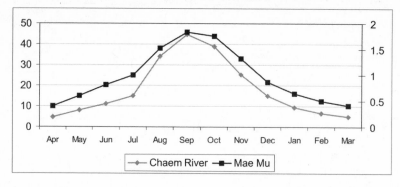

NOTE: The Chaem River (left axis) and its tributary, Mae Mu (right axis), have catchments of 2,175 and 68 square kilometers, respectively. The unit for both axes is cubic meters per second.

FIG. 2.4 *Average monthly streamflow in the Chaem River catchment*

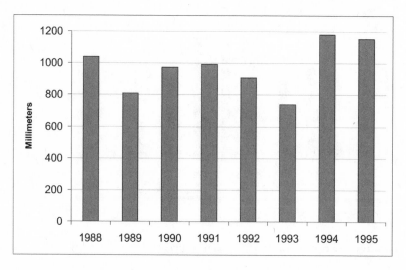

FIG. 2.5 *Variation in annual rainfall in Mae Chaem*

light the extent of variation. Figure 2.5 shows rainfall data for the town of Mae Chaem between 1988 and 1995. Average rainfall was 1,003 millimeters. The minimum for this period was 738 millimeters (26 percent below average) and the maximum 1,377 millimeters (37 percent above average and 86 percent above the minimum). Records from weather stations throughout the region indicate similar volatility in year-to-year rainfall. Unsurprisingly, there is also great year-to-year variation in the level of streamflow in the region's rivers, and some simple statistical tests undertaken by A. Walker (2002:220) confirm that there are high levels of correlation between annual streamflow and annual rainfall.[3] This may seem self-evident, but it is important to emphasize that rainfall and streamflow are highly correlated. Many observers have tended to blame low streamflow on human activities, ignoring the extent of this naturally occurring short-term variation. This issue is discussed in detail in chapters 4 and 5.

REGULATING UPLAND FORESTS

> In the North, watersheds have been decimated by expansion and the encouragement of hilltribe agriculture. The resulting lack of water has led to increasingly dry forests and the immensely destructive effects of uncontrolled fire. This pattern of illegal activity can be found in every major area where large forest tracts still exist, aided and abetted by officials of one stripe or another. It is utterly shameful that, with few remaining natural resources, we take so little care of our lifeblood. (Nok Nguak 1998)

Nok Nguak's statement is a classic summary of the views of many environmentalists, state regulators, and concerned citizens in Thailand about the destruction of the wild *pa*.[4] It also summarizes some of the key elements of the environmental narrative that this book seeks to critically explore. This narrative, however, cannot be understood without reference to the complex history of resource politics in northern Thailand. This vision of forests in Thailand has been reflected in—and helps reinforce—state control of upland areas. Landscape classification and state resettlement programs have been key elements of this project of statemaking.

Classifying Land and Watersheds

In popular imagery and environmental policy discourse, northern Thailand's forests are the central feature of its upland environment. Over the past century, this "wild" zone has been subject to an increasingly rigorous regime of state classification and regulation. According to the categories adopted by the Royal Forest Department, there are three main categories of forest in these northern uplands: tropical evergreen forest, mixed deciduous forest, and dry dipterocarp forest.[5]

- Tropical evergreen forests are mostly found in highland areas above 1,000 meters and they make up about 20 percent of the region's forest cover. Evergreen vegetation is characteristically dense—often with a closed canopy—and evergreen trees reach up to 40 meters in height. At particularly high elevations (above 2,000 meters), some areas of tropical evergreen forest have been described as "cloud forests." These areas of forest have a close association between vegetation and mist and, as such, they often feature prominently in the popular imagery of moist forest zones. However, their extent in northern Thailand is very limited (Bruijnzeel 2004:194).

- A considerably larger proportion (70 percent) of the region's forests is composed of mixed deciduous forest. This forest type, often reaching 20 or 30 meters in canopy height, is located in the intermontane valleys and in the lower and middle reaches of the upland areas, usually below about 800 meters. Traditionally, many areas of mixed deciduous forest were dominated by teak, but this has been considerably reduced by logging. Other areas are dominated by bamboo, an indicator of human activity in the form of logging or agriculture. In the rainy season, there is abundant leaf cover and leaf fall usually begins in January, with much of the forest leafless by the end of March. Forest fires are common during the dry season, partly because of the abundance of dry leaf litter.

- The third category, dry dipterocarp forest, makes up about 9 percent of far northern forest cover. Dominated by dipterocarp species, these forests are usually found on slopes and ridges in hilly areas. This forest may reach canopy heights of up to 35 meters, though some stunted forms may be found at higher altitudes. Associations with pine are common at higher elevations. Again, forest fires are frequent.

The loss of forest cover is the fundamental environmental concern in northern Thailand, and it is around this central issue that many of the other environmental issues cluster. There is no doubt that levels of forest cover have declined significantly over the past century as a result of both logging and agricultural expansion. Data for the entire northern region suggest a loss of forest cover on the order of 50 percent since 1900.[6] Official figures cited by Mingsarn (2004:317) indicate that northern region forest cover has declined from 69 percent in 1961 to 43 percent in 1998. Forest loss was particularly rapid in the 1970s, with forest clearing during this period accounting for about 15 percent of the entire northern land area. While the data indicate that the rate of loss has slowed in recent years—and there are even claims of increasing forest area (Onnucha 2000)—the long-term trend of regional deforestation seems uncontroversial.

This is not a uniform picture, and popular perceptions of rampant forest loss can be misleading in many cases. In fact, the far northern provinces of Thailand are relatively highly forested.[7] Chiang Rai has the lowest percentage for the far north, with 46 percent natural forest cover, or roughly the same as the regional average cited above. But in Mae Hong Son, official data suggest that there is almost 90 percent natural forest cover and in Nan 76 percent. Even in the relatively developed Chiang Mai province, official data suggest forest cover of over 70 percent. Overall, in the nine most northern provinces natural forest cover amounts to about 68 percent (RFD 2004b). While there is some room for skepticism about official data[8]—especially when budget bids are linked to alleged increases in forest cover—there is some confirmation from other sources. For example, a study undertaken by the National Research Council of Thailand (1997) of three catchments to the west of Chiang Mai (with a total area of 6,692 square kilometers) found that total forest cover amounted to 76 percent. In the most remote of these catchments the level was, in fact, 80 percent. And these various provincial and catchment figures include the areas of lowland plain, which are almost completely deforested.[9] If statistics were available purely for upland areas, the percentages of forest cover would be substantially higher.

In other words, the common view that the northern hills are denuded of forests—while often drawing authority from diverse forms of scientific and local knowledge—does not acknowledge that upland forest cover is relatively widespread. Clearly deforestation has occurred. But the assumption that it is rampant—an assumption that drives many environmental interventions—is more indicative of a particular regulatory vision than actual changes in land cover. In this case, "seeing like a state" (Scott 1998) involves the prior definition of an upland "problem" that demands official intervention.

Given relatively high levels of forest cover, it should come as no surprise that national forestry measures have a major impact in the upland areas of these northern provinces.[10] The history of this state intervention, often referred to as "territorialization" (Vandergeest 1996a), goes back to at least the nineteenth century, when the centralizing Bangkok court sought to exercise greater control over the logging agreements between Chiang Mai's traditional "chiefs" and British logging firms. This centralizing mission lay at the heart of the establishment of the Royal Forest Department in 1896 (see "The Royal Forest Department," pp. 40–41). Through a series of legislative measures in the early 1900s, the central

THE ROYAL FOREST DEPARTMENT

The most important organization responsible for forest policy in Thailand is the Royal Forest Department (RFD). It was founded in 1896, an administrative reform influenced by King Chulalongkorn's exposure to forest protection policy on a visit to Europe. Before this time, Thai forests were open for the removal of logs or other products without restriction, except for teak, which required special permits from local authorities known as the chiefs of forest. The creation of the RFD brought forests under the centralized control of the government and replaced logging royalties for chiefs with salaries in return for protecting and properly managing teak forests. The RFD was initially established under the Ministry of Interior and was transferred to the Ministry of Agriculture in 1935, where it remains today (though responsibilities for national parks were transferred to the Ministry of Natural Resources and Environment in 2003).

Since its establishment, the RFD has expanded beyond its initial role of regulating forest extraction. After World War II, the RFD established various forest parks for recreation and habitat protection and created a Wildlife Conservation Division in 1961. Watershed management began in 1953 when four watershed rehabilitation field stations were established in northern Thailand to reforest areas affected by shifting cultivation. The Watershed Research Sub-Division was established in 1965 and eventually become the Watershed Management Division in 1975. Its role became more focused on forest protection after the 1989 logging ban, and today it polices protected areas, reforests new areas, and administers plantations.

There is no doubt that the RFD faces difficult challenges in controlling forest use given lack of funding, corruption, and personal danger to forest rangers. Yet the RFD has been criticized for adopting a conservative, centralized approach to forest management and for resisting the devolution of forest management to localities. Some critics believe the RFD's approach stems from historic foreign influences on how forestry was defined, which excluded local approaches to forest management. Important external influence came from Herbert Slade, a British forester from the Burmese Forestry Department, who became the RFD's first chief conservator of forests. He wrote in 1896: "Forestry is a science and therefore specially trained personnel are required for its management. In the beginning the staff should be recruited from men with experience and if possible with certain other special qualifications, otherwise the forests may easily be ruined and can hardly be reconstituted" (Slade 1896). British officials dominated the RFD for its first twenty-nine years. But even after the appointment of the first Thai conservator in 1927, foresters were still trained in Britain or in British-administered India and Burma. Furthermore, when the first Thai-based forestry training center was established at the Faculty of Forestry in Bangkok's Kasetsart University it was also influenced by European approaches to economic forestry. This foreign influence is still evident. For example, in 1988, a Finnish company, Jaakko Pöyry Oyj, working closely with Kasetsart University and the RFD, was commissioned to write a new national forest plan, and development assistance was provided by Finnaid (the bilateral aid agency of Finland).

Critics have suggested these various Western approaches to forest management have affected both the style and substance of RFD policy. British companies benefited from teak concessions in the RFD's early years. Finnish foresters focused on pine and eucalyptus plantations, especially for pulp and paper. Some critics have argued that the RFD's practice of calling wide-scale monoculture forest plantations "scientific forestry" is a political strategy to legitimize these kinds of plantations and to delegitimize alternative forestry practices promoted by local communities or by people not formally trained in forestry. The RFD has also attracted criticism for resettlement of so-called forest squatters and for its opposition to decentralized forms of community forestry.

Sources: Lohmann 1999, Lang and Pye 2001, Pinkaew 2001, and *Bangkok Post* 1994.

government asserted and consolidated its power over the collection of royalties and the issuing of concessions to foreign logging firms that were active in the region up until the 1960s. In 1941 the Forest Act declared 40 percent of the land area of Thailand as "forest," though the primary objective of the act was to manage forest exploitation rather than conservation. The 1964 Forest Reserve Act, however, emphasized conservation by gazetting so-called permanent forests as forest reserve land by royal decree. And in 1985, the National Forest Policy reinforced the aim of maintaining at least 40 percent national forest cover by setting aside 25 percent of Thailand's land mass as economic forest and 15 percent as conservation forest. This policy was modified after the national logging ban imposed in 1989, following disastrous floods and landslides in the south of the country. The effect of this change, formally adopted in 1992, was to reduce the area of economic forest to 15 percent and increase the conservation forest to 25 percent. Given the relatively high level of remaining forest cover, this policy has a particularly heavy impact in the north, with about 50 percent of the total northern region classified as conservation forest. In some highly forested provinces the disproportionate impact is even greater. In Nan, for example, conservation forest covers 80 percent of the provincial area (Ewers 2003).

"Conservation forest" is a broad administrative category that refers to a wide range of areas where land-use restrictions are applied. One of the main ways the state has sought to control land use in these areas is through the declaration of national parks. Since the National Park Act of 1964 over 110 national parks have been declared in Thailand, with over twenty located in the nine far northern provinces where they take up over 15 percent of the total land area (RFD 2004c; and see figure 2.6). There are also some substantial areas of the north classified as wildlife conservation areas. Another crucially important regulatory tool is the declaration of upland areas as Class 1 watershed. In the mid-1980s a nationwide system of watershed classification was adopted—on the basis of physical and biological criteria—to provide a framework for the management and protection of forested upland areas. In this classic system of "state simplification" (Scott 1998), five watershed "classes" were introduced throughout Thailand, ranging from Class 1 headwater areas that are identified as the highest priority for protection, to Class 5 areas on gently sloping or flat land where intensive agriculture is considered appropriate (table 2.1). These formal categories have been criticized by other researchers who have used different data sources (including data at much finer resolution) and who have attempted to include locally relevant socioeconomic variables (for example Pandee and Maathuis 1990).

Protected Class 1 areas cover approximately 18 percent of the entire country (RFD 2004e) and perhaps as much as 30 percent of the total area of the upper northern provinces (derived from Yanuar 2004: table 5). In fact in some districts the impact is even greater. In Mae Chaem district—the largest district in Chiang Mai province—the Class 1 protection category applies to about 60 percent of the total land area.[11] The Royal Forest Department's Watershed Management Division states that Class 1 areas must be "strictly kept permanently as head water sources" and "immediate reforestation programs must be undertaken on the abundant shift-

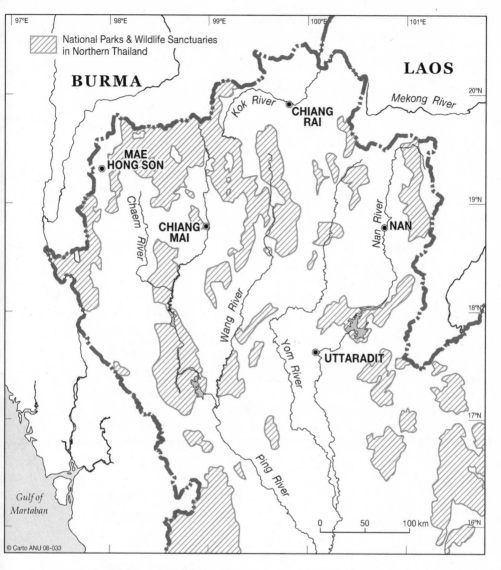

SOURCE: Protected Areas and Development (2005)

FIG. 2.6 *National parks and wildlife sanctuaries in northern Thailand*

ing [cultivation] area" (RFD 2004e). An array of watershed management
units assist in the regulation of these environmentally sensitive upland
zones, and the majority of the country's 189 watershed units are located
in the northern region (RFD 2005). Watershed management units have

TABLE 2.1 Official Watershed Classification Scheme

Classification	Land character	Proposed land use
CLASS 1	Very high elevation and very steep slopes	Protected or conservation forest and headwater source
CLASS 1A: Permanent forest cover	Very high elevation and very steep slopes	Protection. Absolutely no changes to the land permitted.
CLASS 1B: Permanent forest with some cleared areas	Very high elevation and very steep slopes	Should be reforested or maintained in permanent agroforestry
CLASS 2	High elevation and steep to very steep slopes	Use of land for agricultural activities is to be strenuously avoided. Commercial forestry and mining operations may be permitted.
CLASS 3	Uplands with steep slopes	Fruit trees, commercial timber, and perennials. Grazing in some areas. These agricultural activities should be carried out in a stringently responsible manner according to the principles of soil and water conservation.
CLASS 4	Gentle slope areas	Upland farming, with forest and fruit trees on steeper slopes
CLASS 5	Gentle slopes, flat areas	Lowland farming. This land shows high agricultural potential.

SOURCES: RFD 2004a and Bandith et al. 1993

been active in various forms of land-use regulation and, in particular, forest planting. It is estimated that up until 1996 over 1,500 square kilometers of forest had been "restored" in northern watersheds, primarily through reforestation. This represented over 70 percent of the national effort in forest rehabilitation undertaken by the Watershed Management Division (Prasong and Gilmour 1999).

A crucially important point to note—and this is an ever-present issue in much of the discussion of environmental management in northern Thailand—is that "conservation forest," "national park," and "Class 1 watershed" are administrative categories that do not necessarily equate with forest cover. This ongoing problem has bedeviled various systems of forest classification throughout Thailand. While there is, of course, a broad correspondence between areas with substantial forest cover and areas with high proportions of "conservation forest," there is certainly not a perfect match between actual land cover and administrative classification. This is evident even from the most general data where the area of conservation forest in northern Thailand exceeds the area of actual forest cover by almost 800,000 hectares (Yanuar 2004: table 5).[12] The "grossly unrealistic" (Ammar et al. 1991:12) administrative goal of 25 percent conservation forest has generated a massive mismatch between official land classification and actual land use, creating large swathes of "ambiguous lands" (Sato 2000) in which agricultural activities are rendered illegal.

This ambiguity of land classification, coupled with the illegality of certain land uses, has had long-term implications for many settlers within these regions. The impact is particularly intense in the far northern provinces where, in 1990, one-third of villages were found to be located inside forest reserves (Sopin et al. 1990:11). The Land Development Department's land-use plan for upland areas in Chiang Mai province indicates that of 1,400 villages surveyed, almost 1,300 were located in some form of forest reserve (Bandith et al. 1993). Farmers living in these areas have uncertain rights over their land and many lack formal tenure documents. Many upland farmers have found their agricultural or fallow fields taken over for plantation forestry or other activities designed to protect watersheds. The Land Development Department's plan for Chiang Mai province classified almost 600 upland villages as "communities which do not have the potential to become permanent villages and which should be evacuated to more suitable areas" (Bandith et al. 1993:38).

Resettlement and Controlling Upland Agriculture

Resettlement has been one of the strongest forms of state intervention in northern Thailand. Since the 1960s there have been various attempts to encourage or coerce farmers out of the upland forested zones. In 1966, the Royal Forest Department declared that "illicit clearing of the forests for cash crops by local villagers constitute one of the major problems in forestry." To address the problem the department called for vigilant patrol and the "establishment of a number of large settlement areas of the landless cultivators and gradually colonizing them" (Pinkaew 1999:41).

These early resettlement efforts coincided with various military activities in the northern provinces during the 1960s and 1970s aimed at increasing security and reducing the risk of insurgency at the time of the Vietnam War (Hearn 1974). In official eyes, environmental and national security concerns were linked. Field Marshall Sarit Thanarat—the prime minister between 1958 and 1963—declared: "Forests are significant resources for the lives of Thai people and the existence of Thailand. Those who destroy the forests are the enemy who destroy the nation's security" (Pinkaew 2001:75). Escalating tensions in the uplands were marked by sporadic gunfights, some significant battles, and even occasional bombing of villages by government aircraft (*Bangkok World* 1973; Bo Yang 1987; Tapp 1989:36–37; Saiyud 1986; Gua 1975; Mottin 1980:55–59). Many of the conflicts involved settlements inhabited by Hmong villagers, leading some observers to refer to a "Meo (or Hmong) War."[13] Hearn (1974:188–89) lists 101 villages that were resettled or destroyed through so-called refugee programs conducted by the government, aiming to relocate villages considered to be a security risk.[14] He comments,

> The Thai Army's 1967 decision to evacuate large numbers of hill tribesmen from the mountains to the lowlands was a costly mistake for the Thai government, in terms of military strategy, men, and money. . . . The military's stated objective was to separate the "good" tribesmen from the "bad" tribesmen, and then to summarily destroy the remaining bad tribesmen with the Army's superior technology and firepower. It should have been obvious that some of those tribesmen who did not comply with the evacuation order might possibly have been "anti-refugee program," and not necessarily anti-government, or communist. (Hearn 1974:185–86)

forest resettlement justified by calling it a
communist insurgency

It is, of course, unclear how much of this conflict represented a communist insurgency, as it was widely portrayed. Evidence suggests foreign communist agents were indeed present, but most incidents probably represented little more than relatively isolated cases of resistance by upland villagers, especially when subjected to heavy-handed state actions.[15] However these security concerns have had an enduring influence on upland development policy and, during the 1970s and 1980s, substantial portions of the uplands fell within government-declared "pink zones" that were considered to be particularly insecure and that became priorities for more subtle intervention in the form of rural development.

Enforced resettlement was complemented by other techniques of regulating upland populations. The Public Welfare Department took various initiatives to monitor and educate hill settlers, including the establishment of welfare stations (*nikhom*) in strategic locations "at intermediate altitudes in different provinces equipped with stores, dispensaries, schools, and supervisors" (Tapp 1989:34). It was hoped that the welfare, education, marketing, and agricultural extension services provided in these stations would act as an incentive for forest-dwelling farmers—or "squatters" as they were often called—to migrate to the newly established sites, or at least encourage villages to be dependent on, and influenced by, *nikhom*. By the mid-1960s, four such stations had been established in the north, but they attracted few permanent new settlers. According to one observer, the 992 residents of the Chiang Dao *nikhom* in Chiang Mai province "had all been settled there prior to the government's decision to demarcate their sites as settlement areas" (Van Roy 1971:202; see also Tapp 1989:34).[16] In fact, staff efforts at this *nikhom*, which Van Roy (1971:207) studied in some detail, came to be focused on "conspicuous achievements" that would impress the steady stream of bureaucratic dignitaries from the lowlands: "Vying in importance is maintenance of the headquarters' plant and grounds, which are kept well scrubbed and raked, rose bushes watered and pruned and badminton court carefully groomed. The visitor's first impression is incredulity at finding a posh resort in the midst of such a primeval setting."

Another initiative was the Forest Village Program. The general goal of the program was to "establish settlements . . . outside of the watershed for people who had encroached on reserved forests" (Hafner and Yaowalak 1990:336). Households were allocated limited tenure rights to agricultural land in the new villages where basic services were established. Forest village residents were often employed in reforestation programs in "degraded" forest land surrounding the village. By the early 1980s, about fifty such villages had been established in the northern region (Preeyagrysorn 1992).

Since the late 1980s, formal relocation programs seem to have fallen out of favor in northern Thailand (although the issue remained topical in northeastern Thailand where formal government-directed schemes attempted to relocate villages and install forest plantations during the 1990s).[17] Nevertheless, government policies have maintained a strong focus on national security, and the desire to move people out of conservation areas is a regularly stated policy objective, backed by occasional enforcement. Various cases since the late 1980s have created an atmosphere of anxiety and uncertainty among communities in forest conservation areas that lack formal tenure rights. There have been several notable examples of state action:

- In the late 1980s and early 1990s, villages in northern Chiang Rai province were reportedly burned and their inhabitants deported to Burma (*Bangkok Post* 1987, 1991a, 1991b). According to these reports, in 1987 trucks appeared at Akha and Lahu villages near the outskirts of the Doi Tung reforestation project, and the Border Patrol Police forcibly loaded some 160 families onto the vehicles. In 1991, the burning of an Akha village near Doi Mae Salong was also reported. Both of these cases were claimed to be responses to illegal immigration into Thailand. In 2005, the land of three Akha villages in the same area was also allegedly seized and farmers imprisoned for cultivating fields. This action was to make way for a Highland Development Station operated by the Thai Army and the Royal Forest Department (McDaniel 2005). Project proponents stated that the "objective of the station was to serve as a center of knowledge on agricultural occupations for the hill tribe people. They were encouraged to participate in various activities undertaken at the station, including the joint effort to restore the forest and watershed areas to their original abundant condition" (Chaipattana Foundation 2005).
- In the late 1980s, 157 Hmong families from the northwestern corner of Tak province were moved to lowland sites allegedly to protect the headwaters of local rivers and to maintain the integrity of a newly declared wildlife sanctuary (Pratya 1987). Interestingly, this area had been notorious during the late 1960s as a site of Hmong insurgency,

and the government responded by building a road to increase military access. This road became so plagued by attacks that it became known as "The road that cost nine men per mile" (*The Nation* 1973). It is therefore possible that environmental concerns were being used to legitimize alternative means of pacifying this region.

- One famous, and much discussed, case took place in 1994 when four upland villages in Lampang province were moved out of the newly declared Doi Luang National Park, despite claims that they had lived there for forty years prior to the declaration (Pinkaew 2001:1; Anan 1997:217). Various measures were used to coerce the villagers to move: development and welfare budgets to the village were cut; new house construction was forbidden; agricultural expansion was curtailed; farmers leaving the village to sell produce were harassed; and maintenance work on the road to the village was halted. Considerable funds were spent on establishing a relocation site, but farmers found that the agricultural land was poor quality and incapable of supporting their livelihood. As a result, many have been forced to seek employment, and there are serious concerns among local people about the numbers of young girls drawn into prostitution.

- In the late 1990s, there were reports of the destruction of the Lahu village of Tungpaka in Chiang Mai province by Royal Forest Department officials: "thirteen houses, as well as crops were destroyed . . . leaving 60 people homeless" (Gearing 1999:47). According to a Tungpaka resident quoted by Gearing, the village was evicted so that the area could be cleared and a resort built. Gearing (ibid.) goes on to state that the villagers "live in fear they may now be ousted from their refuge at the foot of the hills, an hour-and-a-half's walk from the remains of their 60–year-old settlement."

Nevertheless, during the 1990s it became clear that large-scale relocation of villages in forest conservation areas was simply not practical given the number of villages involved, the strength of political resistance, and the relative shortage of lowland arable land to accommodate relocated upland villages (Aguettant 1996:59). For these reasons, land-use regulation has become a more common and widespread approach than relocation. For some upland farmers longstanding cultivation has been recognized by the granting of various forms of limited tenure, though these schemes have usually only applied to forest reserve lands outside of the more sensitive conservation areas. Sometimes, farmers granted these limited forms of title have been encouraged to engage in what are seen as environmentally friendly practices, such as the establishment of fruit orchards.

Within official conservation areas, however, the situation is considerably stricter. A cabinet resolution of June 1998 on "solving the problems of land in forest areas" rules that communities that have lived in certain conservation areas since their declaration may be permitted to remain, but within strictly demarcated residential and agricultural areas—with no provision for future expansion—and with a focus on subsistence production (Government of Thailand 1998). If the villagers are found to have moved into the area after its declaration they are earmarked for relocation, though if this is not possible they may also be able to remain within similarly demarcated areas and with a similar subsistence orientation. Severe sanctions are authorized in the case of further "encroachment." Pinkaew (2001:31–32) reports that "in the year 1998 alone, there were more than 20 cases of people being charged as 'illegal encroachers' by forestry officials in Chiang Mai." Anecdotal reports suggest that this figure may be rather low and, moreover, that the situation in Chiang Mai province is repeated in many other northern provinces.

The Community Forest Campaign for Farmers' Rights

Increasingly, state action to resettle upland farmers and restrict their agricultural activities has met with vigorous opposition. It is regularly argued that the establishment of extensive conservation areas fails to recognize the resource claims of farmers whose lands fall within their boundaries. As Vandergeest (1996b:262) has argued, "In effect Wildlife Sanctuaries and National Parks have become areas occupied by a non-local armed force, surrounded by an alienated local population." The result of the alienation is that conservation goals are undermined as local residents lose their stake in resource management. A variety of advocacy NGOs have been working with local communities to assist them in regaining this stake. They have encouraged the formation of intervillage networks of farmers, lobbied political leaders, and assisted in the organization of large-scale farmer protests. In 1995, more than 2,000 hill farmers from six northern provinces marched in protest against the Royal Forest Department's desire to evict them from forest reserve land (*Bangkok Post* 1995). A similar protest occurred in May 1999 when some 5,000 lowland and hilltribe farmers formed a Rally for Rights in front of the Chiang Mai provincial hall, demanding better land tenure, less state-sponsored reforestation, and better access to citizenship (Vandergeest 2003; Chayan and Aquino 2000; Subin 1999). Other local disputes about Royal Forest Department systems of land classification, establishment of pine plantations on village land, and the imposition of agricultural restrictions have recently been documented by Roth (2004) and Jonsson (2005).

This grassroots protest action has attracted support from the Assembly of the Poor, which was formed in 1997 as a network of NGOs and trade unions aiming to represent poor people in informal Thai politics (Missingham 2004). Substantial support also came from sectors of the Thai academic community—especially from Chiang Mai University—and a number of prominent public intellectuals (Prawase 1997; Anan 2001; Kultida 2002). There has also been some journalistic support. For example, Sanitsuda (1999), the assistant editor of the *Bangkok Post*, has been a vigorous critic of "gun toting rangers, at the invitation of forest authorities" who seek to evict "peasants from their ancestral homes." But, as potent as this journalistic language is, perhaps the most significant support has come from the position adopted by the hugely influential Thai king, who has shown longstanding support for agricultural and social development in forested upland areas. Even the Royal Forest Department (2004d) has, in theory at least, adopted the royal vision that "the land is still a part of the reserved forest, but people are given permission to use the land."

The issue of community forestry has been central to the recent debate about land management and regulation in upland areas of northern Thailand. Foresters and rural development policymakers define "community forestry" as a form of devolved forest governance that empowers local people to shape forest use within a framework of rules established by the central state (FAO 1978; Gibson et al. 2000). In Thailand, the idea draws on international experience (especially experience with decentralized forest management in India) as well as longstanding local traditions of forest classification, protection, and use. Apart from the various forms of political support mentioned above, the concept of community forestry gained considerable legal legitimacy from provisions of the 1997 Thai constitution, which sought to make environmental policy in Thailand more democratic. In a crucially important provision, the constitution granted the right to "participate in the management, maintenance, preservation and exploitation of natural resources and the environment in a balanced fashion" to "persons so assembling as to be a traditional community" (Government of Thailand 1997: article 46).

The campaign for community forestry has, however, been marked by ongoing dispute. An initial draft bill, prepared by the Royal Forest Department as early as 1990, was criticized for failing to address the needs of villagers. For many observers, this initial draft implied little change to centralized bureaucratic control of forests and offered little chance for villagers to start governing forests locally. Many critics of the Royal Forest Department suggested their proposed legislation was just a pragmatic means to acknowledge the presence of people in forest reserves without giving them substantial resource management rights. In 1999, the director of the Royal Forest Department[18] declared: "we decided to allow villagers to live in forest areas, so we have to give them a chance to make a living from the forest." But to critics, this statement was hiding the truth, with one NGO representative responding: "it's possible that the RFD want to use the community forest law as a new tool for running commercial plantations" (Pennapa 1999). Critics were concerned that the Royal Forest Department believed villagers had no meaningful role in forest conservation. Once again, the department's director in 1999 seemed to acknowledge the realities of upland residence but, at the same time, denied the importance of localized management: "A virgin forest is an untouched forest but that's a utopian notion so we have to find a way to mingle the two [forests and human occupation] with minimum impact. But please don't ever say we need humans in the forest to protect it. That's a lie" (Uamdao 1999).

An alternative approach to community forestry was voiced in a draft prepared in the mid-1990s by the National Economic and Social Development Board, an advisory body composed of both government and public figures including academics and NGOs. This bill was commonly referred to as the "people's version"—given the widespread consultation that went into its preparation—and it sought to provide for many of the elements of decentralization, democratization, and fairness for upland farming groups (including hill tribes) that social critics believed were lacking in previous environmental legislation. Specifically, it would have allowed local villagers to form community forest committees that would be granted extensive management rights over local forest areas. (For details on the draft bill, see "Key Provisions of the People's Version of the Community Forestry Bill," p. 53.) It has, however, been the source of much contention and impasse. In early 2002, Thailand's House of Representatives passed a version of the bill that was broadly consistent with the people's version. However, the Senate rejected key provisions and in

September 2005 a joint House-Senate committee recommended that community forests not be permitted in "special forest zones" defined as areas "with a slope of more than 30 degrees, with high levels of biological diversity, and located in a headwater area" (Kultida 2005).[19]

KEY PROVISIONS OF THE PEOPLE'S VERSION OF THE COMMUNITY FORESTRY BILL

- A national level community forest policy committee will be established to set overall policy directions in relation to community forest administration and management.
- A community forest committee will be established in each province. These provincial committees will be responsible for: receiving applications for the establishment of community forests; inspecting the proposed community forest areas; considering any objections from interested parties; approving the establishment of community forests; setting management conditions; and monitoring community forest performance.
- Representatives of local communities (at least ten representatives who have the support of at least half the community) can propose the establishment of community forests provided they are in a position to take care of the forest. In forest conservation areas, such as national parks, applicants must demonstrate that they have been caring for the forest for at least five years prior to commencement of the act and can demonstrate a "culture of coexistence that favours forest protection."
- Local community forest committees are given wide-ranging powers in relation to management of the community forest. The committee sets down the local regulatory framework for forest management, including the demarcation of conservation and gathering areas and rules for the conservation and use of animals and vegetation. They are able to expel noncompliers from the membership of the community forest; they can require compensation; take legal action; refer matters to the public prosecutors; and are given wide-ranging local policing powers.
- Locally developed plans for the operation of the community forest must be submitted to the provincial committee at the time of application. These plans must set out "protection" and "use" areas within the community forest.

Source: Draft Community Forest Bill n.d.

Despite setbacks in the Thai parliament, this more people-oriented approach to community forestry represents an important challenge to the denial of resource rights of farmers located in forested upland areas. The people's version of the bill is a much-needed response to coercive state policies that have excluded local people from the management of forest resources and have undermined local traditions of sustainable resource management. In asserting the rights of these farmers, and in countering ill-conceived plans for relocation of upland villages, the community forest movement has argued that coexistence of people and forest is possible due to the close relationship between rural livelihoods and forest ecosystems. There is little doubt that the campaign for this legislation has contributed to a softening of the official emphasis on relocation and a greater willingness to explore options embracing local knowledge, decentralized management, and state-community networks.

Yet, the juxtaposition of the people's version of the community forest bill with the state-led vision of excluding local people from forest management has actually reinforced environmental narratives about acceptable forms of environment and society in the uplands. The public debate about community forestry has framed environmental policy and development in terms of (1) legitimate communities, engaged in (2) forest conservation. There is a strong sense in which this reasserts historic state approaches to land classification and upland regulation. As Vandergeest (1996b:266) has argued: "the resource rights specified in the draft bill are so circumscribed . . . that, if enforced, they would fail to address the central conflicts in [protected areas]."

There are two key limitations in the framing of the community forest debate and, in particular, the people's version of the bill. First, the bill states that only "communities" may participate in community forestry. A "local community" is defined in the bill as "the group of people that live together as a society in the same area and pass down their culture together" (Draft Community Forest Bill n.d.). A commentary on this definition suggests communities so defined "must be original local communities" (Anon. n.d.). Under the proposed bill, applications to establish community forests in forest conservation areas must also demonstrate a history of sustainable forest management and a "culture of coexistence that favours forest protection." This emphasis on originality and sustainability is consistent with the key provision of the 1997 constitution quoted above. It also reflects the broader emphasis in much alternative environmentalist literature (in Thailand and elsewhere) on the correspondence between sustainable resource use and communities with strong kinship ties, cultural continuity, and an absence of commercialization.

But perhaps this emphasis on community is somewhat misplaced. In northern Thailand, there are numerous local frontiers where the bill may not operate because histories of settlement are relatively short and local residents have diverse origins (Hirsch 1997b). For example, Del Castillo's study (1990:39) of a fermented tea-producing village near Mae Taeng indicates that resident households came from seven different districts in Chiang Mai province, with eight households arriving between 1980 and 1988, a further six between 1971 and 1980, and eight between 1961 and 1970.[20] By any definition, it is difficult to see how this group of villagers—for whom forest resources are undoubtedly crucial—could validly present themselves as an original local community eligible to apply for a community forest. Indeed, Anan (2000:75), one of the key academic campaigners for community forestry, writes of such recently settled villages as not being old enough "to make their members have a sense of belonging and to create a stable land use tradition," clearly putting them outside the definitions proposed by the community forest movement. Similarly, in Mae Chaem district, 26 percent of household heads surveyed were born outside their current village, with most entering the village because of marriage (field surveys conducted by A. Walker and colleagues in 1999). Given that the self-nominated household heads were predominantly male, the survey did not capture the significant number of in-marrying women. Furthermore, the survey focused mainly on agriculture and hence did not fully capture in-migrating shopkeepers, other local business operators, or government employees. The survey also identified significant numbers of "residents" living outside the village for varying periods to pursue education and nonagricultural employment and to meet geographically dispersed kinship obligations. In brief, there is a real danger that an overly narrow focus on "original" and "local" "community" may exclude many upland residents who have quite legitimate stakes in local resource management

A second crucially important weakness of the people's version of the proposed legislation is that it gives insufficient attention to agricultural land. As discussed previously, large areas of agricultural land are located within forest reserve areas on which tenure rights are ill defined. Yet, despite the fundamental and oft-repeated claims that people and forests can and do coexist—a basic tenet of community forestry and a catch-cry of the campaign in northern Thailand—at no point does the proposed legislation state that agriculture is a legitimate activity within community forest boundaries. In fact, a key provision of the people's version specifically forbids anyone to "control land, farm, live in, build, burn, clear, lop, gather or do anything else that would cause destruction to the forest in the community forest area." In another provision, there are sanctions of five years' imprisonment, or fifteen years if the offence takes place in a conservation area of the community forest.[21] As such, it appears that the proposed community forest legislation would offer no enhanced security for farmers with agricultural lands in the ambiguous zones of forest reserves. The formal status of their fields would not change and the mismatch between formal land classification and actual land use would be unresolved. Despite all the claims about community forest legislation providing a basis for sustainable and secure upland livelihood, the central elements of this livelihood—agriculture and rights to agricultural land— have no clear place within the proposed legislative framework.

How has this situation come about? While the specific motives of those who drafted the proposed legislation are not known, there is a strong sense in which its provisions are framed by the conservationist priorities of the state. As Vandergeest (1996b:266) has suggested, the proposed bill is primarily a "tool for environmental protection and development . . . not for defining and protecting land rights." The key strategy of community forest campaigners has been to demonstrate the credentials of local communities in terms of forest protection, often by promoting rather idealistic images of upland communities living in harmony with nature. As a result, upland agriculture itself has become a much lower priority to the point where it is actually excluded from the community forest framework. The nature of this limitation was highlighted by commentary prompted by discussions in the Thai Senate. Some senators feared the proposed bill would allow upland farmers to "convert the fertile forest to cabbage and other cash crops" and "claim their cabbage plantations as community forest" (Pennapa 2002). In response to this public focus on upland agriculture, the advocates of community rights emphasized the conservationist focus of the bill. An NGO representative responded that the bill "aims to make us responsible for protecting nature in our communities. It doesn't allow a person or group of people to live in, or to make a living in the forest" (Supara 2002b). And a key academic advocate of community forests argued that the bill "gave local communities the right to manage the forests, not to occupy forest land" (Kultida 2002).

In northern Thailand, the distinction between *muang* and *pa* has had long-standing cultural importance. This distinction has been shaped by the region's biophysical realities: lowland valleys surrounded by mountain slopes. There are key biophysical differences, and linkages, between these two zones.

But these distinctions go further than defining the topography and landscape of the region. One of the key objectives of the modern Thai state has been to extend the power of the lowland *muang* into the upland *pa*. It has used a range of strategies to achieve this: waging warfare against its "wild" residents; luring or forcing villagers out of the wilderness into resettlement zones; and, most recently, introducing simplified and legible systems of landscape classification that seek to restrict and regulate human impact on natural ecosystems. Official systems of land-use classification may seem scientifically neutral—based on quantifiable attributes such as slope, soil type, or ecological richness—but they have fundamentally important political implications and are based on quite specific perspectives on the appropriate strategies for protecting the wildness of the upland *pa*. These systems of classification and regulation are gaining increasing support in Thailand from those who seek stronger state action to protect the forest and to maintain the unique ecological values of the uplands.

Community forestry, in many respects, represents a new approach to the forested uplands. Unlike the Thai military or forest regulators, community forest campaigners assert that villagers in the forested zone do not need to be seen as problematic. Their campaign is based on the philosophy that people and forests can live together, thus blurring the idealized distinction between the settled *muang* and the natural *pa*. But this blurring only goes so far. The community forest campaign is, to a significant extent, framed by the predominant preoccupation with forest conservation: indeed this seems its inherent "problem closure." Upland residence is legitimate, provided it can demonstrate a "culture of coexistence that favors forest protection." The wild values of the *pa* predominate—agricultural tenure is not recognized and agricultural activity in community forest zones is declared illegal. The irony is that the advocates of community forestry have ended up promoting the official position that the campaign set out to oppose: that agricultural presence and forest conservation are incompatible. This is the discursive power of narratives. Political interaction between the state and its critics has in effect created a discourse coalition that reiterates the basic narrative that Thailand needs a high level of forest cover in the north; that upland agriculture is a key threat to these trees; and that upland residents can be differentiated according to how far they support this ecological imperative.

3 *Upland People*

FOR YEARS, PEOPLE HAVE BEEN ENCOURAGED to see the uplands of
Thailand as inhabited by "hill tribes"—the Akha, Hmong, Karen, Lahu,
Lisu, and Mien—each with distinctive clothing, traditions, agricultural
practices, and dance.[1] The focus on hill tribes is fed by the literature issued
by tourism companies, government statements about the supposed
problems of dealing with minorities, the persistent focus of many anthropologists on the exotic, and an increasing tendency for environmental
activists to resort to the language of ethnicity (Vandergeest 2003). Visitors to the region are typically advised that "the North is characterized
by densely forested mountainous regions, inhabited by Thailand's many
colourful hill tribe people. Adventurous exploration of this beautiful area
is possible by trekking, river rafting, mountain biking, and even elephant
safaris" (Kaysfeld International 2004). An official government report on
the demography of the uplands reinforces this hilltribe aesthetic (Social
Welfare Department 1995). It features images in all of the sections dealing with the minority hill tribes—all but two of the pictures feature women
in ethnically stereotypical dress—but the sections on the ethnic Thai populations pass without illustration. Describing the largest group of them
as "Thai of the lowlands" compounds the upland invisibility of these Thai
groups. The Thai expression for hill tribe—*chao khao*—has a double meaning that underlines this "othering" of the uplands. *Khao* means both "mountain" and "they," so the *chao khao* are both "mountain people" and "they
people"—the problems of their upland homes symbolically set apart from
the concerns of "we" Thai (Pinkaew 2001:43–44).

Popular representations of "hill tribes" intersect with, and reinforce,

59

environmental narratives of the uplands. Explanations of environmental change cannot be isolated from the representation and participation of different social actors in political debates. This chapter focuses on the two largest hilltribe groups—the Karen and the Hmong—because they occupy very different positions in recent debates about the management of northern Thailand's forested zones. The Karen are often portrayed as sound environmental managers, while the Hmong are equally regularly condemned as destroyers of upland forest. The Karen feature prominently in the campaigns waged by academics and NGOs to increase the role of local communities in upland resource management, while negative images of Hmong agriculture are often drawn upon in justifying the strict state regulation of land use. These are certainly diverse positions, often reflecting the diverse socioeconomic positions and political interests of their proponents. But these differing accounts of upland hill tribes have important commonalities and often share key assumptions about the appropriateness, or otherwise, of different types of upland livelihood.

However, it is important to go further than simply exploring environmental narratives about the hill tribes. It is necessary to interrogate the category itself and its role in creating a selective narrative of environmental crisis. Simplified narratives in Thailand persist partly because they conveniently attribute environmental blame to a group of "others" who reside in the physically and culturally remote uplands (Vandergeest 2003). These narratives contain various simplifications about the livelihoods and environmental impacts of these "other" groups. But they are also highly selective in their focus on hill tribes. In fact, the "lowland" Thai are probably the majority population in the uplands. The people of the *muang* have settled in large numbers in the upland *pa* and, despite their official invisibility, they have a significant effect on the upland environment. And even when they reside in the large lowland valleys they exert a very strong influence on upland policy given their common portrayals as victims of upland degradation. For these reasons it is essential that the narratives about the hill tribes be considered alongside popular representations of the lowland Thai (*khon muang*). Broadening the social focus is an important step in achieving more open consideration of environmental narratives.

THE UPLAND POPULATION

What is the size of Thailand's hilltribe population? Official statistics give some indication, though it is likely that these figures are too low on account of the difficulty of surveying remote upland villages, widespread cross-border movement, and the fact that significant numbers of upland residents are not recognized as Thai citizens. Yet these statistics are a starting point. In 1995, the Social Welfare Department (1995) estimated that there were about 746,000 hilltribe members.[2] This is much higher than the figure of 551,000 reported by the Tribal Research Institute (1989) in the mid 1980s, although it is not clear whether this increase is due to real population growth rather than changes in data collection methodology. The 1995 figures indicate that the largest groups were the Karen (353,000), the Hmong (112,000), and the Lahu (82,000). Their largest concentrations were in the upper northern provinces of Chiang Mai (273,000), Chiang Rai (151,000), Mae Hong Son (102,000), and Nan (82,000). It seems likely that the population has been growing since the mid-1990s largely because of cross-border movement prompted by military conflict in Burma.

Despite popular perceptions, these hill tribes probably make up less than half of the total upland population. While, again, there are real problems with data availability, it seems very likely that there are substantially more lowland Thai in the hills than there are hill tribes. Many of these "lowlanders" are located in small intermontane valleys where, to casual observation, they pursue typically lowland lifestyles based on irrigated paddy cultivation. But many of these farmers also have agricultural fields and fruit orchards on upland slopes, and not uncommonly a substantial percentage of such farmers may be entirely dependent on them. Some of them are what Chapman (1978:122) described as "reluctant swiddeners forced by population pressure to move in increasing numbers away from their traditional base in wet rice cultivation." However, many of those moving upslope have been more enthusiastic, especially as market expansion has created incentives for the extension of cash crops onto hillslopes previously considered marginal. To take just one illustrative example, in a "lowland" northern Thai village in Mae Chaem district, surveying by A. Walker and colleagues found that 25 percent of farmers were entirely dependent on the upland fields they cultivated on the mountain slopes surrounding the village, while a further 33 percent derived some income from these hillslope enterprises.

In another nearby village, surveying was exceedingly difficult, as a large percentage of the working population were "commuting" to their upland soybean plots—located some 20 kilometers to the south—departing in laden pickups before dawn and returning, exhausted, late in the evening. There are also numerous lowland Thai farmers who have moved permanently into these midland zones, cultivating vegetables, raising cut flowers in greenhouses, establishing orchards, or paying other farmers to cultivate cash crops on newly acquired upland fields. Often they are joined by investors from the major urban centers, perhaps running a tourist resort, a roadside gasoline station, or a rustic restaurant complete with karaoke machine and a surplus of waitressing staff.

So, to what extent have the farmers of the lowland *muang* moved into the upland *pa*? Official estimates do not appear very useful. The Social Welfare Department's 1995 survey provides a count of only sixty-seven thousand lowland Thai in upland communities. Longer-term perspectives suggest that this is probably a gross underestimate. Judd's important study (1977:8) of *chao rai* Thai (Thai upland farmers), undertaken in the late 1950s, argues on the basis of field research and statistical analysis that "apart from tribal swiddeners . . . by far the larger number of swiddeners in Thailand are the rural Thai, practicing either integral swiddening or, more commonly, part-time supplementary swiddening." He estimates that "about a fifth" of rural northern Thai households are primarily reliant on upland swiddening and that "many more" have upland fields that supplement their primary focus on paddy cultivation (Judd 1977:6). He suggests that their total numbers are about one million. Chapman (1978:122) put forward a similar argument in the late 1970s when he argued that lowland northern Thai farmers were the "largest ethnic group of shifting cultivators" in Thailand's northern provinces. His estimate is somewhat more conservative than Judd's, suggesting that more than 250,000 nonhilltribe farmers "depend to some extent on shifting cultivation." Another informed estimate from the same period is higher, suggesting that the number is "well over half a million" (Kunstadter, cited in Tapp 1989:36). The effects on upland demography of more recent developments in northern Thailand are not clear. On the one hand, economic diversification in the lowlands has broadened the array of opportunities available to those who may previously have been driven to reluctant swiddening. But at the same time, extensive road construction and expanding markets for upland cash crops have created new settlement opportunities and financial incentives. National estimates (Tongroj 1990:89) suggest that there may be around four million people (possibly substantially more) living in forest reserve areas (most of which are located in upland areas). Given that about half of the forest reserve is located in northern Thailand, this would suggest that the upland population in the north is at least two million. If the estimated hilltribe population is subtracted it still leaves over one million lowland Thai living in the uplands (see also Schmidt-Vogt 1999:79).

For some readers, this may seem an unnecessary diversion into statistical analysis. But it is a very important early step in our critical examination of northern Thailand's environmental narratives. Narratives of environmental degradation in the uplands of Thailand—and narratives about the need for rehabilitation and regulation—typically focus on the problems of the hill tribes (and some tribes much more than others) and resort to naturalized and assumed ethnoecological categories. Alternative approaches that, for example, emphasize the importance of community-based resource management also increasingly rely on stereotypical symbols of cultural difference that tend to associate particular ecological niches with particular forms of culture, knowledge, and identity. Our argument is that the substantial upland presence of "lowland" Thai is just one example of the many ways in which these forms of ecological categorization can be selective and misleading. The old dichotomy between the lowland Thai of the *muang* and the wild "tribals" of the *pa* is a poor basis for understanding recent processes of upland transformation. (See also "Ethnicity and Elevation," p. 64.)

Nonetheless, stereotypical images and symbols of ethnoecological difference serve an important function by underpinning environmental narratives and supporting proposed policies in northern Thailand. The category "hill tribe" is important in constructing a "discourse coalition" in which debate about environmental management in the uplands focuses selectively on certain groups and certain forms of agricultural activity that are seen as problematic. Public perceptions about the typical practices and locations of different upland groups shape environmental debates and support diverse projects of upland statemaking. The three largest groups in the uplands of northern Thailand—the *khon muang*, the Karen, and the Hmong—are selectively brought into environmental narratives, as discussed below. The intention, here, is not to essentialize descriptions of these groups (that is, suggest that these are innate and unchallengeable characteristics of each group). Rather, the intention is to convey a sense of the core imagery on which currently influential environmental narratives draw.

Khon Muang

The *khon muang* are the numerically and politically dominant population of northern Thailand. In terms of broad ethnic categories, the *khon*

ETHNICITY AND ELEVATION

Much popular discussion of highland agriculture in northern Thailand has proposed that there is a clear link between ethnicity and elevation. This view is partly the result of an elegant and influential diagram contained in the groundbreaking book, *Farmers in the Forest* (Kunstadter et al. 1978:8), which showed, for example, that Hmong settle between elevations of 1,000 to 2,000 meters, and the Karen between about 500 and 1,700 meters. Over the years this diagram has been influential in shaping classifications of upland people (Vandergeest 2003:23–24). While the diagram does indicate a wide scale of agricultural activities for different ethnic groups (especially the Karen), it is a poor guide to transformations that have occurred since the 1970s and still presents the image of clearly defined social groups with associated ecological niches. Population growth, expansion of roads and other infrastructure, and agricultural transformation have meant that the distribution of both settlement and land use is often not as neatly defined as this diagram tends to suggest.

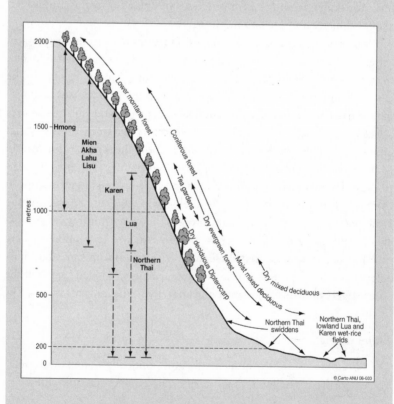

muang are one branch of the larger Tai ethnic group, which includes the central Thai to the south, the Lao, and the Shan. They speak a Tai language that is broadly similar—though with much potential for misunderstanding—to the central Thai of Bangkok. Their religion is predominately Buddhist, but this is a diverse and syncretic form of Buddhism with a strongly animist orientation. The term *khon muang* (people of the *muang*) refers to the stereotypical location of this group in the centralized lowland settlements of the region. Original *khon muang* settlers are thought to have migrated southward into the valleys of northern Thailand as long ago as the eighth century (Freeman 2001:9). The *khon muang* "kingdom" of Lanna (literally, one million rice fields) flourished in the thirteenth to the fifteenth centuries—with its preeminent centers of chiefly power and Buddhist virtue in Chiang Rai and Chiang Mai—but was conquered by Burmese rivals in the mid-sixteenth century. In the following two centuries, the upland valleys of northern Thailand were the site of ongoing contests between Burmese and Siamese centers of power, resulting in large-scale population movements and extensive depopulation. Siamese power was ultimately successful, with Chiang Mai reconquered in 1774, and since the late nineteenth century the region of Lanna has been progressively brought within Bangkok's domain of influence and administration.

Frequently, lowland settlements of the *khon muang* are portrayed as a central residential cluster—almost always focused on a Buddhist temple—surrounded by paddy fields. A river or stream is usually close at hand, given that the classic *khon muang* liveihood strategy is the cultivation of glutinous ("sticky") rice in inundated rice plots, each of which is surrounded by a low mud wall to assist with water retention (figure 3.1). Water is usually supplied by gravity-fed *muang faay* (literally, canal weir) irrigation systems. The most extensive areas of paddy in northern Thailand are located on the major lowland plains (such as the Chiang Mai valley), but there are also substantial stretches in the low slope areas of the intermontane upland valleys and scattered pockets wherever alluvial deposits and convenient water supply provide favorable conditions for cultivation. In the wet season, rice is the preferred crop on these paddy fields, though in many areas more-commercial alternatives are making inroads and some farmers have all but abandoned subsistence rice production. In the dry season—where irrigation is available—many different cash crops are cultivated: soybeans, garlic, tobacco, cabbages, peanuts, peas, sweet corn, maize, eggplants, tomatoes, and potatoes. Given

FIG. 3.1 *Painting of an imagined traditional* khon muang *landscape*

its heavy water requirement, rice is not usually grown in the dry season. Most *khon muang* communities also have gardens and orchards (*suan*) usually located on the fringes of the paddy, on slightly elevated land that is not suitable for irrigation. State conservation policies have encouraged the cultivation of fruit trees on these paddy-fringe gardens, and these grew rapidly in extent during the 1990s. And *khon muang* farmers make extensive use of upland fields, but these don't feature highly in the stereo-typically lowland imagery of *khon muang* livelihood.

How do these *khon muang* farmers feature in the environmental narratives of upland northern Thailand? As noted above, there is a tendency for the *khon muang* to be relatively invisible in environmental debates about the uplands. But they are included in environmental narratives about the region in ambiguous and seemingly contradictory ways. First, and perhaps most influentially at a national level, *khon muang* farmers feature as the victims of upstream and upslope environmental degradation. Most commonly, this takes the form of claims that upland deforestation and agricultural expansion threaten lowland livelihood and health because they cause flooding, drought, siltation, and chemical pollution.

Some of the bitterest environmental disputes in northern Thailand in recent years have been energized by the claim that intensive upland agriculture undermines the sustainability of lowland systems of cultivation and resource management. According to one account of the famous Chom Thong dispute, "the livelihood of some 12,000 Khonmuang (ethnic Thai) villagers was threatened by the cash-cropping of 650 hill-tribe villagers" (Nelson 1990:9).[3] These sorts of claims are popular in conservationist calls for much stricter regulation of upland agricultural activity, but the image of the *khon muang* farmer as victim of upland degradation also features regularly in much more liberal accounts of the importance of community-based resource management. For example, an important paper by Chusak and Dearden (1999), which reviews community forestry initiatives in the north, documents a series of cases where *khon muang* forest protection measures were motivated by the perceived environmental impacts of upslope cultivation. In the Ban Luang area of Nan province, *khon muang* villagers have developed "operational rules" for watershed management that prohibit forest clearing by hill tribes. Enforcement is strict—"the last village that tried to locate there was burned down by the villagers, along with all the crops" (Chusak and Dearden 1999:679). Similarly, in Thung Kao Hang village in Lamphun province they note "efforts to exert more control over local resources began only after the richly forested areas around the village had been mostly destroyed by logging and shifting cultivators and the villagers began to experience severe water shortages" (Chusak and Dearden 1999:682).

These accounts of *khon muang* farmers suffering from upland degradation are reinforced by increasingly popular imagery that promotes the ecologically benign nature of authentic *khon muang* livelihood. In this context, the *muang faay* irrigation systems of northern Thailand have considerable symbolic power (Uraivan 1995). In accounts of *khon muang* agricultural systems, these weir and canal gravity-fed irrigation schemes have come to represent a desirable ideal of decentralized communal management, equitable resource distribution, and locally appropriate agricultural technology. While earlier descriptions of these systems placed primary emphasis on their technological and institutional aspects, in more recent years *muang faay* systems have been identified as lying at the heart of *khon muang* environmental sensitivity. Specifically, watershed forest protection by northern Thai irrigation groups is said to be one of the key antecedents of the modern community forestry movement, and farmer concern about the sustainability of *muang faay* irrigation systems is widely reported to be a key component of contemporary community forestry initiatives (Apinyaa 2001:34–40; Anan 1999:35; NDF 2000a; RFD 1998:23–28). Various forest-oriented ritual activities, such as those that "pay respect to the spirit of the headwater" have been "resurrected" (Chusak and Dearden 1999:11) to add strength to the conservationist claim that *khon muang* agriculture is inseparable from longstanding traditions of watershed management. More generally there is an upsurge of interest in numerous aspects of Lanna tradition, and in this cultural movement the indigenous ecological knowledge of the region's farmers features prominently. Ekawit's account (2001:21) of Lanna "local wisdom" describes the ways in which the subsistence production of *khon muang* farmers is based on technologies and practices that "harmonize lifestyle with the natural environment." For example, forest product collection is governed by "local wisdom that comes from villagers' observation of nature and environmental cycles" (Ekawit 2001:77). Other publications have documented the precepts, ritual prohibitions, and taboos that reflect the sympathetic relationship between *khon muang* culture and the encompassing environment: "You should not cut down big trees. It is not good to make paddy fields or gardens, or to build a house in those areas. If you live there, there will be no happiness" (Khomnet et al. 1996:49).

But there are also competing images. At times, *khon muang* farmers are portrayed as rapacious users of natural resources whose increasingly urbanized settlements and commercialized agricultural systems place unsustainable pressures on local resources and drive both the desperate poor and the entrepreneurial rich to seek advantage in previously unsettled zones. Often these claims about the *khon muang* are motivated by a desire to refute the popular claim that hill tribes are the primary cause of upland environmental degradation. Consider the following description by the prominent journalist Sanitsuda (1994:50–52) in which she describes her journey to a Karen village in Mae Chaem district of Chiang Mai province:

Last year, the route offered a panoramic view of green mountains. Now, the scene is one of a vast, barren terrain strewn with ash. The sky is hazy with smoke from burning trees. The smell of fresh destruction hangs heavily in the air. . . . The shocking site . . . exemplifies the intensity of the deforestation going on in Mae [Ch]aem as a result of the authorities' turning a blind eye to the cash crop invasion. The [*muang faay*] dam masters in the valley are complaining about the decline in water flow that follows deforestation.

But the forest dwellers up in the hills have their own complaints. "It's the town people from the valley who are responsible. They want land to grow soybeans and other crops. Some come up to clear the forest themselves. Others hire the Karens to do it." . . . The days when the Thai townspeople and the Karen forest dwellers each minded their own business are over. Low-lying land for farming is scarce in Mae [Ch]aem, and all is used for rice growing. So eyes are turned to the forest . . . Longpong, an area of more than 10,000 rai [1,600 hectares], is Mae [Ch]aem's biggest cash crop zone. It used to be the area's lushest teak forest. During the cultivation season, the smell of chemical pesticide travels for kilometers outside the area. Most of the pesticide-soaked vegetables are sent directly to Bangkok.

Sanitsuda's crisis narrative represents an alternative imagery of *khon muang* malevolence. There has long been a perception that the *khon muang* are unskilled hillslope farmers with "haphazardly felled and poorly burned" upland fields (A. R. Walker 1992:11). These "lowlanders" are also seen as being key contributors to the "intermediate-zone" resource crisis as they have progressively moved upslope, acquiring the farmlands of less entrepreneurial hill farmers and encouraging, through commercial linkages, unsustainable practices of forest product exploitation (Uraivan et al. 1988). In brief, the perception persists that the authentic and appropriate site of *khon muang* agriculture is the lowland *muang*, where carefully managed irrigation systems provide a basis for sustainable resource management. As these farmers move out of the *muang* into the domain of the *pa*, the mismatch between lowland culture and upland environment results in degradation. A. R. Walker (1992:11) provides a nice summary of this common narrative: the "masters of irrigated-rice technology in their traditional lowland homes . . . are among the least skilled of the hill farmers."

Karen

The Karen are the largest hilltribe group in northern Thailand. Numbering over 350,000, their numbers are largest in Chiang Mai (123,000), Mae Hong Son (77,000), and Lamphun (25,000) (Social Welfare Department 1995). The history of Karen settlement in the region is uncertain, but many researchers believe the Karen have lived in northern Thailand longer than the *khon muang* (Rajah 1986; Renard 1979; Keyes 1979). Most Karen villages are located in the middle zones of the uplands (between about 600 meters and 1,000 meters) though there are also numerous Karen communities in the lower reaches of intermontane valleys.[4]

The Karen have featured prominently in the political campaigns of NGOs and academics who seek to defend the rights of upland peoples. Karen traditions of forest management are referred to regularly by those arguing for the introduction of community forestry legislation, and Karen livelihood is often held up as an environmentally friendly alternative to commercialized agriculture. In order to contextualize this contemporary narrative about the Karen it is necessary to briefly review the ongoing local and international debate about the impacts of shifting cultivation.

Shifting Cultivation. Shifting cultivation is a form of agriculture classically employed in the humid tropics by people living in relatively remote upland regions. It is sometimes called "swidden" agriculture, based on the Old English word used to describe areas where land is cleared of vegetation and crops grown (Grandstaff 1980; Fox et al. 2000). In Southeast Asia, the first stage of shifting cultivation is usually to cut down the trees and the undergrowth and allow the plant matter to dry out in the last month or so of the dry season before it is burnt. It is this land-preparation technique that gives rise to the pejorative label "slash-and-burn." The fertility of the system is strongly dependent on the nutrients released from the forest biomass by the process of burning, which also assists in disease and pest control. Crops are grown on the cleared fields for one or more rainy seasons, but rapid fertility decline and intrusion of weeds soon necessitates a move to another site, where the cycle begins again.

Shifting cultivation has often been targeted by forest regulators and development agencies as a wasteful and inefficient system of agriculture.[5] In colonial eastern India early foresters regularly condemned *jhum* (a local word for shifting cultivation), and many of these ideas found their way into Thailand as modern European systems of forest management were adopted. Government agencies in Thailand have long been hostile to shifting cultivation—first because it was seen as competing with the commercial exploitation of forests and later because it was seen as anathema to forest conservation. Van Roy (1971:198) writes that as early as the 1950s "the belief gathered force that the form of swiddening practiced by the hill tribes is destructive of watersheds, that it causes flash flooding as well as altered climatic and rainfall conditions." He reports that flooding in the 1950s made the upland shifting cultivators "scapegoats of Northern Thai public opinion," a popular view backed by government reports that 40 percent of deforestation in Thailand was the result of shifting cultivation.[6] "There arose a cry within the Ministry of Agriculture, particularly among forestry officials, that the hill tribes were deforesting the Northern uplands and thus endangering agricultural prospects in the lowlands" (Van Roy 1971:198).

As a result of these sorts of claims, regulations were introduced that "demanded the immediate cessation of such practices" with provision for "five years' imprisonment and a fine of 20,000 baht on illicit forest clearing" (Van Roy 1971:199). Van Roy comments that "typically these strictures are raised against the hill tribes; nowhere have I found Thai swiddening . . . and other Thai peasant uses of the upland proscribed." This negative attitude against shifting cultivation has continued until the present day with numerous development projects and regulatory interventions aiming to bring it under control (ICRAF 1999). Popular environmental wisdom continues to single out shifting cultivation by hill tribes as a major cause of deforestation, biodiversity loss, smoke haze, and even climate change.[7] These negative sentiments are nicely summarized by one of the Royal Forest Department's main upland catchment researchers:

> There are almost 700000 shifting cultivators in the highlands. . . . As a result the hill evergreen forest has been widely destroyed by shifting cultivation. The farmers have cut and burnt the forest with slash and burn systems to grow annual crops without using soil and water conservation methods. . . . This practice has caused deforestation and destruction of the ecosystem of catchment areas and decreased biodiversity in the hill evergreen forest. . . . As a result, there is now a large area of wasteland on the mountains and a lack of water in the summer, with floods and landslides occurring in the rainy season. (Pornchai n.d.: section 1.4)

Many anthropologists and cultural ecologists who have undertaken detailed studies of shifting cultivation systems have come to quite different conclusions. The pathbreaking and influential study by Conklin (1954, 1957) in the Philippines describes the shifting cultivation of the upland Hanunoo as a sophisticated and highly complex agricultural system that sustainably supported subsistence livelihoods and enabled long-term residence in permanent settlements. Far from the popular imagery of forest destruction, Conklin describes a system in which fallow areas are strictly protected, areas of sacred forest are carefully preserved, and in which farmers undertake "systematic enrichment of forest and fallow vegetation" (Conklin 1957:87). He calls the system "integrated" swidden given its multifaceted links to a "traditional, year-round, community wide, largely self-contained, and ritually-sanctioned way of life" (Conklin 1957:2). Similarly, Geertz (1963:25) famously argued that swidden farming can be viewed as a system in which "a natural forest is transformed into a harvestable forest." He suggests that the "most distinctive positive characteristic of swidden agriculture . . . is that it is integrated into and . . . maintains the general structure of the preexisting natural ecosystem into which it is projected" (Geertz 1963:16). Overall, much anthropological research has concluded that shifting cultivation can provide a basis for meeting the dual goals of livelihood security and conservation. As Moran (2000:280) writes, shifting cultivation "is a conservative measure that when practiced according to tradition, preserves forest complexity and provides sustained yields."

The "Karen Consensus." Over the past decade or so, much of the writing on the Karen has been framed in terms of this defense of shifting cultivation.[8] Karen shifting cultivation is referred to in Thai as rai mun wian (rotating upland fields) and, as A. Walker (2001b:146) has argued, a "Karen consensus" has emerged whereby rai mun wian is promoted as representing a "fragile ideal of mutually beneficial interaction between culture and nature." Classic Karen shifting cultivation cycles between numerous land parcels on a year-to-year basis, with each plot only being recultivated after a long fallow period of up to twenty years. Typically, rai mun wian focuses on the production of upland rice, though this rice is often intercropped with numerous vegetables, creating a remarkable level of biological diversity within the agricultural and fallow fields. In the tradition of Conklin, Geertz, and others, recent writing on Karen agricultural practices has drawn attention to their distinctive ecologically friendly and sustainable characteristics: careful site selection; short cultivation periods combined with long fallow periods; painstaking management and control of burning; maintenance of large tree stumps; minimal soil disturbance; and preservation of ridgetop and watershed forest cover (figure 3.2 shows schoolchildren exhibiting this environmental attitude). These actions convey various environmental benefits: protection of biodiversity; vigorous forest regrowth (which some believe may create biological diversity superior to undisturbed forest); very limited soil erosion; good water quality and quantity in downslope streams; limited weed infestation; and maintained, or even enhanced, wildlife diversity.

Recent accounts of Karen livelihood argue that the sustainability of rai mun wian is underpinned by a cultural preference—said to lie at the

FIG. 3.2 *Karen schoolchildren with a sign that says "Forest is water; water is life. Return life to the forest, return life to yourself."*

heart of genuine Karen identity—for self-sufficient and subsistence-oriented production. Much of the recent work on the Karen seeks to demonstrate that the economy is based on producing rice and vegetables for household consumption, and that cultural precepts and cautionary tales reflect the "highly-regarded value of self subsistence" (Montree et al. 1992:167). For example, one account argues that "Karen society, both in the past and at present, is a society that concentrates on production for consumption in the household. . . . Farmers thus plant rice or protect rice varieties according to their own likes and dislikes" (Thirayut and Phonphana 1996:36–37). This account explicitly contrasts Karen cultivation with other agricultural systems where decisions are "determined by market fluctuations." This subsistence orientation is also commonly linked to sophisticated systems of local ecological wisdom and an array of customs, prohibitions, and rituals that carefully regulate the selection of land for *rai mun wian* cultivation. The overall outcome of Karen cultural values is that "land is used in a way that is consistent with the forest ecosystem and which also protects long-lasting systems of production"(Kunlawadi 1997:29).

"A LOVE OF THE LAND"

NGO activists have often used the image of Karen environmental benevolence in popular media. The following is an extract from a 1997 article in the *Bangkok Post*:

> The life of Karens is closely linked to nature. Our traditions, beliefs, and tales all reflect our respect for nature. . . . By reviving our folk wisdom and practices that enhance forest conservation, the hill communities won't have to be uprooted and the forest can thrive. The Karen's respect for nature is evident in their farming-related ceremonies year round to pay homage to the spirits of fire, water, soil, mountain, trees and ancestors to protect their crops and bless them. The Karen's legends, which are often told at bedtime to children, are rich in stories concerning nature and wildlife with a stress on the necessity for humans and nature to live in harmony. According to the Karen's customs, newly-wed couples are prohibited from shooting birds and the husbands of pregnant women cannot hunt animals or cut down trees. It is believed such acts may harm the babies. Many trees and animals in their folktales cannot be harmed either for fear of bad luck. (Karnjariya 1997; see also Supara 2002a and Sanitsuda 1999)

> And in 2003 the Thai Airways in-flight magazine carried an article entitled "A love of the land" (Mecir 2003). The article, which was lavishly illustrated with Karen in traditional dress, concluded: "Thus to the Karen, the dictates of conservation and those of the world beyond merge: a tree cannot be cut down because it embodies a person's soul, a patch of forest in an environmentally sensitive watershed area must not be cleared because the resident spirit would surely be angry. And as an old Karen poem says, all things under the sky are bound together."

Of course, it is now well recognized in the literature on the Karen that there have been significant changes in these "traditional" forms of production as a result of both market penetration and state intervention. The process of market penetration into the Karen villages of the Mae Khan catchment is described in the seminal study by Uraivan and colleagues (1988). Early on in the process, they suggest, cash-starved Karen were drawn into the market economy by the lure of consumer goods offered on credit by "shop keepers and merchant traders aspir[ing] to optimize market potential" (Uraivan et al. 1988:101). Cash crops were grown to repay the debts incurred and to provide the wherewithal for future purchases. Subsistence rice production was undermined as rice fields were converted to cash crops such as taro and soybeans. Villagers could now buy rice and consumer durables from traders. Debts mounted as fertilizer and pesticide were poured into the production of cash crops in the hope of realizing higher levels of market income. Ultimately, many Karen lost their land to moneylenders, local investors, or commercially successful and expansive cultivators in neighboring communities. Those who retained their land faced declining productivity under new regimes of intensive cropping. "Despite despair and indebtedness," they conclude, "commodity production is increasing among Karen villagers who are seeking new cash crops with higher market prices" (Uraivan et al. 1988:102).

The state has been blamed for enhancing this upland crisis of commercialization and impoverishment. While Karen communities have received less state attention than their upslope opium-growing neighbors, they have nevertheless received considerable quantities of development aid, especially in districts identified as national security risks. State extension efforts, often aimed at curtailing shifting cultivation, have included a range of subsidies and incentives such as the creation of cash crop demonstration plots; provision of seed, seedlings, and other agricultural inputs; provision of marketing services; construction of paddy fields and irrigation infrastructure; and road improvements. Other statemaking projects have been more coercive. As a result of state forest regulations, many long-resident Karen communities have found themselves located in areas now formally classified (or being prepared to be classified) as forest reserve, conservation forest, or even national park. This has had a dramatic impact on shifting cultivation systems, with the clearing and cultivation of fallow lands greatly restricted in many areas. The effect of state regulations forbidding the felling of trees above a certain minimal girth is that Karen farmers are forced to recultivate fields that have only been fallowed for short periods and where soil fertility is not fully restored. Worse still, local tenure over fallow fields has often been disregarded, as these supposedly "degraded" areas are taken over by reforestation programs run by state watershed management units.

The narrative that has been constructed around the Karen has, then, two major elements. First, there is the idea that genuine or authentic Karen livelihood is based on rotational shifting cultivation, a "forest friendly" system that is underpinned by cultural values that valorize self-sufficiency. Part two of the narrative is a tale of social and environmental decline, as indigenous systems of resource management are disrupted by "externally imposed socio-economic transformation" (Uraivan et al. 1988:86). For many, the future for the Karen lies in a return to more subsistence-oriented forms of economy, a return that is dependent on state recognition of the legitimacy of rotational shifting cultivation and of the resource-management capabilities of Karen communities. Again, as in accounts of the *khon muang*, there is the strong sense that commercial agriculture is fundamentally out of place in the forested upland zones of northern Thailand. Agricultural activities are appropriate in the *pa*, but only when they are subsistence oriented and mimic the ecological diversity of the forest itself. But a central question remains. The key finding of classic anthropological research is that subsistence-oriented systems of shifting cultivation are sustainable "when practiced according to tradition" (Moran 2000:280; see also Vayda 1998). But is a return to tradition viable in the contemporary context?

Hmong

The Hmong are the second-largest upland ethnic minority in northern Thailand, numbering some 73,000 in the far northern provinces, according to government statistics. Hmong farmers have been migrating into northern Thailand—predominantly from Laos—since the latter decades of the nineteenth century and their villages are now scattered throughout the region (figure 3.3 pictures Hmong farmers). A substantial recent in-migration occurred after the 1975 communist victory in Laos—many Hmong having sided with the ousted royal Lao government—and while most refugees ultimately settled overseas, a significant number moved into established Hmong communities in the northern Thai uplands. In the upper north, the largest populations of Hmong are now in Chiang Rai (22,000), Chiang Mai (20,000), and Nan (18,000). Hmong farmers are often resident in the most elevated villages in northern Thailand's upland catchments, though downslope movement in pursuit of economic advantage in the form of paddy fields, fruit orchards, tourism, and rural enterprise is increasingly common.

If the Karen have come to represent the romantic, and sometimes tragic, heroes of the upland environmental narrative, the Hmong are undoubt-

FIG. 3.3 *Hmong farmers in Chiang Mai province*

edly its villains. One of the main reasons for this is the association of the Hmong with the sporadic insurgencies and military conflicts that occurred in northern Thailand in the 1960s and 1970s. The Hmong have found it very hard to shake off the image that they are outsiders whose loyalty to the nation is questionable.

Another important reason is their reputation as opium cultivators. As documented by Geddes (1976) in his classic account of Hmong economy, *Migrants of the Mountains*, poppy cultivation has been a core element of Hmong agricultural practice and the mainstay of Hmong farmers' engagement with external commercial systems. He describes an upland agricultural system in which over 80 percent of the fields were cropped with poppy (often planted after the harvest of a prior maize crop) and about 17 percent with the subsistence rice crop. In a striking contrast to the recent representations of traditional Karen economy, Geddes (1976:131) argues that "direct subsistence agriculture is only a small part of the [Hmong] economy. The major part is the production of opium as a cash crop." Opium was, in many respects, an ideal crop for this upland system. As Renard (2001:3) points out: "Poppy grew well in the hills despite the poor tropical soils there. It required no advanced production technology nor did it need agricultural inputs such as chemical fertilizers or pesticides. . . . Furthermore, opium as a crop had advantages in terms of marketing and handling. No cold storage or sophisticated protection against spoilage was required."

But opium cultivation has long been tainted by illegality and cultural stigma: "The white sap of the opium is collected by the Meo [Hmong] women for pleasurable consumption by the men and also for sale. This is the means by which the selfish husbands are kept as happy as kings" (Boonchuey 1963:99). In the uplands, cultural stigma was compounded by the tendency for Hmong to hire members of other ethnic groups (Karen in particular) to work as laborers in the poppy fields, often paying the addicted workers with opium (P. Cohen 1984a; Cooper 1984:107). Although various branches of the Thai state have, at different times, played a key role in processing and marketing opium, a series of legislative measures have sought to regulate and control its production, and in 1955 a formal ban on the sale and consumption of opium was introduced (Renard 2001:4). Enforcement of anti-opium laws in northern Thailand intensified in the early 1970s, when the Thai government came under pressure from the United States to clamp down on the international drug trade at its agricultural source. Hmong production of opium (and the associated supply of opium and heroin through Thailand from Burma and Laos) came to be stigmatized as a blight on the Thai nation's domestic welfare and international reputation.

As with the Karen, the Hmong have been caught up in the widespread antagonism to shifting cultivation. But, unlike the Karen, the stigma of ecological vandalism is one they have found extremely hard to shake off. In academic and popular accounts of upland agriculture, the Hmong are stereotypically associated with pioneer (rather than rotational) shifting cultivation, an agricultural system in which new fields are cleared from "virgin" forest, farmed intensively for a few years, and then abandoned when reduced soil fertility and weed infestation renders the land unsuitable for further cultivation (Grandstaff 1980). This pioneer method of cultivation is triply stigmatized. First, it is strongly associated with opium production. Second, it is seen as being particularly destructive of forest resources, moving ever onward in its pioneering quest for new areas of virgin forest to fell, burn, cultivate, and abandon. In pioneer cultivation there appear to be none of the complex systems of fallow management found in rotational systems:

> The communities remove most of the trees, dig out rootstock and stumps, and burn the entire swidden areas. They then farm these fields for 2–3 years

or until the soil's fertility is badly depleted and weeds such as *Imperata* grass invade. Abandoning the plots in an ecologically disturbed, inhibited state of succession, upland tribals rarely attempt to return one day to reutilize them. Instead they move on to clear new vulnerable uplands, repeating the process of forest overexploitation, degradation, and conversion to grassland. (Poffenberger and McGean 1993)

And third, as the above statement indicates, this is an agricultural system that depends on mobility—it is the antithesis of the irrigated paddy fields of the lowland *muang*. As Pinkaew (1999) has argued, the Thai term *rai luan looy* (literally, moving and floating upland cultivation) conveys the sense that this is an ungovernable, unstable directionless and disordered form of agricultural activity, and this imagery resonates with broader security concerns about the loyalty of minority upland groups.

Given both of these upland ills—opium production and pioneer shifting cultivation—the Hmong have come to be a key target for development intervention. Reforming the agricultural practices of the Hmong (and others using similar techniques) has been a key justification for many projects of statemaking in the hills. Since the 1960s, a series of development projects run by Thai government agencies, the Thai king's Royal Project Foundation, the United Nations, international bilateral aid agencies, and NGOs have sought to transform Hmong agricultural systems (Renard 2001). While there is considerable diversity in their specific objectives, methodologies, and philosophies, an overriding goal has been to promote the production of opium-replacement cash crops on permanent, rather than shifting, fields: "The long-term policy was to provide development and welfare service to highlanders to stabilize their residence and livelihood, discourage them from growing opium poppy and replace opium with other crops, cease deforestation and contribute to the nation in a manner expected of citizens" (Wanat 1989:16).

State incentives such as the provision of local education and welfare services—sometimes combined with military or police coercion—have sought to encourage residential consolidation in relatively accessible fixed settlements. Agricultural extension efforts have promoted an array of cash crop alternatives (such as kidney beans, cabbages, potatoes, cut flowers, and strawberries) and have provided a suite of agricultural inputs to support their production. And infrastructure initiatives have provided roads, school buildings, fishponds, paddy fields, domestic and agricultural water supply systems, erosion control measures, and highland research stations. Of course the Hmong have not been the exclusive target of upland development, but they have received a disproportionate level of attention and their agricultural practices are, for many, representative of the "hilltribe problem" that development interventions have set out to address.

There is a considerable diversity of views in relation to the impact of these upland development programs. Some argue that the programs have been successful because they have dramatically reduced opium production. Since the 1960s, opium production has plummeted from an estimated peak of almost 18,000 hectares to a relatively trivial 330 hectares in 2000 (Renard 2001:36). It is also clear that pioneer shifting cultivation has almost completely disappeared and that Hmong agriculture is now characterized by intensive cultivation in fixed fields. At a more specific level, some writers have claimed development programs have helped Hmong farmers adapt from a shifting cultivation system already facing critical resource and demographic constraints in the 1970s to the intensive production of high-value fruit and vegetable crops. Teerparp (1996), for example, eloquently describes how the Hmong's quality of life has improved because of the foresight and benevolence of the Royal Project Foundation's opium replacement initiatives. Describing vast fields of cabbages and carrots in a Hmong village near Khun Yuam, Teerparp (1996:42) notes: "Many families have pickup trucks (which they bought with cash, they do not make partial repayments like we do) to take their produce to market. The children have a school and their standard of living is in some ways better than that enjoyed by many children who live in large towns." Similar sentiments are conveyed in an assessment of "sustainable highland agricultural systems" undertaken by Kanok and colleagues (1994:56). In their discussion of the Hmong village of Pah Poo Chom, they refer to the "extreme poverty" of the village in the 1970s with low opium yields—resulting in part from land competition with neighboring villages—and high levels of opium addiction. By contrast, "Pah Poo Chom is today a relatively prosperous village" supporting almost double its 1970s population. This is attributed in significant part to external agency support for the development of flat-land agriculture—on a site where irrigation was possible—and the introduction of agricultural alternatives, especially lychee trees.

But there are strongly contrasting perspectives. A common criticism is that opium replacement initiatives caused substantial hardship when "extension work preceded market planning" (Chupinit 1989:69) and crop

substitutors found that there was no market, or even means of trans-
portation, for their newly adopted crops. "It became very clear," Tapp
(1989:59) observed, "that these crops, such as beans or potatoes, many
of which the Hmong have always grown, cannot be called 'cash crops'
if there is no market for them." He goes on to suggest that the "arbitrary
markets" established by development agencies were unsustainable given
the dependence on "massive external subsidization." But there is also a
more fundamental critique. Some have argued that the "assimilationist"
logic of upland development efforts reflect a chauvinistic lowland Thai
perspective about appropriate forms of livelihood and the desired attributes of a loyal citizenry. Tapp (1989:64) writes that the disproportionate
focus of government policy on the Hmong is interpreted by the farmers
themselves "as evidence of a fundamental ethnic hostility and antagonism towards them." The "underlying aim" of development projects,
according to Tapp (1989:38)—and this is an influential view shared by
many other critics of upland development—"has been to integrate and
assimilate, if not destroy, the culture which differs from the majority of
the state, and to deprive it of its economic base." At the same time, the
argument is made that the transition away from opium was largely an
internal Hmong initiative and that many of the most successful opium-
substitution crops were adopted as a result of farmer-to-farmer extension rather than development intervention (Renard 2001:61; Tapp
1989:58–59)

Furthermore, many critics have alleged that the upland development
programs have negatively affected the upland environment as well as
Hmong society. Since the 1990s, commercially oriented Hmong agriculture has come to be stereotyped as a consumptive assault on fragile
mountain ecosystems with the pejorative imagery of "cabbage mountains"
often deployed. Hmong cash cropping is regularly blamed for ongoing
deforestation, destruction of upstream water sources, erosion, and downstream siltation and contamination of both water sources and agricultural produce. Ironically, the Hmong—having made the transition away
from opium and shifting cultivation—are now accused of continuing,
and even intensifying, the environmental degradation that upland development policy sought to avoid. Charges of catchment degradation have
been taken up with passion—and occasional violence—by some lowland
farmers' groups and are often supported by conservation groups and arms
of the Thai state less sympathetic to the cause of upland development
than some of their colleagues:

Hmong tribespeople who have resettled in Phop Phra district [in Tak province] are destroying forests and dealing in drugs, the government claims. Ladawan Wongsriwong, deputy labour minister, said problems were reported at 19 villages among those which had developed on a 125,000-rai [21,000 hectares] area of deteriorated forest land along the Phop Phra-Umphang highway since 1987 . . . the Hmong were resorting to their "old tricks" at their new home, she said. Her Majesty the Queen had seen the forest destruction in the area during her visit to the villages, and asked Prime Minister Thaksin Shinawatra to take care of the problem. Mrs Ladawan said the locals had destroyed their land with excessive use of chemical fertilisers and pesticides, and in their search for new fertile plots for cultivation had destroyed forest areas around their villages. State agencies must act swiftly to protect the forest which was the villages' only source of water, she said. (Supamart 2001)[9]

In separate incidents in Nan province during 1999 and 2000, lowland Thai people blocked a road leading to Hmong lychee orchards and then eventually burnt many of the trees and a number of dwellings, on the grounds that they were responsible for watershed degradation. The lowlanders were assisted by the Chom Thong Conservation Group from Chiang Mai, which has also been involved in long-term campaigns to relocate upland Hmong farmers (Ploenpote 2000).

Many NGOs and academics sympathetic to the Hmong rightly claim that activities and statements like these are based on ethnically stereotyped and inflammatory rhetoric. But there is often a surprising degree of agreement on basic claims about environmental degradation. This is a clear contrast with the NGO treatment of the Karen. One of the primary objectives of the discourse on Karen rotational shifting cultivation (*rai mun wian*) is to distinguish it from the expansive and mobile pioneer shifting cultivation previously practiced by Hmong opium farmers. While pioneer shifting cultivation of opium is now in the past, this symbolic marking of the Hmong as less ecologically benign adds force to more currently relevant critiques of their commercially oriented "monocropping." For example Pinkaew (2000:60)—one of the most prominent academic critics of state policy in the uplands—argues that "profit striving mono-cropping agriculture" promoted by development schemes in Hmong villages near Chiang Mai "not only separated hill people from the traditional farming, but has also driven them to use extensively the forest lands and chemical pesticides." Of course, comments such as these—made by people who are undoubtedly sympathetic to Hmong interests—attempt to place the blame for the ills of monocropping on external intervention, portraying the Hmong (like the Karen) as victims of inappropriate state development policy. This is another example of the persistent theme that commercialization in the uplands is socially and environmentally inappropriate.

However, the image of Hmong as victim, rather than villain, is problematic. It has to confront the considerable evidence that agricultural transformations such as the adoption of cabbages are the result of internal Hmong initiatives rather than external intervention. It also sits uneasily with the philosophical position held by many activists that emphasizes farmers' agency and adaptive ability in the face of changing conditions. One way that activists have attempted to deal with this dilemma is to adopt the familiar strategy of emphasizing Hmong environmental knowledge and to generate positive ecological images of Hmong communities. As one recent publication states: "in managing forest and natural resources, the Hmong have a life that has always been connected to nature for as long as the Hmong have been people on this earth" (Sawang et al. 2002:110). Paiboon (2003) argues that Hmong farmers have well-established traditions of forest protection. He describes the *ntoo xeeb* ritual as a "sacrifice . . . to ask all the gods to inhabit the trees, own the trees, protect the village's well being" while the *ten hao de* ceremony "aims to extend life of the watershed, beg the guardian spirits to protect the village's watershed and its forests from destructi[on]"(Paiboon 2003:18–19). Hmong villages have also become involved in widespread programs of upland tree "ordination,"[10] emphasizing their links with other upland communities in programs of locally initiated watershed conservation (Paiboon 2003:18). And, perhaps most importantly, some Hmong leaders have emphasized how their communities have adopted supposedly more environmentally benign forms of agriculture:

> We changed our fallow cultivation and poppy fields to fruit orchards because we wanted to faithfully follow Thai state policies. Forestry officers and the government cannot find poppy fields anymore because we transformed our poppy fields into tree orchards, following their objectives. We have done as they wanted. They wanted to see the greenness in the mountains; we have followed that policy by growing our fruit orchards to create forest for them. We think that our fruit orchards in the mountains are no different from the state forestry reforestation of teak or whatever. Moreover, our fruit orchards not only create "greenness" and extend the green areas on the mountains,

but also make people happy with their earnings. That goes along well with what developers and the government want—to improve our living conditions. (Aranya 2006:77)

CONCLUSION

"Hill tribe" is a powerfully selective category that associates the upland environment with ethnic minorities that have culturally distinctive lifestyles. But lowland Thai also play an important role in the upland environment, though these lowland Thai are differently situated in the region's environmental narratives than are the Karen and the Hmong. Three main stereotypes are at work: the paddy cultivating *khon muang*, the forest-dwelling Karen, and the cash-cropping Hmong. These are simplified narrative constructions that reflect underlying values about desirable (and undesirable) upland lifestyles. The stereotypical images of ethnic groups support the simplified messages of environmental narratives and these, in turn, feed back into ethnic representations.

OTHER GROUPS IN THE UPLANDS

Besides the Karen and the Hmong, the other main upland groups are the Lawa, Mien (often referred to as Yao), Lahu, Akha, and Lisu. Lawa settlement in the region is thought to have predated the arrival of the *khon muang*, whereas the other groups are more recent settlers, having migrated from Burma and Laos over the past 150 years. The combined population of these various groups is estimated at about 285,000 (Social Welfare Department 1995). These upland groups are also associated with various forms of shifting cultivation, in some cases intermediate between the rotational agriculture of the Karen and the pioneer cultivation of the Hmong. However, the recent trend toward more intensive permanent cultivation is as evident among these groups as it is among the Hmong and Karen. Though less prominent, these smaller groups are also brought into environmental narratives in varying ways. For example, one recent coffee-table book about the Akha was romantically called *Akha: Guardians of the Forest* (Goodman 1997), referring to their reputation for protecting forest zones close to their villages for spiritual purposes.

To a large degree, the stereotypical ways these groups have been represented are still informed by the persistent cultural distinction between *muang* and *pa*, outlined at the beginning of chapter 2. In the narratives informed by this distinction the lowland *muang* are the appropriate places for intensive agriculture, supported by long-term investment in irrigation systems. The paddy field, covered in a lush green carpet of rice, is the central image of desirable agricultural activity. By contrast, views about agricultural presence in the upland *pa* are much more ambivalent. A hardline view is that agricultural presence is unacceptable, as reflected, for example, in the longstanding suggestion by some observers that any form of shifting cultivation is unacceptable, and a persistent policy emphasis on relocation or strict demarcation of agricultural lands. By contrast, a much more moderate view argues that agricultural presence is not only acceptable but desirable given its contribution to complex systems of ecological diversity. This is the alternative imagery that has been constructed around the Karen in response to official condemnation of shifting cultivation systems. But, in this alternative perspective, the emphasis on forest-friendly activity remains—and it seems likely that this has been deliberately exaggerated to avoid the accusation that supporting upland residence implies a tolerance of environmental degradation. The uplands are still seen as the domain of the *pa* and agriculture is acceptable provided that it blends in with the forested environment. There is little place in this vision for commercial agriculture, which is regularly condemned as disrupting the delicate upland balance between cultural and natural systems. Commerce, it seems, belongs in the lowland *muang* and is out of place in the wild *pa*.

Of course, this is the narrative that has proved so challenging for the Hmong. The strongly commercial orientation of many Hmong agricultural systems is under attack from conservationists, state forest regulators, and advocates of subsistence-oriented upland livelihoods. Belated attempts have been made to recast the Hmong in more environmentally friendly terms, but this has had little impact on altering widespread stereotypes.

So, how can upland people be viewed in less predetermined ways, relying less on stereotypes and more on a recognition of the diversity of environmental cause and effect in the uplands? This book argues that environmental narratives and the social and political positioning of upland peoples are mutually connected. Reevaluating how environmental change is seen will affect the classification of social groups, and changing narrative-driven views of social groups will result in different forms of environmental knowledge. A vital step forward is to look critically at some of the key debates on environmental management in the uplands. There is a pressing need to examine the popular narratives about the impacts of upland agriculture in its various commercial and noncommercial forms. This involves looking critically at the different elements of environmental debate to determine what political objectives derive authority from simplified narratives; how environmental blame is selectively attributed to certain social groups; and how complex environmental processes are reduced to assured statements of cause and effect.

4 *Forests and Water*

IN TRADITIONAL THAI WORLDVIEWS the wild forest (*pa*) was perceived in largely negative terms as a place of danger, illegality, and cultural lack. The *pa* was a place physically and symbolically remote from the lowland settlements (*muang*). Of course, this imagery has not been erased, but there is now much more frequent emphasis on the desirable attributes of the forest and on the interrelationship between *muang* and *pa*. In the reframing of the *pa*, the forested uplands are now seen as a source of natural resources and environmental services. In the popular imagination the key resource provided by the forest is water.

Motorists on mountain roads in northern Thailand are constantly reminded of this relationship between forests and water. Numerous roadside signs—many erected by the Royal Forest Department—remind those passing of the environmental and livelihood benefits to be derived from forest protection in the uplands. In this discursive project of statemaking, particular emphasis is given to the role of forests in maintaining the nation's hydrological health (figure 4.1). On a spectacularly forested and winding section of road to the west of Chiang Mai, for example, a series of rustic signs declare: "if you love the country you have to love forests"; "if the soil loses forest, the sky loses rain and people lose their hearts"; "if the forest is destroyed the soil is dry—the forest is the source of water"; "if the forest disappears the earth is dry, rain disappears and the rice dies"; and "the streams will dry out if the covering shade of the forest is lost" (A. Walker fieldwork 2003). The roadside exercise in civic education is interrupted somewhat by advertisements for fertilizer and agricultural chemicals, but it climaxes in a ridgetop display of nationalist symbolism at the

87

FIG. 4.1 *"The people and the state cooperate to return clear water to the Sa River." Note the water cascading out of the forest and the very traditional village.*

entrance to the Royal Forest Department's watershed management unit. Beneath a cluster of Thai flags and the royal crest, passing motorists are reminded of the role of forest cover in ensuring a "sustainable Thailand."

Various forms of knowledge underlie claims about the relationship between forests and water supply. Clearly, there is considerable disagreement about the best strategies for the management of upland forests in northern Thailand. But, at the same time, there are also broad agreements on certain environmental assumptions (or narratives), especially the importance of forests in maintaining the hydrological health of local and national catchment systems. A strong discourse coalition has emerged, based on the notion that there is a symbiotic relationship between forests and water supply. This relationship has become a widely accepted part of the knowledge and aesthetic of upland Thai landscapes, and the road-side claims of the Royal Forest Department are echoed in the statements of academics, NGOs (both "conservationist" and "people-oriented"), and many farmers. There are two key elements of this hydrological knowledge to explore critically: the claim that forest cover ensures reliable rain-fall; and the claim that forests are catchment "sponges" that store wet-season rainfall and release it steadily during the dry season. These particular forms of knowledge have played a significant role in northern Thailand's most famous environmental dispute.

ELEMENTS OF HYDROLOGICAL KNOWLEDGE

Forests as a Source of Rainfall

At a conference in Chiang Mai in 1999, the director general of the Royal Forest Department spoke of the national importance of forest conservation.[1] One of his main arguments was that, unlike countries in South Asia that could rely on Himalayan snowmelt, Thailand's water supplies were secured by its forested upland catchments. His argument can be summed up in the popular environmental slogan *mi pa, mi fon* (literally, have forest, have rain). Specifically, the argument is that forests create a climatologically moist zone in which rainfall is relatively abundant. In more technical terms this can be expressed as the claim that relatively high rates of evapotranspiration from forested areas enhance local precipitation.[2] This climatological knowledge is backed by popular imagery in which upland forested zones are regularly portrayed as environments of mist, low-lying clouds, and steady rain, with abundant streams coursing through verdant landscapes (such images are also used in television advertisements for products such as Thai beer when the advertisers want to invoke heritage and national pride).

The belief that forest clearing reduces rainfall has widespread appeal. To start with one local example, a taxi driver in Chiang Mai spoke vividly about how he had given up agricultural work and come to look for a living in the city due to the lack of rain (A. Walker fieldwork 2002). "When I was young," he reported "there was no dry season at all, it used to rain all year and we could grow two crops. The irrigation canals were open all year, now they are only open sometimes." Looking around at the dry and dusty urban landscape of concrete buildings and car parks he commented: "in the past everything was green, now all we have is dryness." But why has the weather changed? His answer was unambiguous: "lots of forest has been cut down to build houses; now all we have is development." This sense that forest loss brought about by modernization has resulted in regional desiccation appears to be widespread. Farmers consulted about changing agricultural conditions in northern Thailand regularly suggest that rainfall is no longer as reliable as it used to be, often failing to arrive "according to the season." In Samoeng district, to the

A reading primer distributed by the Ministry of Education in upland areas declares in one of its lessons: "The forest helps the rain fall. When the rain falls the plants become beautiful." The message is reinforced later in the book when a "cooperative thinking exercise" asks: "Is it true that a lot of forest makes it rain a lot? What is the reason?" The lessons are accompanied by illustrations of appropriate upland Thai lifestyles (Damri et al. 1999).

west of Chiang Mai, farmers comment that the local area is warming up and drying out, becoming more like the city of Chiang Mai and losing its cool and moist ambience (A. Walker fieldwork 2003). Hirsch encountered similar views during his 1980s fieldwork in the lower north of Thailand:

> According to the reports of early settlers, rainfall in Lan Sak before defor-estation was fairly consistent and extended over more months of the year than it does now. . . . Deforestation has caused a radical change in the local hydrological cycle. Locally rainfall is now inconsistent and, according to vil-lagers, extends over a shorter period. . . . As a result agriculture has become a marginal and risky activity where previously there was a great deal more certainty. (Hirsch 1990:75)

And the claim is circulated in various forms of popular culture. A 1999 Chiang Mai magazine for tourists, for example, had an article sensa-tionally titled, "There's no doubt—it's a drought!" which claimed that, "the bottom line is forests decimated by excessive tree felling and land denuded by slash-and-burn agriculture severely reduce cloud forma-tions—and thus rainfall, the main cause of Thailand's drought" (Tham-masak and Hardy 1999).

A number of scientific studies have lent their support to the view that rainfall has declined. Nipon (1994), for example, cites a study that found "sharp decreases" in annual rainfall in northern Thailand. Giambelluca and Ziegler (1996:18) cite another study that concluded that annual rain-fall may have declined by as much as 15 percent in the northern region between the 1950s and 1990s. Similarly, a study by Wongvitavas found that there had been a "sharp decrease" in rain in a number of regions of

Thailand, including the north (cited in Mingtipol et al. 2002:31). And, finally, a major Japanese-Thai research project also links deforestation with rainfall decline, suggesting there has been a "remarkable" decline in September rainfall between 1951 and 1994 (Matsumoto 2003).

The Forest Sponge

A second element of popular hydrological knowledge is that forested upland soils act as a "sponge"—absorbing and storing water during the wet season and releasing it slowly during the dry season. This particular version of hydrological knowledge has been expressed in many different contexts, and in many other countries as well. In Chiang Mai province, a prominent, and royally sponsored, forest protection project adopts this version of hydrological knowledge, framing it in explicitly nationalistic terms:

> Everyone knows that forest is the source of water for all people who live on Thai soil. We do not have any other source of water in Thailand . . . [the forest] provides for underground water storage, making the ground moist as a benefit for all people. . . . The result of cutting forest is the destruction of the water source of the Thai people. (Suan Pa Sirikit 1999)

A similar account, though focusing on the community rather than the nation, is provided by a prominent northern NGO, the Northern Development Foundation:

> Vast humid forests bring rain. Some of the water from the rain washes fertilizer from decomposed leaves down into the fields, paddies, and orchards. The rest is absorbed by the forest and slowly released for the community to use all year, forming streams and creeks that flow unhindered into rivers. (NDF 1996:9)

And the International Board for Soil Research and Management (1997:51) adds some scientific authority to this particular hydrological model in their report on one of their case study subcatchments:

> The catchment is under high forest cover and the soil is covered by grass, bark, and litter, that is, it is well protected. Soils are very spongy with a lot of organic matter (>3.5%). . . . This watershed functions like a sponge, absorb-

ing water during the rainy season, and with a long period of seepage into streams during the rest of the dry season.

Flood and Drought as the Sponge Is Destroyed

The flip side of the "forest as sponge" theory is the view that forest clearing has caused both wet-season flooding and dry-season water shortage. Intensive agricultural cultivation is seen as having a particularly negative impact on the forested soils that comprise the catchment sponge. It is regularly argued that as agricultural activity expands at the expense of forest, the absorptive spongelike property of the humus-rich forest floor is lost. This argument claims that exposed and chemically treated soils become compressed and intensive cultivation causes them to lose much of their organic content. Accordingly, rates of soil infiltration decline and rates of surface runoff increase, often causing flooding in the wet season and leaving less soil moisture available to contribute to dry-season flow:

> Northern farmers who depend on the downstream flow of water for their livelihoods claim the rivers are drying up and they point the finger of blame at the hilltribe farmers. . . . Dr Suchira Prayoonpitack, a Chiang Mai University sociologist, said the watershed forests of the North can no longer absorb and hold water. "Several decades ago, fertile forests served as natural water catchments and reservoirs," Dr Suchira explained. These catchments prevent floods during the rainy season, and are a source of water during the dry season. But the rapid diminishing of the forest has caused floods in the rainy season and drought in the dry season. (Supradit 1997a)

Flooding. Over the past twenty years a number of widely publicized events have contributed to the belief that hydrological imbalance arises from forest clearing. Probably the most famous, and influential, case occurred in Nakhon Si Thammarat in southern Thailand in November 1988 when torrential monsoon rains triggered disastrous flash flooding and mudslides. Torrents of water, mud, and trees—many of which were already felled logs awaiting transport—cascaded down from the mountains, sweeping away villages in the unfortunate Phiphun district. The United Nation's humanitarian report on this event was stark: "430 people dead, over 1,000 still missing, 958 injured, 600,000 affected. Damage to 435,000 houses, over 300 government offices including hospitals, 550 schools, 139 temples. Heavy damage also on bridges, irrigation, mines and roads. 300,000 ha of farmland destroyed and 137,000 animals dead" (United Nations Department of Humanitarian Affairs 1988).

This occurred at a time when many politicians and NGOs had been campaigning for a ban on logging, and the shocking events in Nakhon Si Thammarat gave activists an added opportunity to target deforestation. As one report noted, "uncontrolled logging was blamed for many of the deaths caused by recent floods" (quoted in Dartmouth Flood Observatory 2003). The report stated that in the areas where most of the casualties occurred "mud, logs and trees cascaded down denuded hills, slamming into houses and burying villages." The event had major national repercussions, prompting the national logging ban that was declared in January 1989 and the government decision soon after that 25 percent of the country would be set aside as conservation forest. Many observers claimed the logging ban would also improve water supply and address concerns about rainfall (*Bangkok Post* 1989b). When the logging ban was passed, the *Bangkok Post* welcomed it as a "welcome reprieve for [the] nation's forests" and stated,

> People . . . tended to regard forests as something given free by Mother Nature. . . . It was only when Nature struck back that the country was violently shaken out of its state of complacency and naivete. The devastating floods which wrought havoc in the southern provinces, especially in Nakhon Si Thammarat, late last year served as a dire warning of climatic change, partially attributable to massive deforestation in the region. Elsewhere, in the Northeast, drought has struck several provinces successively over the past few years, driving tens of thousands of young men and women out of their impoverished villages and into the cities to look for new hope. (*Bangkok Post* 1989a)

Despite the national conservation measures, a similar disaster occurred in 2001. During the wet season there was widespread flooding throughout northern Thailand, but the situation was most severe in Phetchabun province where about forty people were killed when flash floods and mudslides again swept through downstream villages. Villagers received little warning, saying that they heard a sound like an "elephant screaming" before houses were swept away (BBC News 2001). Again, deforestation was quickly identified as the prime culprit; however this time the target was not rampant logging but agricultural clearing undertaken by upland farmers:

A forestry officer yesterday blamed shifting cultivation by Hmong villagers in Phetchabun's highlands for deforestation leading to this week's flash floods in Lom Sak district. "The forest covers only 30% of the province's area while a large area was occupied by the hilltribes who have farmed on the mountains for a decade. Nan, Chiang Rai, and Phayao are also flood-prone areas because they have no more than 30% of forest cover left, compared to 70% in Tak and Mae Hong Son, and 68% in Chiang Mai" said Mr. Thavee yesterday. The provinces where hilltribe people lived usually do not have much forest left, so these provinces were the most at risk. (Kultida 2001)

A team of researchers sent to survey the impacts of deforestation in the area concluded that "mountains forming the Pa Sak valley as well as waterways originating in Phrae have undergone drastic changes. . . . The water-absorbent terrain on high slopes has been cleared of trees that held top soil to allow the cultivation of seasonal crops. The whole river valley is at a high risk of potentially fatal landslides" (*The Nation* 2001).

Dry-Season Water Shortage. Over the past decade there have also been a series of drought events that have heightened public concerns about the scarcity of water resources. Throughout the country's major irrigation districts, dry-season farmers have been urged to grow water-saving crops or to abandon cultivation altogether given concerns about low dam levels (Pennapa 2004; Kultida 2004a; Ward 2002). What is notable is how readily these concerns about lowland water supply have been linked to upland deforestation. In 1999, the director general of the Royal Forest Department argued that flows in the Chao Phraya River, "the central region's lifeline," could decline "drastically over the next seven years unless there is a quick end to deforestation in upstream watershed areas." He predicted that deforestation in the Nan catchment could reduce flow in that major tributary from 11 billion cubic meters to around 7 billion cubic meters and that annual waterflow in the Yom River could decline from 3.7 billion cubic meters to a little over 2 billion (cited in Prasong and Gilmour 1999). During the drought of 2004, the head of the Royal Irrigation Department expressed similar sentiments, arguing that "mother nature's" message was that "the only way to stop this is to bring back the forests." He argued that the alarmingly low water levels in the major northern rivers were "because there is no water flowing from the forests, where a large amount of water is absorbed and stored." He concluded by urging the forestry officials to "work harder on reforestation" (Kultida 2004b).

These national-level concerns are echoed in more localized accounts of water shortage compiled by academics and activist NGOs. Almost invariably, water shortages experienced by downstream farmers during the dry season are attributed to the loss of the forest sponge in upland areas. Accounts of local water shortage regularly assert that watercourses have ceased to flow and springs have dried up due to the clearing of upland forests. Apinyaa (2001:35–37) provides a typical account of local forest protection in Lamphun province:

> The villagers came to be aware of the importance of water and protected about 60 *rai* [10 hectares] of forest as watershed forest around the irrigation weir and near where water flowed from the base of the large *takian* tree throughout the year. . . . [But later] the forest became degraded and there were no forest products as before and drought started to visit the villagers . . . again. . . . So the villagers agreed to expand the areas of protected forest for their children and grandchildren.

Chusak and Dearden (1999:682) provide a similar account:

> Thung Kao Hang is a village . . . in the upper part of the Li watershed, an important source of water for the fertile rice growing areas downstream. . . . Efforts to exert more control over local resources began only after the richly forested areas around the village had been mostly destroyed by logging and shifting cultivators and the villagers began to experience severe water shortages.

And, again, this time from Phayao province to the north:

> Meanwhile, local people in the downstream areas were threatened by water shortages, brought on by the earlier reduction in forest area. This raised awareness of the importance of the forest as a source of water for agriculture. . . . Most villagers in the area know that the natural forests remaining within the boundary of the Sritoy commune have been protected and managed by villagers to conserve water for agriculture and domestic consumption. . . . Community-based programmes for forest protection aimed at water conservation were established primarily because of the need to control water supplies for paddy and cash crop production in the downstream communities, as their survival was threatened by water scarcity resulting from deforestation and watershed degradation. (Jintana and Routray 1998:283, 286, 289)

The political potency of this popular narrative about forest clearing and water shortage has been highlighted in the case of the famous—and now iconic—dispute between *khon muang* and Hmong farmers in Chom Thong district of Chiang Mai province. One of the leaders associated with this dispute was the controversial monk Phra Phongsak Techadhammo, who is said to have spent some time in the 1970s meditating in a cave in the Mae Soi valley—in the uplands of Chom Thong—near where the Hmong village of Pa Kluay had recently been established. This was said to be an area that was "covered with dense forest [and] seamed with watercourses" (Nelson 1990:8). These forests were said to have "matched some of the greatest in the whole Doi Inthanon mountain range, and the water flowed in the . . . streams all year round" (Anon. 2003). However, returning in the 1980s Phra Phongsak was shocked by the level of forest clearing and the "dire effects" on downstream farmers. The Mae Soi had "dried out completely" and "crop failure was almost universal, livestock died of starvation and dehydration, and farmers were forced further into debt" (ibid.). These problems were quickly attributed by Phongsak and lowland farmers to upland farming by Hmong villagers. This farming had intensified during the 1980s as a result of the opium substitution activities of the Thai-Norwegian Church Aid organization combined with independent Hmong adoption of cabbage cultivation.[3]

As a response to the crisis, Phra Phongsak dedicated himself to watershed forest protection: "When we began to instruct the villagers in 1985," he wrote, "their future was hopeless, because the water was completely gone. All of their land was unfarmable. If we hadn't started caring for the forest . . . it would have been a desert" (quoted in Anon. 2003). It soon became clear where Phongsak stood in the emerging debate about the appropriate role of upland communities in forest management: "Man coexisting with the forest: that's a romantic idea, little more than wishful thinking. People still talk about it because that's the way they'd like things to be. The hill tribe population is growing rapidly. They don't just farm to live, they farm to sell and with the support of vested interest groups. They have TVs, motorcycles, and cars" (Phongsak, quoted in Fahn 2003:145).

Phra Phongsak rapidly built up a support base among lowland villagers who complained about water shortages in their orchards and paddy fields (see figure 4.2). The membership of the Watershed and Forest Conserva-

FIG. 4.2 *Farmers in Chom Thong showing a dry and sediment-filled stream to visiting researchers*

tion Group he formed in 1983 is said to have expanded dramatically from only 2,000 in 1986 to an implausible 90,000 in 1989 (Anon. 2003). In 1984, a group of his supporters, including M.R. Smansnid Svasti,[4] a member of the extended Thai royal family, formed the Dhammanaat Foundation for Conservation and Rural Development (Pinkaew 2000:63; Normita 1989). With international backing, and practical support from the Royal Forest Department, Dhammanaat has put in place a wide range of watershed protection measures: tree planting, forest patrols, firebreak construction, and fire-fighting programs along with construction of small dams and irrigation systems (Nelson 1990:9). The foundation's activities in one of the Mae Soi subcatchments have been hailed as a "model for watershed restoration projects elsewhere in Thailand" (Julian 2003) and have been featured in highly positive and somewhat romantic terms by some Western media.[5] Some observers claimed that the hydrological effects of forest protection and restoration were dramatic: "For the past two years, the Mae Soi River has flowed, even in the dry season. This is in contrast to the eight other rivers in the district that all dried up during the same period" (Julian 2003).[6]

Forest conservation activities have been combined with more overtly political action that has been directed primarily at the Hmong, whose agricultural activities were seen as the main cause of catchment degradation. Political activities have concentrated on calls for relocation of the Hmong village of Pa Kluay which is located in the mountains above Chom Thong (Nantiya 1990). As Pinkaew (2000:60) has argued, Dhammanaat's core concept of *sinlatham*, "which focuses on the balance of all living things and their mutual dependence and coexistence," does not seem to extend to upland farmers. This is especially the case when those farmers are practicing intensive commercial agriculture. As early as 1986, lowland villagers were reported to have become "so angry that some made threats to burn down the village [of Pa Kluay]" (Renard 1994:663) and, around this time, Hmong villagers suspected lowlanders of being responsible for the theft and killing of upland livestock (Nantaa and Supamaat 1999:22–23). That year, Phongsak led some five hundred villages to build a 14–kilometer barbed-wire fence around forest in the upper Mae Soi catchment as a basic means of protecting it (Pongpet 1990). Sometimes, lowland concern was mixed with resentment that foreign aid had contributed to a damaging transformation of upland agriculture. As M.R. Smansnid Svasti said (quoted in Normita 1989): "These so-called experts come to Thailand to help the country, but what they do is destroy it by abetting the destruction of its resources through their ecologically unsound opium poppy crop substitution programmes."

In the late 1980s and 1990s the dispute in Chom Thong heightened. Intensive lobbying by the lowlanders led the director general of the Royal Forest Department to declare in 1989 that Pa Kluay was the top national priority village for relocation, and that the Hmong farmers in this and two nearby villages would be resettled to Tak province (Panida 1989; Renard 2001:63). Following this, further action was taken to strengthen the barbed-wire fence in Mae Soi, which then surrounded more than 300 hectares of forest and agricultural land, including the fields of almost thirty Hmong farmers (Nantaa and Supamaat 1999:23).[7] Some years later, the fence posts were painted in red, white, and blue stripes—the colors of the Thai flag—as an indication that the fence and the enclosed forest represented an irresolute part of Thailand. In 1998 the campaign for relocation climaxed with the distribution of leaflets accusing the Hmong farmers of destroying the watershed. There were sporadic roadblocks of the roads leading to the upland areas. This active campaign has been backed by "research papers" demonstrating that the Hmong community "damaged the forest and created problems for downstream farmers" (Kamol 2000; see also Pinkaew 2000). Despite such pressures, however, the Hmong villages were not relocated, partly as a result of growing concerns about the effectiveness of resettlement, and partly because of opposition from the highly respected Royal Project Foundation that had sought to achieve sustainable upland agriculture without resettlement.

The Chom Thong dispute is an iconic dispute for various reasons. It is mostly associated with lowland farmers' fears about the impacts of upland agriculture on water supply, but also refers to disputes about soil erosion and sedimentation. The dispute has also highlighted different approaches within the highest echelons of Thai society toward upland minorities: both the Dhammanaat Foundation and the Royal Project Foundation have been administered or supported by members of the extended Thai royal family, yet each has taken radically different approaches to resettlement and upland agricultural development.[8] There are also deeper themes about the way environmental change is presented and environmental knowledge used. For example, the Chom Thong dispute has tended to divide observers into two mutually exclusive camps— one emphasizing the ecological fragility of upland watersheds and the other focusing on the rights of highland farmers. The conservationist followers of Phra Phongsak have used nationalism as a metaphor for the need to protect fragile upland forest and to dismiss the expertise of national or foreign advisers. According to some observers, this nationalism has readily slipped into racism against the Hmong (Lohmann 1999). Meanwhile, international environmentalists (Van Beld 1991 and Fahn 2003:143) have tended to represent the campaign in romantic terms as representative of a "local" grassroots response by lowland farmers to environmental degradation. Both international and Thai environmentalists further legitimize their campaign by accusing opponents of seeking to weaken national forest protection. Most fundamentally, however, the Chom Thong case is an important illustration of the way in which popular hydrological narratives are deployed in political disputes, focusing blame selectively and justifying repressive action. These hydrological narratives draw on, and reinforce, popular ethnic stereotypes that paint the Hmong as the villains of upland degradation and the *khon muang* as its victims.

QUESTIONING CONVENTIONAL BELIEFS

The Chom Thong dispute is well known, but it is certainly not an isolated case. Condemnations of upland agriculture are routinely linked to concerns about the hydrological impacts of forest clearing. Similarly, the nationwide system of watershed classification is motivated primarily by a desire to preserve forested upland water sources. This system of classification renders vast areas of upland agriculture illegal in the interests of watershed conservation. Given these various political implications it is important that narratives of hydrological crisis be subjected to some critical scrutiny, particularly concerning three related issues: (1) the effects of forests on rainfall; (2) the effects of forests on total streamflow; and (3) the effects of forests on the seasonal distribution of flow (in other words, the impact of forest clearing on wet-season flooding and dry-season water shortages). The resulting contrasting forms of knowledge highlight the selectivity of popular hydrological narratives and show some of the ways in which narratives reduce complex processes to simplified statements of cause and effect.

Forests and Rainfall

The environmental narrative linking forest loss to reduced rainfall draws on memory, recent experience of rainfall unreliability and drought, the apparent dryness of the concrete city, and some scientific research. But despite regular reference to a past period of more abundant rainfall, it is surprising that there is usually very little consideration of long-term rainfall data, even though this information is readily available from, for example, Thailand's Royal Irrigation Department.[9] These data have to be treated with some caution given incomplete record keeping and, in many cases, rather short-term data series. Nevertheless, there are a number of locations where relatively complete data series dating from the 1920s are available (figure 4.3). What does this information suggest about trends in rainfall over this period? Consistent with popular claims about deforestation, the data from some locations do suggest a long-term decline in rainfall. This is evident in the minor downward trends in the data from Doi Saket and Chiang Mai. However, the data from other locations such as Fang, Khun Yuam, Mae Hong Son, and, interestingly, Chom Thong suggest a long-term increase. Taken as a whole, the data suggest long-term stability in levels of precipitation, despite very substantial reductions in forest cover. Only a very selective reading of the data could support the claim that deforestation has led to reductions in levels of rainfall. Enters (1995:95) has arrived at a similar conclusion, arguing that there were "no statistically significant changes [in precipitation] between 1927 and 1989." Similarly, Nipon (1994:28) cites a study conducted in northeast Thailand to the effect that "yearly statistical analyses showed an insignificant relationship between monthly, seasonal and annual rainfall patterns and the remaining forest areas. In other words there was no correlation between the rainfall parameter and the percentage of remaining forest area." And a further study found no changes in rainfall totals or patterns in the 12,100–square-kilometer Nam Pong basin in northeastern Thailand between 1957 and 1995, despite a decrease in forest area from 80 to 27 percent since the 1970s (Wilk et al. 2001).

Forests undoubtedly contribute to atmospheric moisture (due to high rates of evapotranspiration compared to other land uses). So why does considerable forest clearing apparently not lead to a significant reduction in rainfall? The answer to this important question lies in the passage cited from Donner (1978) in chapter 2: the rain that falls in northern Thailand is predominantly monsoonal and derives not from evapotranspiration in northern Thailand itself but from marine sources to the west. Climatological research suggests that the strong maritime influence in Southeast Asia generates a significant degree of climatic stability, which greatly moderates the impact of reduced evaporation caused by forest clearing (Tinker et al. 1996:17–19; Henderson-Sellers 1993:351; Polcher and Laval 1993:118; Calder 1998:3; Chomitz and Kumari 1998).

However, these data do not completely undermine the popular claim that forest clearing has reduced rainfall. Two factors need to be considered, one temporal and the other spatial. In temporal terms there is some evidence that a relatively drier period occurred during the 1980s and 1990s and that this followed a relatively wetter period during the 1970s.[10] Shorter-term analyses of rainfall patterns—and popular recollection—are likely to highlight this declining trend. Importantly, the dryer period during the 1980s and 1990s coincided with a dramatic increase in concern about forest policy in Thailand and it is not surprising that these two key environmental issues—water supply and forest loss—have become linked in public debate and policy discourse. The recent dryer period, however, is by no means unprecedented, with the longer-term data showing a long-standing oscillation between relatively wetter and relatively dryer periods, seemingly independent of the progressive decline in forest cover. The ten-year moving average data in figure 4.3 illustrate this pattern.

Spatial factors are also likely to be important in accounting for the strong cultural association between forests and rainfall. Forested areas in northern Thailand tend to be located at higher altitudes and, as noted in chapter

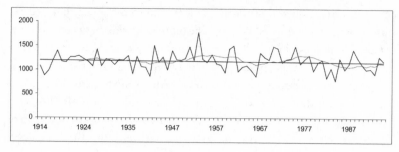

CHIANG MAI

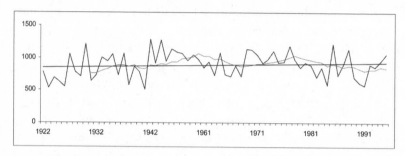

CHOM THONG

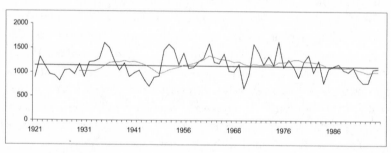

DOI SAKET

NOTE: Rainfall data (in millimeters) were obtained from the Web site of the Royal Irrigation Department (www.rid.go.th). In compiling the graphs, years for which the data are incomplete or clearly erroneous have been deleted.

FIG. 4.3 (pp. 102–3) *Rainfall data from northern Thailand, with long-term trend and ten-year moving average*

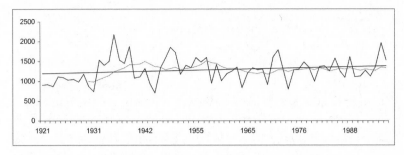

FANG

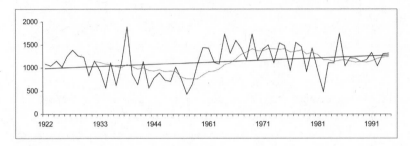

KHUN YUAM

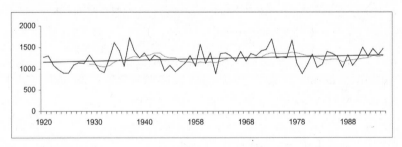

MAE HONG SON

2, these are also the areas that receive the highest rainfall. Why do these areas receive higher rainfall? Primarily because rainfall occurs as warm moist air masses rise to higher and cooler altitudes. The dramatic influence of altitude on rainfall can be demonstrated by a comparison of the rainfall records of Mae Chaem village and Doi Inthanon, which is located only 11 kilometers to the east but almost 2,000 meters higher. In Mae Chaem, rainfall averages around 920 millimeters per year while at the peak of Inthanon the average annual rainfall is over 2,200 millimeters. Clearly, then, the belief that "where there is forest there is rain" has a strong basis

(where there is rain,
there is forest' is more correct

A number of international studies using time-series data or climate simulations have suggested that there is little evidence of a clear relationship between levels of forest cover and rainfall (Bruijnzeel 2004:187–94). One of the earliest studies (Bernard 1953) found no evidence for forests influencing rainfall in the Central Congo basin. Similarly, in Southern India, annual rainfall over the last hundred years has not decreased, despite the general conversion of the dry deciduous forest to agriculture (although long-term data suggests a decline in the number of rainy days) (Meher-Homji 1980). Research in Brazil found that the partial conversion of *cerrado* vegetation (shrubs and scattered trees) to pasture had no effect on rainfall in the Tocantins basin (Costa et al. 2003).

However, some simulation studies suggest that forest clearing of areas between 1,000 and 10,000 square kilometers may cause delays in the formation of clouds (for example, in southwestern Amazonia: Cutrim et al. 1995). But others have suggested that modeled reductions in rainfall in the Amazon "apply only to extreme conditions of complete replacement of forest by grassland over very large areas" (Tinker et al. 1996:19). Global circulation models have suggested that removing forest cover in the entire

in common-sense experience and observation, and the persistence of the narrative is unsurprising. But the higher levels of rainfall in highland areas are a function of altitude rather than forest cover.

Forest Cover and Total Streamflow

For many years, hydrologists have challenged the conventional belief that forests increase total water runoff. They have pointed out that this belief is highly selective and tends to disregard the role of evapotranspiration (consumption of water by the trees) within forests as an important source of water demand (Calder 1999; Bruijnzeel 2004). The level of forest water demand, and the tendency for it to be ignored in popular narrative, is well illustrated in one of northern Thailand's classic forest and water case studies.

In the pathbreaking and influential edited collection, *Farmers in the Forest* (Kunstadter et al. 1978), Thiem reports on an experiment under-

Amazon basin (were it to occur) would result in reduced rainfall in some areas but only by an average of about 0.5 millimeters per day (Rowntree 1988).

Hydrologists have argued that one important factor influencing the relationship between forest cover and rainfall is albedo, the amount of energy reflected back into the atmosphere by vegetation. In most cases, albedo does not change greatly with conversion of forest to other forms of vegetation (Houghton 1990).

There is one situation where local forest clearing does appear to have a clear effect on local precipitation. "Cloud forests" are a type of evergreen mountain forest found in tropical areas where local climatic conditions cause cloud and mist to be regularly in contact with the forest vegetation. In such cloud forests in Asia, cloud-water interception may account for some 5 to 20 percent of ordinary rainfall, and even more in exposed sites such as on coasts (Bruijnzeel 2004:194). Clearing of these forest formations may reduce local precipitation and water supply. However, these forests have very limited distribution in northern Thailand, occurring only at very high altitudes (over 2,000 meters) and perhaps contribute only an additional "50 mm per year of additional annual rainfall in forested areas over and above cleared areas of the same altitude" (Nipon 1994).

taken in Huay Kok Ma, a small forested watershed in Chiang Mai province. He notes that this small 65–hectare watershed, with a rainfall of 1,938 millimeters, was able to deliver 481,825 cubic meters of water to the Ping River network. "This suggests," he writes "the importance of preserving permanently all the forests in the land category as watershed protection in the source areas of essential water supplies" (Thiem 1978:68). At first glance, the numbers look impressive, and statistics like this are often drawn upon to support the widespread claim that forests help to secure downstream water supplies. However, some simple mathematics raise intriguing questions. Assuming that precipitation is uniform over the watershed area (a reasonable assumption given the small size of the catchment), the total amount of rain falling on the watershed amounted to 1,259,700 cubic meters (650,000 square meters of catchment multiplied by 1.938 meters of rainfall). With a discharge of only 481,825 cubic meters (only 38 percent of the total rainfall) it seems that Huay Kok Ma has almost 800,000 cubic meters worth of explaining to do.

Where did all the water in Huay Kok Ma go? The usual culprits in the hydrological crisis narrative—forest-clearing upland cultivators—have the perfect alibi: this was a fully forested catchment "covered with dense vegetation of the Hill Evergreen (Lower Montane) type" (Thiem 1978:68). So what is the answer? Perhaps the forest itself may have an important role to play.

A solution to the mystery of Huay Kok Ma can be found by examining the route from rainfall to streamflow. As rain falls in a forested catchment such as Huay Kok Ma, a significant percentage is "intercepted by the forest canopy . . . [and] evaporated back into the atmosphere during and immediately after the storm" (Bruijnzeel 1997:126). Clearly the amount intercepted varies according to the type of forest and the timing and intensity of rainfall events, but average levels of leaf interception typically range from 10 percent to 30 percent (Bruijnzeel 1997:141–44; Witthawatchutikul and Suksawang 2000; Klinge et al. 2001:92). According to Bruijnzeel (1997:144), teak trees, for example, have an interception rate of about 20 percent "over a range of climatic conditions," though studies undertaken by the Royal Forest Department found average interception rates in Nan province of 36 percent (Charoensuk et al. 2000) and, for a mixed deciduous forest with teak, 39 percent in Chiang Mai province (Chanpaga and Watchirajutipong 2000). In some cases very high rates of interception (around 70 percent) have been recorded, for example, in dense bamboo forests (Saengkoovong et al. 2000).

Once the rain reaches the ground (as direct throughfall, leaf drip, and stemflow), it can either soak into the soil or run across the soil surface. As noted above, it is widely believed that rates of infiltration in forests are very high (sometimes as much as 100 percent of the rainfall that has escaped leaf interception). This is a crucially important issue in relation to the timing of streamflow and is discussed further below, but for now it is reasonable to accept that very high rates of infiltration are achieved. Once rainwater has soaked into the soil, it then has to contend with the extensive root systems of forest trees. Compared with other forms of land cover, forests have deep root systems and high rates of root production, especially in the drier montane forests of northern Thailand (Holbrook et al. 1995:245). Though precise measurements are lacking, it is clear that a large percentage of the rainwater that enters the soil is captured by the forest root systems and returned to the atmosphere in the form of transpiration. The combined effect of canopy interception-evaporation and transpiration is substantial. Analysis undertaken by Giambelluca and

Ziegler (1996: figure 3) provides a figure of 850 millimeters per year out of an annual rainfall of 1,170 millimeters. This is consistent with model estimates derived from the work of Perez and colleagues (2002) in which the level of forest water use ranges from 720 millimeters (out of 900 millimeters of rainfall) to 1,160 millimeters (out of 2,000 millimeters of rainfall). Significantly higher rates of water use—about 1,500 millimeters, or 90 percent of total rainfall—were reported for a study area of forest, cassava field, and fruit trees in Rayong province (in eastern Thailand), with forest having higher rates of water use than the other land covers (Witthawatchutikul and Jirasuktaveekul 2000).

So, on the basis of research on the hydrological properties of forest cover, it should come as no surprise that of the roughly 2,000 millimeters of rainfall in Huay Kok Ma only 38 percent ends up as streamflow. Canopy interception-evaporation and transpiration can easily account for the balance. The crucial point that the popular hydrological narrative excludes is that natural hydrological processes in forested catchments account for very significant losses of moisture from the catchments without any human intervention at all. Alford (1992:267), working with catchments on a much larger scale than Huay Kok Ma, suggests that the

INTERNATIONAL RESEARCH ON FORESTS AND STREAMFLOW

International hydrological research questions some common beliefs about the impact of forest clearing on total lowland water yield. Lal's study (1983) from Nigeria estimated the increase in streamflow following the conversion of forests to crops to be 140 millimeters per year (that is, 140 millimeters more of annual rainfall over the catchment area flowed into the stream rather than being lost to evapotranspiration). A similar study in Tanzania found the increase to be substantially higher, at 410 millimeters per year (Edwards 1979). In the Amazon region, annual streamflow increases of 150 to 300 millimeters have been observed following forest conversion to pasture (Fritsch 1992; Jipp et al. 1998). Many other international studies have found similar results. Hydrologists explain these observations by pointing out that total evaporation and transpiration from forests are usually much higher than from alternative land cover, leading to a net increase in annual water supplies.

mountain catchments of northern Thailand have an "extremely low 'runoff efficiency'" averaging, from his data, approximately 20 percent (that is, only 20 percent of the water that enters the catchment as rainfall leaves the catchment as streamflow). His conclusion that "the mountain catchments of northern Thailand are among the most 'arid' on earth, when considered solely from the standpoint of specific runoff" (Alford 1992:268) may seem somewhat extreme, but it is a sobering reminder of the alternative forms of hydrological knowledge that are excluded by the dominant narrative. These alternative accounts suggest that while forests may be effective "sponges" they are also very effective catchment "pumps" (Hamilton 1987:258).

Focusing on the water consumed by forests disrupts the narrative of hydrological crisis in other ways too. It suggests there is considerable hydrological potential to increase annual streamflow by lowering the level of interception and transpiration in upland catchments. The most common way in which the evapotranspiration profile of a catchment is lowered is by clearing forest and replacing it with grasslands or crops. In other words, some elements of hydrological science suggest that forest clearing—and replacement with land covers that have lower rates of evapotranspiration—may increase the annual streamflow of catchments and, in terms of total annual rainfall, the percentage increase can be very significant (Bruijnzeel 1997:133). Indeed, Vincent and colleagues (1995:9) report that "trends of increasing annual stream flow have been found in many tributaries after deforestation occurs." And Bruijnzeel (1990:84) asserts that "removal of forest cover leads to higher streamflow totals and reforestation of open lands generally leads to a decline in overall streamflow." So, when senior government officials argue that deforestation is reducing total streamflow in the Chao Phraya River (see "Dry-Season Water Shortage," p. 94), they are drawing on a simplified narrative of environmental crisis that excludes other forms of knowledge put forward by hydrological scientists. Their appeal to science is highly selective.

Forest Soils and the Seasonal Distribution of Streamflow

But what about the impact of forests on the seasonal distribution of waterflow? What do hydrological studies suggest about the common argument that the forest sponge helps even out the seasonal flow of water? Does forest clearing encourage wet-season flooding and dry-season water shortages?

The Effect of Forest Cover on Wet-Season Flow. Good evidence supports the claim that many forested areas act as sponges in the sense that forest soils often have high rates of infiltration that can absorb high levels of rainfall. These high rates of infiltration are said to be facilitated by the "thick layer of natural debris" (Vincent et al. 1995:6); the relatively high organic content of forest soils; and the presence of numerous small and large "tunnels" (or macropores) in forest soils created by tree roots. One study in Thailand suggests that some forest soils can absorb a remarkable 280 millimeters per hour (Vincent et al. 1995:8). These infiltration rates often decline when forested areas are cleared for agriculture, as the most absorptive surface soil and litter are removed, and as soils become hardened by cultivation practices and the effects of direct rain splash. In a study in northeast Thailand, Takahashi and colleagues (1983) found that rates of infiltration on forested land were significantly higher than those on nearby cultivated plots. Rates of infiltration on cultivated plots were particularly low—with runoff sometimes exceeding 60 percent of rainfall—early in the cultivation cycle, before crops and weeds provided ground cover. By contrast, they found that runoff from the high-infiltration forest plots rarely exceeded 10 percent.

However, a somewhat more complex and nuanced picture that sits less comfortably with the popular narrative emerges from a study undertaken by Ziegler and colleagues (2001) in Chiang Mai province. They suggest that the most effective sponges were actively cultivated fields with infiltration values of well over 90 percent of all rainfall. They found that these fields have infiltration rates approximately five times higher than forest, a finding consistent with that of a similar study undertaken in northern Vietnam (Ziegler, Giambelluca, Plondke et al. 2000). There was, however, some evidence that infiltration rates on upland fields decline during the cultivation period and, in particular, rates of infiltration on recently abandoned fields were found to be relatively low, with runoff up to 40 percent during storm events (Ziegler et al. 2001; Ziegler, Giambelluca, Plondke et al. 2000).[11] These studies also acknowledge that infiltration rates in forest may have been underestimated, given that sampling took place in flat, relatively accessible and probably somewhat trampled areas of forest. A key finding of this research is that paths play a key role in generating overland flow during storms. The studies found that these paths have very low rates of infiltration and that rates of storm runoff can be very high indeed. Given the close association between paths and cultivated fields at a landscape level, the very low rates of infiltration on paths may significantly compromise the relatively high rates achieved on cultivated surfaces.[12]

Research reported on by Nipon (summarized in Enters 2000: table 11) lends support to the view that differences in infiltration rates between forested areas and cultivated areas may not be dramatic. In mixed deciduous forest and dry dipterocarp forest, Nipon reports rates of runoff of 5.5 and 3.6 percent of total rainfall respectively (in both cases, with a slope of 15 percent). These rates increase somewhat (10.9 percent and 6.1 percent) when the forest is burnt. For upland rice fields, Nipon reports rates of runoff ranging from 2.9 percent to 12 percent (across a range of slopes), and for bare soil he reports rates ranging from 1.8 percent to 12.7 percent.[13]

What implications do these studies have for the view that forests mitigate flooding or that forest clearing increases its likelihood? Clearly this is a highly complex issue, with the influence of land-use changes controlled by locally specific factors such as soil characteristics, management practices, slope morphology, and the intensity of rainfall events. International hydrological research suggests that, in some cases, forest clearing can increase stormflows, particularly where such clearing is associated with poor soil management. As Bruijnzeel (2004:201–4) points out, this increase in "peak flows" can occur in situations where cleared and compacted soil is less absorbent and also in cases where the reduced evapotranspiration following forest removal means that the soil is wetter and less capable of holding additional rainfall. However, there are two key points to note in relation to these findings. First, it is well recognized that these effects occur mainly at relatively small scales where there are relatively immediate links between upstream and downstream processes. At larger catchment scales the impact of land-cover change appears to be much less marked. As Bruijnzeel (2004:205) argues, "high stormflows generated by heavy rain on a misused part of a river basin may be 'diluted' by more modest flows from other parts receiving less or no rainfall at the time, or having regenerating vegetation." Simplified hydrological narratives pay little regard to these complex issues of scale.

The second key point is that the ability of forests to reduce peak flows and mitigate flooding appears to apply only to relatively low-intensity storm events. This is an important point because, as shown by the 1988 floods in Nakhorn Si Thammarat, it is the extreme storm events that drive perceptions and policy about the importance of forest cover. What is often

There has been considerable research in the Himalayan region about the relationships between forest conversion, rainfall, and flooding. Research there indicates little evidence for forest cover influencing flooding at the regional scale. Marston et al. (1996:257) studied twenty-two river basins in Nepal and concluded that 82 percent of the variation in river flood discharges could be explained by the topography (or morphometry) of drainage area alone, and that "forest cover did not add explanatory power." Similarly, Hofer and Messerli showed there was no demonstrably significant increase in the monsoon discharge of the Ganges for the sixty years before 1995, a period when deforestation had occurred (cited in Ives 2004:105).

Other studies have highlighted the role of storm intensity, especially when ground conditions are already saturated. About floods in Haiti, Calder and Kaimowitz (2004:8) wrote, "the idea that peasant farmers chop down trees allowing water to run off the hillsides taking the topsoil with it and thus causing floods does not reflect the facts. Studies show that forests do mitigate floods linked to small storms. For larger and more damaging events . . . there is little evidence that forests offer real benefits. Whatever the land use, the rainfall has to run somewhere."

These studies imply that flood management needs to focus less on forest cover as a controlling factor and more on the diverse factors that make specific regions vulnerable to floods. More research is needed on how land management with or without forest cover can reduce flood peaks. Moreover, the perceptions of floods and their perceived frequency may be linked to socioeconomic trends such as the increased financial value of property damaged by floods and the location of housing and economic activities on floodplains, rather than a universal increase in the size and frequency of floods. Enforcing reforestation, or restricting other forms of forest access, might actually increase vulnerability to flooding by forcing land use into more flood-prone areas.

ignored in public discourse is the extraordinarily high levels of rainfall that preceded the tragic flood events that have mobilized public opinion in Thailand. In the Nakhon Si Thammarat event, an estimated 1,051 millimeters of rain fell in the five days before the disaster, with almost 450 millimeters recorded on November 21 (Sureeratna 2001:15). Hydrological research suggests that the ability of forests to prevent flooding in such extreme events is limited; the forest soil quickly becomes saturated and is incapable of absorbing more rainfall. The Nakhorn Si Thammarat disaster took place in November, at the peak of southern Thailand's rainy season when the soil would already have been well soaked. In fact, the sheer weight of water within the soil itself—a product of its spongelike properties—is well recorded as a contributing factor to landslides. Once again the popular narrative emerges as being highly selective in its description of biophysical processes. Dramatic natural variation in rainfall is simply ignored in a narrative that confidently links environmental cause (upland clearing) and effect (downstream flooding).

The Effect of Forest Cover on Dry-Season Flow. So, the forest sponge may play some part in moderating wet-season flow. But what is its effect on dry-season streamflow? Does forest cover help to guarantee dry-season flow by storing wet-season rainfall and gradually releasing it during the dry months that follow? This is a complex issue that has prompted considerable international research (Calder 1999 and Bruijnzeel 2004 provide good reviews). There does, however, appear to be an emerging consensus along the following lines: while absorptive capacities of forest soils are acknowledged (the "sponge effect"), this has to be balanced against the fact that forests are high users of water (the "pump effect"). The overall impact of forest clearing on dry-season flow depends on the trade-off between these two effects. After reviewing a range of international catchment studies, Bruijnzeel (1989:234, 236) concludes that if a reasonable amount of care is taken to maintain the infiltration capacities of cleared land, the positive effect of reduced evapotranspiration will be greater than the negative effect of reduced infiltration, resulting in an increase in dry-season base flow. Obviously, how much care is required will vary considerably depending on local conditions, but as a starting point it seems reasonable to suggest that if the reduction in infiltration is less than the reduction in evapotranspiration then the impact on dry-season streamflow will be very limited.

The work of Takahashi and colleagues (1983) provides one illustration of this trade-off between infiltration and evapotranspiration. As noted above, this study found that infiltration on cultivated upland fields was significantly lower than infiltration in forest. However, when researchers examined the soil itself they found that the cultivated areas had higher levels of soil moisture, which is the basis of dry-season flow. In the forested area, "the soil was drier in deeper horizons and always in the condition of low soil moisture, compared to the other plots" (Takahashi et al. 1983:97). The lower soil moisture under forest resulted from the trees using more water than the crops cultivated on the cleared land.

This single study, however, does not diminish the complexity and uncertainty about the effect of land-cover change on soil moisture. There are situations where very high rates of wet-season runoff may occur following forest clearing, especially when the impact of roads and pathways is taken into account. There is no doubt that some forms of forest clearance are accompanied by factors that make soils lose their spongelike qualities—compaction by roads and machinery, loss of soil faunal activity, paving from settlements, or overgrazing. If these changes occur, then the loss to soil infiltration rates may outweigh the increase in total waterflow resulting from reduced evapotranspiration, and hence dry-season flows will decline. Giambelluca and Ziegler (1996: figure 5), for example, provide model simulations of a hypothetical catchment that suggest that a 50 percent conversion of forest to agriculture may reduce dry-season flow by as much as 30 percent. However, three further aspects of their research highlight the complexity of these processes. First, their simulations also indicate that a 100 percent conversion of forest to agriculture leads to a much smaller impact on dry-season flow (about 15 percent), given that at this level of conversion the impact of reduced water use is relatively more important. Second, their simulations suggest that the impact on dry-season flow is much less when forest is converted to a mixture of agriculture and secondary vegetation (probably a more realistic scenario), with a 50 percent conversion reducing dry-season flow by about 15 percent and a 100 conversion to mixed land cover increasing dry-season flow by about 12 percent. Finally, when their modeling approach is applied to an existing catchment where forest cover has declined from 76 percent in 1955 to 56 percent in 1983, their simulations suggest that wet-season flow increased substantially "while dry-season flow was not significantly altered" (Giambelluca and Ziegler 1996:14). This modeled finding for a small catchment is consistent with the review of actual data on the seasonal distribution of waterflow for the Ping River itself, undertaken by Enters (1995:94), which concluded that "no statistically significant changes between 1927 and 1989 could be identified."

CONCLUSION

One of the central narratives about forests in northern Thailand is that they are a source of water and, as such, their preservation is crucial for the ecological health of the nation. Conventional beliefs about forests and water include the assumption that forests help create rainfall and that the removal of the upland forest "sponge" causes both flooding and water shortage. These beliefs are a good example of the way in which environmental narratives frame complex and uncertain environmental phenomena in terms that are simplified and readily acceptable to a diverse public. The narrative provides straightforward answers to widespread anxieties about climatic variability and uncertainty. The beauty of the "forest as sponge" narrative, and a key factor in its persistence, is that it can explain both excess water (in the form of flooding) and insufficient water (in the form of dry-season water shortage). There is rarely a year when the occurrence of one (or both) of these environmental events does not "confirm" the "truth" of the negative impact of upland forest clearing. This "truth" is deeply political. As the Chom Thong conflict demonstrates, hydrological knowledge is used to justify coercive action against upland farmers whose livelihoods do not conform to the stereotypes of forest-friendly agriculture. The various ways in which "scientific" narratives are used to political effect is clearly evident from some of the statements of the major players in this conflict.

These political factors highlight the importance of critically assessing popular hydrological knowledge. There are good reasons to be skeptical about many of the conventional beliefs about the biophysical linkages between forests and water supply. Regional rainfall data suggest that long-term rainfall trends are relatively stable, despite substantial reductions in forest cover. Hydrological studies suggest that forests are high users of water and that forest clearing can, in fact, increase the annual supply of water to downstream areas. Forests may play a part in limiting some flood events, but the influence of forest cover seems to operate mainly at the small catchment scale and in many cases is greatly outweighed by other factors, such as the magnitude of rainfall and local topography. Forest clearing may also play some part in relation to dry-season streamflow, but mainly in situations where the soil management on cleared land is sufficiently bad to greatly reduce wet-season infiltration. Indeed, as discussed in the next chapter, any such effects on dry-season water supply are probably far less important than substantial increases in water demand.

These alternative perspectives on upland hydrology have some important implications for environmental policy in the uplands. First, some caution is warranted in relation to extensive tree-planting programs, either in the form of plantations, orchards, or initiatives in watershed "rehabilitation." Contrary to popular belief, increased tree cover is likely to reduce the annual water yield of upland catchments rather than increase water supply. If the objective is to secure larger supplies in major downstream hydroelectric and irrigation schemes, the initiatives are very likely to be counterproductive (Aylward 2000:18). There is also a good chance that extensive tree planting will reduce dry-season flow, because the medium- to long-term benefit in terms of enhanced infiltration on reforested soil may well be limited and strongly outweighed by short- to medium-term increases in the level of water "lost" due to the increased evapotranspiration.[14] The popularity of pine plantations in some areas of northern Thailand (Oberhauser 1997) is particular cause for concern, given that a number of studies have indicated that such plantations can have a significant negative impact on both annual and dry-season streamflow.[15] Bruijnzeel's (2004:208) finding should sound a warning note to those committed to upland reforestation: "the conclusion that already diminished dry season flows in degraded tropical areas may decrease even further upon reforestation with fast-growing tree species seems inescapable."

A second implication is that much greater research and policy attention needs to be given to the issue of runoff in cleared areas. As Calder (1998:6) has written, "in general, the role of vegetation in determining the infiltration properties of soils, as it affects the hydrological functioning of catchments . . . remains poorly understood." There is now considerable recognition of the role that farmers can play in conserving the forest itself, but there appears to be much less public attention given to the current and potential role of farmers in maintaining forest functions—high infiltration rates in particular—in agricultural zones. Further research is required on rates of infiltration in cultivated areas and the effectiveness of local and introduced conservation measures—including the maintenance or establishment of forested "filter zones"—in limiting runoff. This research will assist in a more informed assessment of the trade-offs between the costs of soil-conservation measures and the possible off-site benefits in terms of dry-season water supply (see for example, Rao et al. 1996). It will also help in establishing whether or not key hydrological functions can be performed by strategically placed "filter strips" of forest, plantation, or orchard. Ziegler, Giambelluca, Plondke, and colleagues (2000) found that buffers of relatively high-infiltration land cover can significantly reduce the amount of overland flow that reaches the stream network (see also Giambelluca and Ziegler 1996). Research on catchment-scale runoff also suggests that an emphasis on soil and land-cover management needs to be combined with much more attention to limiting the hydrological impact of roads and pathways.

Finally, it is important to emphasize—in case there is any risk of misunderstanding—that the arguments in this chapter certainly should not be read as arguments against forest protection. Clearly there are diverse reasons for forest protection and for more sophisticated (and participatory) forms of reforestation. But conservation decisions should be made on the basis of sound information and discussion, rather than simplified narratives. Unfortunately much of the popular hydrological knowledge discussed in this chapter amounts to a gross simplification of very complex catchment processes and supports land-use policies that may actually worsen environmental problems.

5 *Water Demand*

IT IS STRIKING HOW LITTLE ATTENTION has been given to the water-demand implications of several decades of agricultural transformation in the uplands of northern Thailand. In a classic example of "problem closure" in environmental policy, researchers and government regulators have mainly focused on upland catchment degradation—and the ongoing debate about resource protection—rather than giving attention to rapidly changing patterns of resource use. This has created a focus on the problems of water supply rather than on the impacts of changes in water demand. The lack of attention to water demand is surprising, given the widespread evidence that dry-season agricultural production has increased from a very low level in the mid-twentieth century, to the point where it covers much of the paddy land in the narrow valley bottoms and extends even farther when sprinkler irrigation has been adopted on hillslope fields. Concerted analysis of the implications of this agricultural intensification in the uplands of northern Thailand is long overdue. Broadening the focus of environmental knowledge to incorporate water demand opens the way to a more accurate and balanced understanding of the hydrological challenges faced by farmers in the uplands of Thailand.

The discussion in this chapter is based largely on a detailed case study of the Mae Uam catchment in Mae Chaem district of Chiang Mai province. Some water resource tensions appear to be emerging in this catchment, and the detailed data that is available on local agricultural transformation provides a unique opportunity for examining the underlying drivers of this resource tension.[1] Comparative material is also drawn from other areas in northern Thailand to suggest that the processes observed in Mae Uam are by no means unique. Overall the data from Mae Uam and elsewhere provide an important counterbalance to the predominant narrative that forest clearing has generated a crisis in water supply. In fact, these data suggest that the most likely cause of increased water resource tension is a dramatic and unprecedented increase in the level of demand for water in the dry season. This alternative perspective has important political implications in that it shifts primary attention away from the inhabitants of supposedly sensitive upper-watershed areas and directs attention to the various sources of water demand that exist throughout the catchment system.

THE MAE UAM

The Mae Uam River has its sources on the western slopes of Doi Inthanon, the highest mountain in Thailand. From this high mountain source, the river runs in a southwesterly direction to its junction with the Chaem River, dropping about 2,000 meters in the process (figure 5.1). The total area of the Mae Uam catchment is 43 square kilometers, with elevation ranging from a low point of 480 meters (near the district center of Mae Chaem) to a high point of almost 2,400 meters (near the peak of Doi Inthanon). The average slope is 18 degrees and flat land suitable for intensive irrigated agriculture is confined to narrow strips along the valley floor.

The population of the Mae Uam catchment is approximately 3,500, distributed between seven villages. In the two most upstream villages almost 85 percent of household heads surveyed identify themselves as Karen. As discussed in chapter 3, the Karen are the largest "hilltribe" group in northern Thailand who, in response to official charges of hilltribe natural resource degradation, have developed a reputation in academic and activist literature for their conservationist, forest-friendly, and noncommercial orientation. In the other five villages of the Mae Uam catchment almost all households identify as *khon muang*, the majority lowland population in northern Thailand.

Even though the downstream villages form part of the district township of Mae Chaem, the Mae Uam catchment is overwhelmingly agricultural, with 93 percent of household heads surveyed indicating that farming is their main occupation. Up until the last two decades, the agricultural focus of both Karen and *khon muang* households was the production of rice for subsistence purposes. Rice was grown both in irrigated

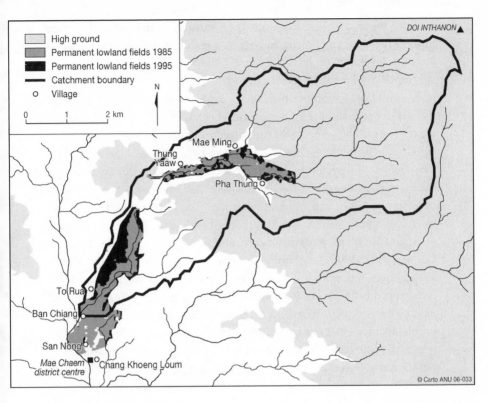

FIG. 5.1 *Mae Uam catchment*

paddy fields and in rain-fed hillslope fields. Rice production was, and still is, supplemented by vegetables grown on the edges of rice fields and in home gardens and by the collection of bamboo shoots, mushrooms, and wild vegetables from surrounding forests. Prior to the mid-twentieth century it appears that Mae Uam formed part of a relatively open land frontier, with satellite communities experiencing little difficulty in opening up new areas of agricultural land. In some cases, villages were established in degraded forest areas that had been opened up by logging operations. Based on experience in other districts of northern Thailand, it seems likely that population growth in the past was accompanied by the gradual expansion of paddy land and the shortening of fallow cycles on upland fields. With the incorporation of the upper reaches of the catchment in Doi Inthanon National Park in the late 1970s, shifting cultivation systems in the upstream Karen villages came under increasing regulatory pressure, as they have in many other parts of northern Thailand.

Since the mid-1980s, there has been substantial agricultural change in the Mae Uam catchment, in part as a result of the activities of agricultural development agencies. During the 1980s, Mae Chaem district was a priority area for development given its relative isolation, poverty, and reputation for opium production and communist insurgency, and the district was the site of the major Mae Chaem Watershed Development Project. The project was supported by a major grant from the U.S. Agency for International Development and was locally implemented by the Ministry of Agriculture. Development activities in the Karen and *khon muang* villages along the Mae Uam included infrastructure support (roads, irrigation systems, and fish ponds); promotion of new crops and farming techniques; construction of terraced paddy fields; marketing initiatives; and distribution of fruit-tree seedlings (Ministry of Agriculture and Cooperatives 1984). Irrigation development was a priority activity and, in the upper reaches of the catchment, a series of concrete weirs were constructed from the late 1970s onward, while in the lower reaches two major irrigation weirs were built in the late 1980s. An aqueduct that draws supplementary—but expensive, given the need for pumping—irrigation water from the main stream of the Chaem River was also constructed to service farmers in the lower reaches of the catchment in the mid-1980s. Agricultural development was greatly facilitated by the construction of a road linking Mae Chaem with the major northern Thai marketing centers during the 1970s and by the gradual improvement of the road through the Mae Uam catchment itself in the 1980s and 1990s. These development initiatives appear to have contributed to a significant increase in the production of cash crops, especially soybeans.

Land-cover data for the Mae Uam catchment from the period 1985 to 1995 provides some interesting perspectives on this recent period of agricultural transformation.[2] First, these data suggest that there has been a modest decline in rain-fed hillslope cultivation over this period—from 425 hectares in 1985 to 393 hectares in 1995—contrary to popular images of rampant hillslope expansion, and associated deforestation, in northern Thailand. Importantly, these data suggest that most rain-fed hillslope fields are now permanently cropped, rather than being left fallow or abandoned. Of the 393 hectares cultivated in 1995, over 336 hectares had been cultivated in 1990, and almost 240 hectares were cultivated in both 1985 and 1990. Discussions with village leaders and household surveys indicate that all upland fields are now permanently cropped, with no extended fallow periods.

The second, and most important, trend in land use in the Mae Uam catchment is the expansion of permanent agricultural fields along the valley floor and on the adjacent gently sloping land. This expansion has included both irrigated paddy fields (assisted by improvements in irrigation infrastructure) and the establishment of orchards and permanent gardens on sloping land immediately adjacent to paddy fields. As can be seen in figure 5.1, this expansion has been most significant in the downstream zone of the catchment, though there is also evidence of paddy field consolidation in the upstream agricultural zone. Land-cover data indicate that in 1985 these areas of permanent valley bottom cultivation covered 203 hectares (4.4 percent of the catchment area). By 1990 this had increased to 256 hectares (5.6 percent) and by 1995 had reached 350 hectares (7.6 percent). This expansion has been facilitated by the construction of irrigation infrastructure and the construction of paddy fields as part of local development initiatives.

AGRICULTURAL INTENSIFICATION AND WATER
RESOURCE TENSION

Since the 1970s, the catchment of Mae Uam, like other areas in northern Thailand, has experienced rapid agricultural change and increasing tensions about access to water. During field surveys undertaken in late 1998, farmers in the downstream *khon muang* villages expressed concerns about dry-season water shortages and the high cost of pumping supplementary water supplies from the main stream of the Chaem River. These concerns are similar to those expressed by downstream farmers in mountain catchments in many areas of northern Thailand where the image of *khon muang* farmers as victims of upstream degradation is widespread. In the Mae Uam catchment, as in many other areas, local concerns about water resources are also informed by a high-profile forest protection and reforestation project that uses the rhetoric of hydrological crisis (discussed in the previous chapter) and continually portrays upper-watershed forest degradation as causing water shortages. Concerns about dry-season water supply have even prompted proposals that dams be built in the middle and upper reaches of the Mae Uam to store "surplus" wet-season flow. These proposals have been contentious. In the early 1990s, activists in the upstream Karen villages campaigned vigorously, and successfully, against a proposed reservoir that would have inundated some of their valuable paddy fields. By the late 1990s, the proposals became more modest, with army engineering teams planning to build small check dams on minor subtributaries within the catchment.

These local debates about access to water have taken place against a backdrop of rapid and complex agricultural transformation. This transformation, however, has not affected all aspects of agricultural activity equally. Agricultural modernization has had a relatively limited impact on wet-season agricultural activity. Both the *khon muang* and Karen villages in Mae Uam cultivate irrigated rice in the wet season for local consumption. During the wet season in 1997, rice was grown on over 80 percent of the cultivated paddy area. The balance was made up of soybeans and maize (about 5 percent each) and small plots of shallots and other vegetables. Over 80 percent of these nonrice crops were grown on rain-fed paddy fields, with irrigated paddy devoted almost exclusively to rice production. It is clear that subsistence-oriented production is by far the highest priority on the relatively high-yielding irrigated fields (over 3,000 kilograms of rice per hectare). During the wet season there is also some cultivation of hillslope rain-fed fields, which in 1997 amounted to about 45 percent of the area of paddy cultivation. During 1997 these fields were cropped with upland rice (73 percent), soybeans (20 percent), and maize (11 percent). Upland rice features prominently—despite relatively low productivity (around 1,200 kilograms per hectare)—largely because there is a significant group who are entirely dependent on hillslope rain-fed fields for their agricultural livelihoods. In the Mae Uam catchment this group comprises about 17 percent of farmers.

By contrast, there have been very important changes in the patterns of dry-season cultivation. Until the 1980s, dry-season cropping in the small upland catchments surrounding Mae Chaem was limited to small areas of vegetable gardens on the banks of streams. Local people report that in these earlier times many households experienced annual deficiencies in rice production, but chose to supplement incomes by engaging in off-farm activities and trading rather than by planting additional crops during the dry season. According to local informants, cattle trading was an important feature of these economic systems, with dry-season paddy fields used as a staging point for cattle in the trade between upland villagers—including villages across the border in Burma—and the larger trading centers close to Chiang Mai. Given the rudimentary state of transport connections, farmers working as dry-season ox traders also played an important part in the basic commodity trade:

Many Mae Chaem people were ox traders. Almost every village went to buy cattle from Lawa and Karen villages. Any village that didn't have cattle was not so rich. One person would have five or ten cattle and they would go in a group of four or five from Mae Chaem to sell betel in Chom Thong and return with kerosene, tinned fish, and salt. They would stay in their village a few nights and then go and sell in Lawa, Karen, and even Shan villages. . . . Mae Chaem people didn't grow enough rice to support themselves. Those who didn't operate as ox traders had to go out to work. (Carupa 1997:152; see also Chusit 1989 and Moerman 1975)

Since the 1980s, however, there have been numerous agricultural changes. Nonagricultural pursuits are still important, but soybean has been widely adopted as a dry-season crop (figure 5.2). Data from household surveys in Mae Uam indicate that soybeans were cultivated on almost 70 percent of the irrigated paddy area during 1997–1998. Soybeans have been widely promoted in northern Thailand—largely as an import substitution initiative—and they now constitute, by area, one of the main nonrice crops in the region (Abamo 1992:15, 26). In the Mae Uam catchment, soybeans have been grown for local consumption over a long period, but commercial production was only introduced in about 1984 when demonstration plots of improved varieties were established in numerous villages as part of the Mae Chaem Watershed Development Project (Ministry of Agriculture and Cooperatives 1984:21). Good yields were recorded and, despite the fact that limited input support was offered to farmers, adoption was rapid, perhaps due to uncharacteristically high prices in the latter half of the 1980s (Kanok et al. 1994:74). Soybeans remain attractive given stable prices, low input costs, and modest labor requirements. Of course, adoption has not been completely unproblematic, with low yields in some areas—possibly associated with declining soil fertility—prompting adoption of other dry-season crops. Maize, which can be readily sold in Mae Chaem, is a popular alternative, though its relatively high water consumption is a major disadvantage in dry years. Other farmers have experimented with higher-value vegetable crops such as sweet corn, carrots, potatoes, and shallots, but none of these alternatives have become as popular as soybeans.

The Hydrology of Dry-Season Cultivation

Popular narratives in northern Thailand suggest that water resource tensions in areas such as Mae Uam are the product of declining water supply,

FIG. 5.2 *Soybean cultivation*

itself a result of catchment degradation. This narrative, by focusing on water supply, draws attention away from the water demand implications of substantial increases in dry-season agriculture. The importance of this increase in demand can be illustrated with some simple hydrological calculations. These calculations highlight the hydrological and social selectivity of the dominant narrative.

First, it is necessary to estimate dry-season water supply. There is no stream gauge in the Mae Uam catchment, and so water supply is estimated by taking eleven years of streamflow data from a nearby catchment with roughly similar aspect, elevation, and morphology and scaling these data according to the specific characteristics of the Mae Uam.[3] The intention is merely to provide an indication of the likely magnitude of water supply in the Mae Uam catchment. Figure 5.3 provides the results of these calculations, which use February as the month of measurement. This month was selected because it is a dry-season month that usually has high water demand. The data represent the total amount of water available for irrigators in the catchment for this month, measured in cubic meters. The graph clearly shows very significant year-to-year variation in

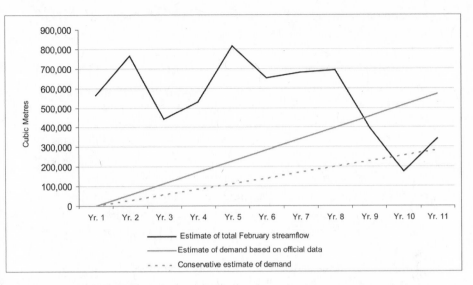

FIG. 5.3 *Comparison of estimated water supply and water demand in Mae Uam catchment*

dry-season water supply. In February of year five (a year of particularly high rainfall) the catchment is estimated to have yielded over 800,000 cubic meters, while in year ten (a drought year) the amount is less than 200,000 cubic meters.

The estimate of water demand is based on the water consumption (evapotranspiration) of the soybean crop. The calculation uses the internationally standard method of combining an estimate of evapotranspiration from a reference crop (for Chiang Mai) with a crop coefficient for soybeans (which varies according to the stage of growth of the crop.) Using the Royal Irrigation Department's reference crop data and their crop coefficients for soybeans, the total water consumption of 1 hectare of soybeans during February (assuming a planting date of mid-November) is 1,340 cubic meters.[4] However, this represents crop water consumption under ideal and well-fertilized conditions and, if achieved, would result in levels of yield significantly beyond those typically achieved by farmers in the Mae Uam catchment. A more conservative estimate of 670 cubic meters is provided by Perez and colleagues (2002) based on an estimate of likely agronomic conditions in Mae Uam. Given the significant difference, both estimates of water consumption have been used: the official estimate and the conservative estimate. These estimates of water demand for the month of February have been added to figure 5.3. In year one it is assumed that none of the paddy area is cropped with soybeans, with the percentage steadily increasing to 80 percent in year eleven.[5] Of course, this is not intended to be an accurate reflection of the history of soybean cultivation in Mae Uam. Rather, the purpose is to provide a broad indication of the hydrological magnitude of past, and possible future, dry-season agricultural trends within the catchment. (In the survey year approximately 70 percent of the paddy area was cropped with soybeans.)

The findings from this simple analysis are striking. At the higher levels of soybean cultivation the potential for water deficit in dry years is clearly evident, even if the more modest levels of crop evapotranspiration are used. Put simply, in these dry years there is not enough water in the stream to support the water consumption of an extensively planted soybean crop.

In fact, the water constraint is probably even more critical than the graph indicates. Remember that water demand is estimated only on the basis of water consumption by the crop itself. But, given irrigation inefficiencies, significantly more water has to be extracted from the stream in order to get this amount of water to the crop. In these types of irrigation systems considerable amounts of water are lost through canal seepage and evaporation, deep percolation (below the rooting zone of the crop), and drainage back into the stream. While much of this additional water can be reused within the catchment, the relatively inefficiency of conveyance and delivery systems compounds timing and coordination problems. Second, technological constraints place limits on the percentage of water that can be extracted from the stream—some estimates provided by local farmers and agricultural development workers are as low as 50 percent—given that pumps are generally not used to extract water from streams or canals during low-flow periods. Moreover, irrigation weirs have no capacity to store water to meet water demand in peak periods. For all these reasons it is likely that substantial water resource constraints and tensions are likely to emerge well before the supply and demand lines intersect. In brief, the complaints of downstream soybean cultivators about water shortages in drier years are unsurprising.

This simple hydrological analysis highlights the potential for the hydrological limits of catchments to be reached—and exceeded in drier years—as a result of relatively unremarkable processes of agricultural intensification and where the irrigated land comprises a modest percentage of the total catchment area. Data from Mae Uam suggest explanations for water resource tensions that lie outside the framework of the popular narrative linking declining water supply with declining forest cover. In fact, in Mae Uam the decline in forest cover has been modest, from 78 percent of the catchment area in 1985 to 72 percent in 1995. The data presented above suggest that the most dynamic element in this upland catchment system is water demand and, combined with significant natural variation in water supply, this is the key driver of resource tension. Exploring the nature and distribution of this water demand helps in highlighting the political selectivity of the dominant narrative and provides a basis for a more democratic framing of water resource challenges.

The Sociology of Dry-Season Agriculture

Dry-season cultivation of soybeans is now widespread in both upstream and downstream areas of the Mae Uam catchment, and in both Karen and *khon muang* villages. Among all the households surveyed in the Mae Uam catchment almost 60 percent cultivated soybeans in the previous dry season. They devoted, on average, almost 80 percent of their household paddy fields to this pursuit. What are the key sociological dimensions of this substantial agricultural change? And what are the implications for environmental management in the uplands?

Access to Irrigated Paddy Land. In the debates about forest cover and water supply it has become very easy for government officials, conservationists, and lowland irrigators to point the finger of environmental blame at upland cultivation. Shifting cultivation and, more recently, intensive commercial cultivation undertaken by "hill tribes" is regularly condemned as compromising the hydrological health of catchments. However, if the focus of the debate is shifted to water demand it becomes evident that irrigated paddy fields are, in fact, a key driver of resource tension. In the Mae Uam catchment, all dry-season soybean cultivation takes place on irrigated paddy fields. Upland fields simply lack the irrigation infrastructure that is essential for any dry-season cultivation. Within the Mae Uam catchment, development project support for irrigated agriculture has contributed to a high level of paddy ownership, with about 80 percent of households in the catchment owning irrigated paddy fields. Among dry-season soybean cultivators the level of ownership of irrigated fields is about 0.7 hectare. It might seem obvious that all dry-season soybean cultivators are irrigated paddy owners, but this point is worth reinforcing given the popular narrative that upland hillslope farmers are the primary agents of catchment transformation. (Remember that in Mae Uam there has been a decline in hillslope cultivation.)

A few statistics illustrate the central role of irrigated fields in supporting agricultural intensification. Irrigated fields result in higher and more stable yields during the main rice-growing season. Survey data indicate that those who cultivate soybeans in the dry season are relatively successful wet-season rice cultivators, with average production of about 2,200 kilograms of rice per household. This generously covers subsistence requirements and permits the sale of about 15 percent of irrigated rice production. Revenue from wet-season rice sales facilitates investment in dry-season agricultural inputs; in turn, fertilizer residue and nitrogen benefits[6] from dry-season cultivation have a beneficial effect on wet-season rice yields. For some farmers (about 15 percent of dry-season soybean cultivators), cash incomes and investment potential is further supplemented by the ownership of rain-fed hillslope fields on which they can grow wet-season cash crops (soybeans and maize), which they are able to do because their chief supply of subsistence rice is provided by their irrigated paddy fields.

The contrast with the 17 percent of households totally dependent on rain-fed hillslope fields is striking. Contrary to widely held stereotypes this is not just an upper-catchment hilltribe phenomenon. The Karen village of Mae Ming has the highest incidence of households that are completely dependent on upland fields (44 percent of households). But the second-highest incidence occurs in the downstream *khon muang* village of Ban Jiang (24 percent). And in the highest-elevation Karen village of Pha Thung, the incidence is relatively low (only 14 percent). These households, of course, have no impact at all on dry-season irrigation demand, and none of these farmers indicated that they could rent irrigated paddy fields during the dry season. (This is unsurprising, given that these fields are already heavily used).

It is worth considering the precarious position of these households in order to understand their relative inability to benefit from processes of agricultural intensification within this catchment. During the wet season these households farm, on average, 0.6 hectare of hillslope fields on which rain-fed rice is the predominant crop (almost 90 percent of the cultivated area). This is a strongly subsistence-oriented system, with all households indicating that they consume (or keep for seed) all the rice they produce. But this production of rice is highly unlikely to provide enough rice to live on. The average rice production is only about 650 kilograms per household, and the average household size is five. Some 75 percent of these households cannot meet their subsistence needs from rice production, and an estimated 40 percent have difficulty meeting subsistence needs even when income from nonagricultural sources is taken into consideration.[7] These households can also be described as being disadvantaged by other indicators: they have by far the lowest level of spending on agricultural inputs; the lowest household labor input; the lowest use of hired labor; and the lowest ownership of consumer durables. Given the precarious position of many households in this category, it is unsurprising that they find it hard to invest in hillslope irrigation systems (such as sprinklers). It is also highly unlikely that they will be in a position to purchase or construct irrigated paddy fields that have higher levels of food production than the nonirrigated slopes.

Ethnicity, Catchment Location, and Soybean Cultivation. Can any conclusions be drawn about ethnicity and dry-season cash crop cultivation? Overall, the data from the Mae Uam catchment challenges commonly drawn distinctions between commercially oriented lowland villagers and subsistence-oriented uplanders. Many popular discussions of upland farmers paint somewhat idealized images of Karen livelihoods, emphasizing subsistence rice production and detachment from commercial relations. However, survey data from Mae Uam indicate that Karen are actively engaged in commodity production. In the village of Mae Ming, almost 80 percent of Karen households that own paddy fields grow soybeans in the dry season. In the other Karen village, Pha Thung, the percentage is lower, but still very significant at 53 percent. In fact, the lowest rate of soybean cultivation (38 percent of households surveyed) was not found in the more isolated Karen villages but in the downstream *khon muang* village of Chang Khoeng Loum, which is, in many other respects, the most commercialized village in the catchment given its proximity to the district center.

This is not to suggest that there are no differences in the patterns of agricultural activity within the catchment. While the Karen are active participants in soybean production, a good number of the downstream *khon muang* farmers appear to be even more heavily involved. But this appears to be due to a number of locally specific geographic and infrastructural factors rather than any innate cultural preference. What are these factors?

First, some of the downstream villages have particularly high rates of irrigated paddy ownership, which is the key to dry-season soybean cultivation. In the *khon muang* village of To Rua where there is relatively abundant flat land, 94 percent of farmers own irrigated paddy land (and almost all of them grow soybeans). This is substantially higher than the rate of paddy ownership in the Karen village of Mae Ming (56 percent).

Second, the soil in the downstream areas, particularly near the village of To Rua, is said to be particularly suitable for soybean cultivation, requiring minimal fertilizer input. During surveying, farmers in other villages often spoke enviously about the quality of the soil in the lower reaches of the catchment.

Third, it appears that as a result of good planning or topological good fortune, the two weirs built in the lower reaches of the catchment in the 1980s have provided the opportunity for a substantial increase in permanent cultivation around the *khon muang* villages of To Rua and Ban Jiang. Analysis of the land-cover data indicates that the largest area of expansion of permanent lowland cultivation in the catchment occurred on the northern fringes of these villages' paddy fields (see figure 5.1).

Fourth, the downstream villages have very good access to marketing infrastructure in the town of Mae Chaem. Of course, the upstream Karen villages are not particularly inaccessible, but less regular visits by traders and higher transport costs mean that "farm-gate" soybean prices in these villages are about 10 percent lower.

Finally, downstream farmers appear to have more secure land tenure than their upstream counterparts. In To Rua, for example, only 20 percent of agricultural plots have no formal title, while in the Karen village of Pha Thung this figure is 72 percent. The relationship between land tenure and agricultural strategy is complex, but it seems likely that more secure tenure improves the chances of downstream farmers receiving cheaper, formal sources of agricultural credit from local banks and lenders.

In brief, it appears that the superior resource endowments of some of the *khon muang* villages mean that they can achieve particularly high rates of dry-season soybean cultivation. Farmers in these villages complain about the adequacy of dry-season water, but they are the highest water users in the catchment. Of course, the water used by the upstream Karen farmers is not hydrologically insignificant: the Karen also plant substantial areas of soybeans, and if they did not use water the situation for the downstream farmers would be much alleviated. But, of course, the Karen farmers would see little reason why they should forgo their water use to help more favorably located farmers in downstream villages.

Are these findings relevant to experiences elsewhere in northern Thailand, or is the Mae Uam catchment unusual? Two sources of information are useful in considering this issue. First, remotely sensed (satellite) data of land-cover change provides indirect evidence that the land-use trends in Mae Uam are widespread in the region. Second, the existing research on agricultural transformation in upland areas, while fragmentary, provides some key case studies that suggest increasing demand for water, rather than declining water supply, is the main factor in recent resource tension.

Land-Cover Change

Remote-sensing data show that the small catchments close to Mae Uam experienced broadly similar patterns of land-use change since the 1980s.[8] For example, in the Mae Pan catchment, immediately to the south of Mae Uam, the area of forest cover is also about 80 percent (in 1995), a decline of 4 percent since 1985. As in Mae Uam, this decline has been associated with a 36 percent increase in the area of permanent lowland fields and a slight decline in the area of upland fields. Local surveys indicate that, as in Mae Uam, investment in irrigation infrastructure has played a key role in this process of lowland intensification. For the Chaem River catchment as a whole—of which Mae Uam is one small part—the percentage of forest cover is the same (80 percent, a decline from 88 percent in 1985). This finding underlines the point that there are still substantial areas in northern Thailand with very heavy forest cover, although these data do not provide a clear indication of forest quality, which may have improved or worsened during this period. In the Chaem River catchment, the area of permanent lowland fields increased by 74 percent between 1985 and 1995 (from 3,660 hectares to almost 6,500 hectares), while the area of upland fields increased by only 11 percent (from 20,700 hectares to 23,000 hectares). Upland cultivation—some of it irrigated with sprinkler systems—clearly has a much more important role within the Chaem River catchment as a whole than it does in Mae Uam, but the trend toward valley-bottom agricultural intensification is equally evident.

The more developed Mae Khan and Mae Klang catchments have land-cover trends that are even closer to those in the Mae Uam catchment (see their location in figure 2.1). The level of forest cover in 1995 was

72 percent, a decline from 80 percent since 1985. During the same time, permanent lowland fields increased by 32 percent and the area of upland fields declined by 11 percent. In these two catchments, permanent lowland cultivation has grown substantially faster in small, relatively isolated catchments (43 percent)—such as those similar to Mae Uam—than in the extensive and highly developed paddy region along the Ping River to the south of Chiang Mai (18 percent increase). In some of these catchments, the rate of increase appears to have been dramatic. In Mae Laan Kham (the site of Waraalak Ithiphonorlan's 1998 study on shifting cultivation, which is discussed further in chapter 8), the area of permanent lowland fields has increased by 396 percent, while in the upper Mae Waang watershed the increase has been a more modest 234 percent.

Some other studies of land-cover change have produced similar results. For example, a study undertaken in the Karen communities of Wat Jan dramatically indicates the expansion of paddy fields. In 1954, aerial photographs indicate that there were only 77 hectares of paddy in a group of four Wat Jan villages; by 1973 this had doubled to 154 hectares and by 1994 had almost tripled to 215 hectares (Panomsak 1997:43). In a nearby district of Mae Hong Son province, Puginier (2001: table 2) found a similar pattern, with the areas of paddy field increasing from 114 to 354 hectares between 1983 and 1994, largely as a result of substantial population growth. An even more dramatic picture emerges from a study by Jintana and Routray (1998) in Phayao province. Though they provide no figures, their land-use maps demonstrate an extraordinary increase in the extent of paddy cultivation in the downstream reaches of the Mae Chai catchment. In the 1950s they say that the downstream area "was dominated by forestland with a few patches of rice fields" (Jintana and Routray 1998:283). By the 1990s there had been "an increase in large patches of paddy fields, followed by large areas under natural water reservoirs, few settlements, and very small patches of idle land" (ibid.). Yet despite this evidence of a very significant increase in irrigated cultivation, they adopt the dominant narrative and attribute water shortages to the "reduction in forest area" (ibid.).

Of course land-cover data have to be treated with considerable caution, as results are highly dependent on the resolution of the images and the methodology used for interpretation. Nevertheless, the various studies cited above strongly suggest the value of explanations of water resource tension that lie outside the framework of the "forest clearing produces water shortage" narrative.

Secondary Sources

These broad data can be supplemented by some more localized accounts of agricultural transformation. Once again, the impression gained is that Mae Uam is far from an isolated case. Kanok and others' *Assessment of Sustainable Highland Agricultural Systems* (1994:xxiv, xxxi) notes that water consumption in northern Thailand tripled between 1980 and 1989 and that "competition for water between neighboring villages, between highlands and lowlands, and between agricultural and urban areas will intensify." Their case studies of agricultural intensification provide evidence of substantial increases in the dry-season cultivation of vegetable crops (cabbages in particular) on both irrigated paddy fields and on upland fields (the latter made possible by the introduction of gravity-fed sprinkler irrigation systems) (Kanok et al. 1994:53, 62, 83). The researchers also point to increasing use of irrigation to support establishment of temperate fruit orchards.

The local impacts of these general trends are evident in some specific case studies. Recent reports on the Mae Wak catchment (Ukrit 2001; Ukrit and Isager 2001)—which is located just to the north of Mae Uam—describe water resource conflict between the upstream village of Mae Ma-lo and the downstream village of Mae Wak. The details contained in these reports indicate that agricultural development in the Mae Wak catchment has been very similar to that in Mae Uam: a substantial decline in shifting cultivation, an increase in permanent cultivation, and, in particular, an expansion of paddy fields. In the upstream village of Mae Ma-lo, evidence suggests that dry-season water use has increased to support the cultivation of carrots and onions. Mae Ma-lo is a relatively small village (58 households), but its total area of paddy land is large at 91 hectares—giving an average of about 1.6 hectares per household (Ukrit and Isager 2001:25–26). There is also extensive reliance on paddy in the downstream village of Mae Wak, where the 70 households cultivate a total of 104 hectares of paddy land. Recent infrastructure support provided by the Royal Irrigation Department has improved water supply to this paddy land and has "facilitated an increase in agricultural productivity in the village" (Ukrit and Isager 2001:22). An important aspect of this improvement appears to have been the adoption of dry-season cropping of soybeans and corn (Ukrit and Isager 2001:23). The outbreak of water resource conflict in this small catchment during the 1990s suggests that dry-season cultivation may be exceeding the hydrological capacity of the catchment in relatively dry years. As one of the reports concludes, "the question is, will the conflict rear its ugly head again if the vagaries of nature bring back another dry spell in the future?" (Ukrit 2001:30).

A brief examination of the much more famous conflict in Chom Thong similarly suggests that water demand may be a key contributing factor. In the early 1980s there appears to have been a significant and rapid increase in upstream water demand in the Hmong village of Pa Kluay, largely as a result of opium eradication initiatives and adoption of alternative crops, especially cabbages. By the years 1985–1986, some observers were blaming the widespread introduction of upstream sprinkler irrigation systems used for cabbage production for declines in downstream flow (Renard 1994:663). However, as a number of advocates for the villagers of Pa Kluay have pointed out, this was only one side of the hydrological story. A process of agricultural transformation was also underway in the downstream areas of Chom Thong district: "At the same time the agricultural system of the lowlanders was changing to a system that required increasing use of water, for example, cultivation of longan orchards, off-season cultivation on paddy fields, and cultivation of onions, soybeans, peanuts and garlic in the dry season" (Atchara 1998:95).

So it appears possible, even likely, that the underlying cause of the conflict in Chom Thong is a substantial increase in demand for water throughout the catchment. And given the distribution of population and irrigated farmland it is likely that this increase in demand has been most substantial in the lower reaches of the catchment. This fundamentally reframes the dispute—not as one between forest destroyers and forest protectors but as between groups making competing claims on a limited water resource. With farmers in downstream areas experiencing, for example, substantial reductions in soybean yields (Atchara 1998)—probably as a result of water demand exceeding supply in dry years—it is not surprising that they would seek to delegitimize the agricultural water use of their upstream rivals. The popular narrative of environmental crisis brought about by upland degradation is very effective in this delegitimizing process.

CONCLUSION

Environmental narratives are commonly heard and simplistic accounts of environmental change through which "actors are positioned, and through which specific ideas of 'blame,' 'responsibility,' 'urgency' and 'responsible behaviour' are attributed" (Hajer 1995:64–65). Common explanations of water shortages in northern Thailand certainly achieve these effects. State agencies, some conservation groups, and associations of lowland irrigators vigorously, and sometimes violently, argue that forest clearing undertaken by upland farmers causes water shortages. This draws on a long tradition of blame in which upland cultivation, especially shifting cultivation, is portrayed as one of the primary causes of northern Thailand's deforestation and environmental degradation. The fact that many of these upland farmers are members of ethnic minority groups— some of whom are relatively recent arrivals in northern Thailand— provides fertile material for the combination of ethnic prejudice and environmental blame. These hilltribe groups are all too easily portrayed as undermining the ecological basis of irrigated agriculture, one of the stereotypically core elements of Thai national culture. As such, there is widespread support for an array of watershed regulatory measures put forward by government agencies that seek to preserve and restore forest cover in upland catchments and restrict, or even relocate, the agricultural activities of upland groups.

Responses to the charges of forest destruction and water source depletion have been vigorous. Activist academics and NGOs in northern Thailand, as in many other parts of the world, construct a counterdiscourse in which upland minority communities are portrayed as having well-established traditions of forest management and sustainable land use that provide a basis for sustainable community presence in forested watershed areas. This defense has been particularly enthusiastically mounted in relation to the Karen. Attention is drawn to forest-friendly cultivation techniques; ritual forms and belief systems that prioritize forest protection; indigenous systems of watershed protection; and local knowledge systems that reflect local understanding of the crucial links between upper catchment forest cover and healthy streamflow. To challenge negative stereotypes of the impact of upland cultivation on hydrological health, NGOs have worked with upland villagers to form "watershed networks" that promote the capabilities of local institutions in protecting forest cover and maintaining water supply (NDF 2000b). As one report notes, "the lowland people receive water because their brothers and sisters in the upland areas work together for conservation" (Saengdaaw et al. 2000:67).

Despite the contention of this debate there is an underlying narrative agreement that forests are the key to sustainable water resource management. The debate is about the appropriate way of protecting forest cover—essentially, the internationally familiar debate between state regulation and local management—but it is not a debate about the relationship between forest cover and water supply. There is a widely shared consensus that forest cover maintains water supply and that deforestation causes water shortage. In the large and contentious literature on environmental management in northern Thailand, this persistent focus on forest protection and water supply has diverted attention from the important issue of water demand. In conceptual terms, this represents a "problem closure" that focuses only upon water supply rather than the interaction between water supply and water demand. Very little attention is given to the greatly increased quantities of water that new agricultural systems consume. Water shortages are regularly and consistently attributed to a reduction in supply caused by deforestation. The debate is framed by a preoccupation with water resource preservation (which is equated with forest protection) rather than a focus on contemporary patterns of water resource use.

The dominant hydrological crisis narrative's focus on water supply is also highly socially selective. As long as the focus of public debate is on maintaining and protecting water supply, the regulatory focus will be on those residents in the forested upstream areas who are seen as being crucial in securing downstream flows. The impacts of these regulatory measures aimed at forest protection often fall most heavily on farmers who are completely dependent on the cultivation of rain-fed hillslope fields. It is this upland hillslope cultivation that has come to be the key site of claim, counterclaim, regulatory intervention, and institutional mobilization. Information from Mae Uam suggests that these upland hillslope farmers are the most disadvantaged and economically vulnerable and—ironically—are the farmers whose agricultural activities make the smallest call on water resources. Addressing the needs of these farmers, rather than seeking to regulate their agriculture for presumed impacts on lowland water supply, is one clear alternative to the problem closure currently adopted by many of those involved in the management of upland natural resources.

There is good evidence that conflicts over water resources are driven by substantial increases in water demand rather than a decline in water supply. The case study from Mae Uam suggests that more attention should be focused on the water resource impacts of paddy expansion and increased dry-season cultivation throughout upland catchments. The research presented here is preliminary and from one particular location—and there is clearly much potential for further field surveying and more sophisticated hydrological modeling—but there does seem to be substantial evidence that water resource conflicts are primarily driven by substantial increases in water demand placed against a backdrop of substantial natural variation in water supply. This is a very different perspective on environmental change than that contained in the forest-focused narrative presented in the previous chapter.

Disrupting the narrative of water supply crisis has important political implications. If the water management focus is shifted to water demand, then attention must shift to the diverse causes of demand that exist throughout the hydrological system. Suddenly, upper-catchment farmers are not the only focus, but lowland irrigators are also brought into the picture along with industrialists, tourist resort operators, and urban water consumers. The study of Mae Uam suggests that hydrological pressures are emerging from agricultural activities throughout the catchment and that, in fact, the demand pressures are likely to be most intense in downstream areas. The study suggests that there is no reason for regulatory mechanisms targeting hydrological issues to be focused on relatively forested upstream areas. Rather, socially and environmentally sustainable initiatives in catchment management must surely involve attention to the water demands of upstream and downstream farmers. Of course, this broader regulatory focus may well be unwelcome, and it should come as no surprise if supply-based arguments continue to be mounted in order to maintain the geographically and socially restricted focus on upstream forested catchment areas. This selective application of the principles of catchment management, combined with simplistic narratives of hydrological crisis, clearly serves the interests of the relatively more developed and sociopolitically influential communities in downstream areas.

A shift in emphasis to water demand may also prompt some rethinking of the current strategies used to defend the rights of upland farmers. At present, this defense is framed largely in terms of the farmers' ability to protect forests and maintain water supply. This defense has been mounted in very particular terms with considerable emphasis placed on the desirability of subsistence-oriented, low-input forms of forest-friendly cultivation. But, as the Mae Uam case study demonstrates, many of these upland minority farmers are becoming heavily engaged in commercially oriented production, especially in the dry season when the use of irrigation water is essential. In such contexts, sharp dichotomies between high-water-using downstream farmers and subsistence-oriented upstream farmers are simply not tenable. Some may consider it to be politically risky to draw attention to increasing water use by upstream farmers, especially when they are members of minority groups subject to various forms of discrimination. However, environmental policy reform in northern Thailand should be based on a revised perception of hill farmers and their agricultural transformations. A more democratic and environmentally effective approach to policy is to assert the rights of these relatively marginal farmers as legitimate users of catchment resources rather than as guardians of resources for those in downstream areas.

In future negotiations about water resources, it would be unfortunate indeed if upstream irrigators found their resource claims constrained or even undermined by narratives of catchment guardianship, forest protection, and subsistence orientation. It is surely relevant that those most virulently targeted in recent catchment disputes—such as the famous dispute in Chom Thong—are upland farmers whose intensively commercial practices are inconsistent with official and alternative images of appropriate upland livelihoods. A defense of their rights may best be framed in terms of their legitimate claim to a fair share of scarce and valuable resources, a claim that needs to be liberated from the normative imagery of the hydrological importance of upland forest guardianship.

6 Erosion

MANY OF THAILAND'S NARRATIVES about forests and water are intricately connected to beliefs about soil erosion. Visitors to the uplands are often struck by how farming seems to cling to steep slopes, and how villages perch precariously on narrow ridges. Popular notions of soil erosion suggest careless agriculture will wash soil downhill, where it is then deposited on roads, on rice fields, and in irrigation channels. And erosion on the hillsides is believed to reduce agricultural productivity and diminish the water-holding properties in upland soils. According to one United Nations report in 1988,

> there is now ample evidence of degradation and erosion of soils in Thailand. Changes in physical and chemical properties of soils have made many more susceptible to erosion and it is now estimated that about 107 million *rai* [18 million hectares] nationwide suffer from a medium to high degree of soil erosion, particularly in upland areas where slopes are greater than 5 percent. . . . The eroded topsoil, itself, of course, causes further problems downstream. (UNEP 1988:6–7)

And the conservationist NGO, the Dhammanaat Foundation, that was influential in the Chom Thong dispute, argued that "heavy rains wash away the soil, which quickly silts up dams, reservoirs and rivers. . . . Every rainy season now, lowland paddies are buried under 2–3 meters of sand. . . . The evergreen headwater forest should be areas of strict conservation as their removal brings about environmental disaster" (Svasti 1998).

As a result of these concerns, various development programs, government initiatives, and scientific research projects have focused on soil conservation. The Land Development Department (2004) reiterated the relationship between environmental "crisis" and statemaking by describing soil erosion as an issue of national importance and proposing a wide array of regulatory interventions to manage it. One of the most common approaches is to limit cultivation on vulnerable hillslopes (figure 6.1 shows a steep slope under cultivation), often by replacing smallholder agriculture with pine or teak plantations. In the 1970s, the Land Development Department adopted a policy that stated that "soils that are either too steep . . . or that are too gravelly or stony . . . or that are too shallow . . . for cultivation of most upland crops . . . can be best used for timber production" (Scholten and Wichai 1973:89). In many upland areas where commercial reforestation is not possible, farmers have been encouraged to plant fruit trees. Grass "filter strips" have also been widely promoted as a means of reducing soil erosion on upland slopes. The Royal Forest Department's watershed management units are reported to have distributed over forty million vetiver grass seedlings between 1993 and 2000 (RFD 2004e). And various government agencies have also encouraged the terracing of sloping land or the development of paddy fields in low-slope valley bottoms. These various interventions in upland landscapes and livelihoods are seen as crucial in maintaining upland soil quality, reducing downstream impacts, and avoiding the need for further deforestation in search of undegraded soils.

But these common cause-and-effect statements about soil erosion are not always confirmed by research findings. Moreover, some of the proposed solutions to problems of soil degradation may not necessarily address complex issues of soil management. There is a need to look more closely at common beliefs about erosion and sedimentation in Thailand and to assess how far popular conceptions have been "stabilized" by social and political factors.

POPULAR CONCEPTIONS OF EROSION

Soil erosion is the removal of soil by wind or water. It is an important cause of declining agricultural fertility because erosion removes soil nutrients, or the soil particles that hold nutrients and moisture. By and large, wind erosion is not a common problem in Thailand. Water erosion, however, can occur in a variety of ways. Sheet erosion is the removal of soil

across the surface of the land, while gully erosion involves the development of deep trenches. Rills, or rivulets, are smaller indentations that can
occur simultaneously with sheet erosion or that can lead to the formation of gullies.[1] Under intense rainfall the overland flow along rills and
gullies can resemble temporary streams. Tillage on agricultural land can
contribute to erosion by making the soil easier to wash away, and can
also be a source of erosion in itself as the action of digging on sloping
land gradually moves the soil downslope (Turkelboom et al. 1999). River
erosion can also contribute to riverbank soil loss.

Erosion is an everyday occurrence in most landscapes. But in extreme
cases, it has been blamed for dramatic collapses of civilizations such as
Angkor in modern-day Cambodia or the Mayan civilization in what is
now Mexico—although some analysts have claimed economic and military factors were also relevant.[2] During the twentieth century, the most
famous example of severe erosion occurred in the so-called Dust Bowl
of the mid-western and southern plains of the United States during the
1930s. In this case, a period of rapid agricultural expansion was followed
by dust storms and erosion that enhanced economic depression and caused

FIG. 6.1 *Cultivation on steeply sloping land*

many farmers to move out of the region. These international experiences reverberate in the policy imagination of the Thai government. In one report on soil erosion in Thailand, the Land Development Department (1989:1), issued this dire warning: "Soil and water, the two natural resources are vital to the welfare of the nation. The loss of these resources has led to the destruction of many world civilizations."

The uplands of northern Thailand have become a particular focus of concern about soil erosion for a number of reasons. First, shifting cultivation—and especially the so-called pioneer form—has been associated with high rates of soil loss. The British colonial scientist O. H. K. Spate (1945:527), writing about upland agriculture in Burma, commented that "naturally, these practices are attended with serious deforestation and soil erosion." These views are apparent in later writings too. In 1987, the Thailand Development Research Institute (1987:296), a Bangkok think tank, wrote, "Whereas slash and burn agriculture was once more closely attuned with the ecosystems exploited, it now causes untold ecological damages. . . . In the process, major watersheds are being denuded, with increasing silt loads washed down into the nation's rivers [and] silting up dams."

Usually, "slash-and-burn" deforestation is seen to lead to erosion because clearing trees disturbs the soil and removes the "binding" action of tree roots. The absence of forest canopies also exposes soil to greater splash action from rainfall, which can then further enhance erosion if it forms overland flow. The effect of rainfall is said to be particularly marked during the heavy showers at the onset of the wet season when the soil is freshly tilled and crop cover minimal. Deforestation also reduces local evapotranspiration and hence can increase the volume of water available to travel over the soil surface. There are also said to be impacts on soil fertility. Deforestation means a reduction in the supply of nutrients from decaying leaves and, moreover, degraded soils are vulnerable to invasion by *Imperata cylindrica* (a grass) and other weeds, which make agricultural production difficult (Thiem 1978; Hurni and Sompote 1983).

Second, the pattern of population growth and cultivation on steep slopes has been considered especially erosive. Several authors have proposed that demographic pressures mean that upland agriculture will take place on steeper and steeper slopes, and hence will increase erosion by using land that is inherently unstable. This argument has become internationally famous as a result of writings on the Himalayan region. Writing about the Middle Hills of Nepal, Eckholm (1976:77) commented,

"Population growth in the context of a traditional agrarian technology is forcing farmers onto even steeper slopes, slopes unfit for sustained farming even with the astonishingly elaborate terracing practiced there."
These arguments also influenced thinking about northern Thailand. In 1980, Ives (1980:10) wrote, "Serious land shortage has reduced the traditional periods of forest fallow so that the old systems are on the verge of collapse. Soil erosion, decreasing soil fertility, progressive deforestation and spread of *Imperata* grasslands are all contributing to a critical situation in the mountains, which also has increasingly heavy impacts on the settled agricultural systems of the lowlands." And this vicious circle of population growth, deforestation, and erosion was echoed in other reports. The Thai-Australia World Bank Land Development Project (1985) estimated that hilltribe populations were growing by 3 percent per year; swidden cycles had fallen from fifteen years to under four years; and 2 percent of forest cover was lost to agriculture each year. The project estimated that these changes produced soil erosion rates of between 50 and 100 tonnes per hectare, or 10 to 20 times the sustainable limit.

Third, both historical and current crops grown in the uplands have been associated with erosion. The most famous of these has been linked to national security concerns. During the 1960s and 1970s, some observers argued that opium tended to be cultivated on the steepest or most erodible soil in northern Thailand. A United Nations report in 1967 asserted that some hill tribes selected soils susceptible to erosion because this allowed greater ease in planting poppies (UN 1967:18). Farmers also encouraged erosion by using fire to remove vegetation and to make the soil friable before cultivation (UN 1967:18; Cooper 1984:61). Another report by Japanese anthropologists observed that the best opium crops came from poppies that had poorly developed flowers, and hence farmers tended to locate poppy fields in cool high-altitude fields, often with steep slopes (Shiratori et al. 1973).

Crops introduced more recently have also been blamed for causing erosion. Since the late 1970s, a combination of farmer initiative and intervention by agricultural development schemes has resulted in the replacement of opium cultivation with alternative cash crops such as cabbages, potatoes, and strawberries (Renard 2001). Some have argued that commercialization has exacerbated erosion by encouraging more land clearing and more intensive land use on currently cleared lands. Some argue that many of the new crops offer little leaf cover to protect underlying soils, while others argue that there has been little accompanying investment in soil conservation (Hoare 1984; Hurni and Sompote 1983). A *Bangkok Post* article in 1990 summed up the concerns by stating in its headline that "cabbage is worse than opium" (Sanitsuda 1990:164). It is also often argued that the high chemical use required to cultivate cash crops in upland areas has compromised soil quality and composition, making it even more fragile and erodible. Sometimes, the cultivation of cash crops is described in terms of lost tradition and an assault on the fragile balance of nature: "Traditionally, the hill tribes used slash and burn tactics in a limited way—just to produce food for their families. But in trying to produce cash crops and satisfy the demands of the market, the tribes surpassed the natural capacities of the land, degraded by deforestation and erosion" (Tuenjai 2000:1).

And, fourth, analysts have claimed that the hill farmers in northern Thailand might not understand the threats posed by erosion, and therefore might not take steps to prevent it. One familiar claim is that farmers who are making a transition from shifting to nonshifting forms of cultivation do not necessarily perceive erosion as a threat because they have never experienced it as a long-term problem. Previously they have been able to abandon degraded lands and start afresh without seriously confronting the problem. Consequently, it is argued that upland development and extension workers need to persuade such farmers to protect soil. In the late 1980s, Harper and El-Swaify (1988) found that 37 percent of farmers studied explained that the reason they did not use conservation was because they did not believe erosion to be a serious problem, partly because a lot of farmers expected to relocate cultivation on a regular basis. Similarly, Pahlman (1990:99) noted that 43 percent of the upland (*khon muang*) farmers she interviewed in Nan province "did not perceive they had a problem of soil erosion at all," while only 23 percent considered it to be a serious problem. To illustrate the argument, Pahlman (1990:82) showed how farmers were keen to identify problems such as weeds, insects/pests, and lack of water or land, whereas soil erosion came last in problems mentioned by farmers. Consequently, Pahlman proposed that upland development programs should make farmers more aware of erosion hazards.

REASSESSING EROSION IN THE UPLANDS

It is clear, then, that soil erosion is an important component of the broader narrative of environmental crisis in northern Thailand. It is also clear that erosion is one of the main challenges facing upland farmers in the region. But do these popular conceptions really help in the understanding and effective management of soil problems? An increasing number of analysts now question whether the simple cause-and-effect linkages of erosion and upland agriculture contained in these popular narratives are helpful in explaining the complex soil-management challenges faced by upland farmers. It is becoming increasingly clear that these narratives overgeneralize and simplify these challenges, and give insufficient attention to biophysical variation and the great diversity of farmers' soil management strategies. An important initial question to consider is how far common approaches to describing and measuring "erosion" fairly represent the kinds of soil problems experienced in northern Thailand.

The "Universal" Soil Loss Equation

There is a growing debate about whether the word "erosion" is a fair description of all the diverse processes of soil degradation and sedimentation experienced in complex landscapes (Blaikie 1985; Hallsworth 1987; Zimmerer 2004). Part of this is a debate about current approaches to measuring and estimating erosion. For much of the twentieth century, governments and researchers used the so-called Universal Soil Loss Equation (USLE) as a standardized model for estimating erosion rates. This equation was formulated in the United States after the Dust Bowl of the 1930s and was intended to predict levels of erosion, and hence allow farmers to keep soil loss to within acceptable levels (USDA 1961). The model has been used in Thailand to provide general estimates of soil erosion at a regional level, providing support to claims of an environmental crisis. For example, Jantawat (1987:13) estimated soil erosion in northern Thailand to be "higher than the world and Asian averages" at the remarkably precise figure of 933.67 tonnes per square kilometer per year. Manu and Ard (1980) estimated less precise categories of "severe" and "very severe" erosion on 16.9 percent and 5.8 percent of land in northern Thailand respectively.

But is the USLE really universal, and can a model based on experience in the American Dust Bowl really be effective in explaining erosion in other parts of the world? In relation to northern Thailand, there are a number of important issues to consider. First, there are the various components of the USLE itself. In particular, the USLE may exaggerate the importance of slope length when applied to complex farming landscapes.

Topographic surveys in northern Thailand may, indeed, indicate considerable slope length in many areas (figure 6.2 shows hillslope cultivation). But these surveys ignore how slopes are divided into different plots, which may have different crops or which may be divided using barriers or areas of trees, bamboo, and grass. Research indicates that these surface vegetation "filters" may play a very important role in interrupting the erosive flow of water across the land, causing soil to be deposited at each interruption (a point also made in chapter 3 concerning waterflow). Regional-level applications of the USLE may also underestimate soil protective measures. In northern Thailand, many farmers adopt practices such as covering soil with leaves of crop residue to protect newly planted seeds and seedlings. Many hillslope farmers also practice minimal tillage, planting seeds in individual holes (made with a wooden stake) rather than plowing the entire area. The USLE may also fail to acknowledge differences between rainfall patterns in America and the humid tropics. The USLE was based on average rainfall figures, whereas in the humid tropics rain tends to fall in high-magnitude storm events during one long wet season. This difference means that the highest risk of erosion is reduced to short periods in the tropics, and these may or may not coincide with local cropping cycles that determine when crops are most vulnerable to erosion (Hallsworth 1987:145). Finally, one further significant source of error is the lack of attention to soil formation rates in the tropics and subtropics (which are likely to be greater than in temperate zones). Consequently, it is difficult to determine acceptable levels of soil loss rather than just focusing on absolute rates of soil loss. These limitations raise many questions about the applicability of the USLE in upland areas of northern Thailand. One indication of this lack of relevance is provided in a study undertaken by Thitirojanawat and Chareonsuk (2000) in Nan province. They found that the USLE, with standard soil erodibility factors, predicted rates of soil loss 104 times greater than those actually observed in runoff plots.

Apart from its internal structure, a second general weakness of the USLE is that it focuses primarily on erosion from agricultural land, and the definitions used in the equation imply sheet erosion, or erosion that occurs more or less evenly across agricultural plots. But much erosion in upland areas, especially those with high levels of monsoon rainfall, occurs in the form of gully erosion and landslips, which may be related to previously existing geomorphological processes and hence are not necessarily primarily affected by agriculture. Much erosion or sediment movement

FIG. 6.2 *Hillslope cultivation in Chiang Rai. Note the soil protection, the natural gully, and the healthy rice field under the slope.*

in the uplands may therefore result from nonanthropogenic biophysical processes rather than from agriculture. This has particular importance for understanding the causes of lowland sedimentation. Research in the Middle Hills of Nepal, for example, has argued that hillside gullies called *pahiros* result from long-term geological processes of erosion rather than recent human activity (Smadja 1992:7). The importance of these nonanthropogenic factors is underlined by Bruijnzeel (quoted in Calder 1999:29): "in situations of high natural sediment yield as a result of steep terrain, high rainfall rates and geological factors, little, if any, influence will be exerted by man."

Third, the USLE does not indicate where sediment may be delivered. There is a common belief that soil eroded on hillsides will be quickly transported into rivers and deposited in the lowlands. However, research suggests this process may be much slower and that much eroded soil may not even leave local basins. Classic research on sediment yield—or the amount of sediment removed from a basin by a river—has indicated that surprisingly small amounts of sediment removed from hillsides by erosion are transported outside of the basins (Trimble 1983). Rather, much sediment may be deposited farther down slopes (often in traps formed by vegetative landscape filters) or in storage zones such as valley floors or floodplains. In other words, soil is often moved, but not lost from basins. Moreover, sedimentation in the lowlands is not simply a product of sediment supply (such as from upstream erosion), but also reflects river discharge. Discharge is the power exerted by a water mass and represents the capacity for rivers to carry sediment. Large rivers, with high levels of discharge, can carry immense quantities of sediment without depositing it. But reducing a river's discharge (through activities such as extracting water for dams or irrigation) can increase rates of sedimentation. There has been a major increase in the extraction of water for irrigation throughout northern Thailand since the 1980s, and consequently sedimentation problems are likely to have been partly caused by increased water extraction rather than an increase in sediment supply. Lowland farmers complaining about sedimentation, such as those in Chom Thong, should consider the extent to which their own irrigation practices are contributing to the problem.

In fact, studies in northern Thailand suggest that there has been no medium- or long-term increase in sediment in the region's river systems. Research by Alford (1992:267–68) suggests there is significant year-to-year variation in sediment yield, matching year-to-year variation in streamflow, but that "volumes of suspended sediment moving through the rivers of northern Thailand are among the lowest of all river systems worldwide." A similar review of data by Enters (1995) suggests that sediment loads in the Ping River increased somewhat from the 1960s to the mid 1970s but declined again to the mid 1980s, despite ongoing deforestation and agricultural transformation including the introduction of opium-substituting crops. As with the study undertaken by Alford there is a clear correlation with short- and medium-term variation in streamflow, suggesting "a sediment source within the stream channel . . . rather than sheet erosion" (Enters 1995:97–99). These results suggest that much erosion occurring on hillsides in the uplands is likely to be trapped in numerous landscape filters and points of redeposition before reaching the main river network. Consequently, using aggregated estimates of on-site upstream erosion (such as the USLE) to predict downstream sedimentation is likely to lead to vastly inflated results (Chomitz and Kumari 1998:17; Bruijnzeel 1997:140).

A related weakness with the USLE approach is that the focus on "soil loss" can divert attention away from the reality that soil is, in fact, relocated and a proportion of this relocation can be very beneficial. Sedimentation that results from erosion may reduce agricultural productivity

IN-STREAM SEDIMENTATION: COST OR BENEFIT?

Sediment carried to streams and rivers may serve some useful purposes. Enters (1995:102) has argued that the dredging of riverine sediments has played an important part in the development of the northern Thai construction industry. Local observations by A. Walker (in 2004) near Chiang Mai add some support to Enters's argument. Here, in the middle reaches of the Mae Khan catchment, a river-dredging business (operating within a national park) is the main source of sand for the local construction industry. There are some local concerns about the impacts of the dredging, but these are focused mainly on the impacts of the sand-filled trucks on the road running down to the river. Some local residents oppose this economic activity and want to close the businesses down. But these views are consistently outweighed by others who highlight the economic benefits of dredging both in terms of local employment and reduced construction costs.

if it clogs streams and rice terraces, but it may enhance productivity if it deposits nutrients on agricultural land. As Blaikie and Brookfield (1987:4) famously wrote, "one farmer's erosion is another's soil fertility." In northern Thailand, it is often forgotten that the rich alluvial soils favored by lowland agriculturalists have resulted from long-term erosion and deposition of upland soils. Even at more local scales, it has been observed that soil eroded from higher slopes can significantly improve the fertility of lower slopes. There is some evidence that this process is actively managed by farmers to assist, for example, in the formation of paddy fields (Turkelboom 1999:257; Chomitz and Kumàri 1998:21). This process has also been observed in Nepal (Kienholz et al. 1984). As Enters (1995:104) notes about Thailand, "Farmers are aware of the positive effects of light to moderate soil erosion and are able to use it to their advantage." Indeed, in 1939 the British colonial soil scientist Robert Pendleton (1939:43) argued that Thailand's greatest agricultural problem was insufficient erosion to remove infertile weathered soil:[3]

In Thailand . . . particularly between the hills and productive lowlands . . . there has not been sufficient, normal, geological erosion in this country to remove the weathered-out residual material left after the decomposition of rocks into soil. . . . Farmers will cross from five to ten kilometers more of such poor, infertile soil if they can plant upland crops such as peppers and cotton on the hill slopes which are less infertile because the soil has gradually eroded from them.

Because of these various limitations, many critics have suggested that the only thing universal about the USLE is its name. Critics do not suggest that erosion is not a problem; rather, the USLE wrongly gives the impression that the causes and management of erosion are universal. Some soil scientists now believe the USLE should be modified for each location (Harper 1988). Others suggest it should be abandoned in favor of more meaningful work on improving soil fertility such as restoring soil nutrients, and local soil protection practices. One critic wrote, "[The USLE has] probably absorbed too much of the relatively slim resources available for conservation work, with the inevitable neglect of work that would have been more relevant" (Hallsworth 1987:145).

Erosion and Shifting Cultivation

The presumed causes of erosion can also be questioned. Quite apart from concerns about the applicability of the USLE, there is also considerable evidence that shifting cultivation may not be as degrading of soil as commonly portrayed in popular erosion narratives. Many studies of shifting cultivation (in its various forms) in areas of low population density have questioned popular stereotypes. Conklin's pathbreaking work (1954, 1957) on shifting cultivation in the Philippines concluded that cultivators adopted a variety of practices to minimize impacts on soils and forest. Nye and Greenland (1960, 1964), working in Africa, recorded that soil carbon content and organic matter did decline rapidly when forest was converted to shifting cultivation, but that levels recovered sufficiently following fallow periods and the input of ash.

These findings have been supported by later research (for example, Palm et al. 1996; Murty et al. 2002). In Borneo, researchers have claimed that local agriculture has been unduly blamed for causing sedimentation in rivers and that nonanthropogenic causes of erosion also need to be considered (Hatch 1983; Douglas et al. 1992). And in Papua New Guinea, anthropological work has demonstrated how some farming groups prolong soil fertility by adopting conservation practices such as "soil mounds," where farmers carefully maintain soil quality and hence maintain high levels of cultivation (Sillitoe 1983:1998).

Similar work has been carried out in Thailand. A United Nations survey in 1967 reported, "It can be freely stated that the hill tribe people have an amazing grasp of soils and their potential. . . . Contrary to a widespread belief, the shifting cultivation as practiced by the hilltribes does not lead to any grave soil deterioration. . . . soil erosion is rare, and we have as yet not observed any serious accelerated wash-off or gully erosion" (UN 1967:127, 128).

Other international research undertaken in the 1960s and 1970s (Kunstadter et al. 1978) found that erosion was less apparent than expected in Thailand's hill-farming areas, although trails and villages were occasionally sites of obvious erosion or soil compaction (Sanga 1978: 169–70). One researcher from this period reported that "erosion is another matter that obviously warrants attention in the uplands, because cultivation of the steep slopes would appear to be a direct invitation to disaster. Surprisingly, however, there is little dramatic evidence of erosion other than that associated with road building" (Charley 1983:395).

Further work also identified various means by which some farming groups, such as the Lawa and Karen, carefully selected land to burn and set fires in locations that minimized resulting erosion (Kunstadter 1978; Zinke et al. 1978). Excessive erosion is also prevented by minimal tillage; the preservation of tree stumps and associated root systems; and the use of vegetation strips, logs, and plant residue as filters to prevent the downslope movement of soil. In Mae Hong Son province, Chanphen (1998) found that such practices in association with upland rice cultivation helped to minimize soil erosion. On six observed plots, levels of erosion were below officially accepted standards while on four plots there was minimal erosion. Once again, locally grounded research has provided evidence that challenges the common beliefs that dominate official and popular statements about environmental degradation in the uplands.

Soil Erosion and Modern Commercial Agriculture

Clearly, then, there is considerable research that questions the simplistic association of upland agriculture with high levels of erosion. Many of these studies of shifting cultivation have been undertaken in areas characterized by low population densities, relatively abundant land, and regular long fallow periods. But what happens when such systems are placed under land pressure because of internal population growth, in-migration, and increasing state restrictions on the clearing of forested lands? Many narratives of environmental problems in northern Thailand assume that permanent and commercially oriented agriculture will increase upland degradation. But is this the case? As shifting cultivation is progressively transformed into permanent cultivation, is soil degradation the inevitable result?

Perhaps not. One indication of this is provided in a survey of catchments in northern Thailand by the International Board for Soil Research and Management (IBSRAM), in search of suitably degraded case-study sites. Some of the observations in this report provide important reminders that recent trends in upland cultivation, even on steeply sloping land, have not led inevitably to degradation:

> In [one possible case study] catchment no severe erosion problems could be observed even on extremely steep, cleared soils. . . . In the lower part [of the catchment] cultivated plots on steep slopes showed a surprising stability of the topsoil and there was no evidence of erosion in these fields. . . . No severe soil erosion could be observed [in a second catchment] even on steep slopes under cultivation. . . . There is no evidence of surface runoff or erosion in this catchment. (IBSRAM 1997:54–55, 58, 59)

Some other more detailed studies provide somewhat less rosy conclusions, but equally raise important questions about the popular narratives that link recent agricultural transformation and increasingly unacceptable levels of erosion. Important questions emerge about the extent of agricultural impacts, the supposed inevitable relationship between population growth and degradation, and the perceptions of farmers themselves.

The Mien in Chiang Rai. In one study in Chiang Rai province, Forsyth (1994, 1995, 1996) assessed how an upland village had reacted to land shortages and declining soil fertility. The study asked the question, Does population growth lead to increased cultivation of steeper slopes? As discussed above, many discussions of environmental degradation in upland areas of Asia have suggested this will occur. A second question was, How do farmers, who have historically relocated villages regularly, respond to erosion problems under new conditions of sedentary agriculture?

The study was based in the Mien (Yao) village of Pha Dua, in the north of Chiang Rai province, on granite and sandy-clay soils at an altitude of about 700 meters. Historically, the Mien—like the Hmong—were "pioneer" cultivators who relocated villages every ten to twenty years in order to find more fertile farming land. This village, however, was founded in 1947, and the farmers have stayed since then. The population has grown from 110 in 1947 to about 1,200 in 2005. The staple crops of the Mien were rice, maize, and opium. Since the 1980s, however, opium cultivation has been abandoned, and farmers have cultivated new commercial crops such as soybeans, ginger, and peanuts, with limited amounts of coffee, oranges, and lychee.

The study used aerial photographs and a geographic information system (GIS) to analyze to what extent steep slopes had been used over time. Six sets of aerial photographs and one land survey were used to create maps of where agriculture had been most concentrated over time. These maps were then integrated with a topographic map to show whether agricultural land use had increased on the steepest slopes. The extent of soil erosion was then estimated using a basic model that assumed erosion would be highest where agriculture had occurred most frequently on the steepest slopes.[4] This divided the landscape into areas of predicted "most" and "least" eroded land, which were then measured for the existence of erosion.

The study used the cesium-137 method to measure soil erosion, which is a useful way to show historic soil erosion on agricultural land since the 1960s. The technique is based on the assumption that cesium-137 isotopes were deposited evenly on soil following the thermonuclear bomb tests of the 1950s and 1960s. Soil erosion (or deposition) since this era can therefore be measured by comparing the amount of isotopes in soil on agricultural land with other sites that have remained relatively uneroded. The advantage of this technique is that it permits a historic measurement of cumulative erosion from 1963, the peak of the bomb tests.[5] This approach is more attractive than experimental soil plots because it measures actual erosion on-site and because it summarizes years of erosion, rather than relying on short-term experimental conditions. Finally, the study used interviews and participatory discussions with farmers over a period of some months to identify perceptions of soil fertility and erosion. These interviews were combined with observation of farming practices and visual surveys of the landscape and soil degradation.

The study provided four important findings. First, population growth had encouraged farmers to use flatter land more frequently rather than moving onto ever steeper plots. This finding contradicted the concern of Eckholm (1976:77) that population growth forced farmers onto steep slopes unfit for farming. Figure 6.3 shows the relative sizes of the "most" (4) and "least" (1) eroded land categories, which indicate the relationship between steep land and historic frequency of agriculture. As figure 6.3 shows, the "most" eroded category is significantly smaller than other categories, indicating that relatively little cultivation has taken place on the steepest slopes. Farmers also confirmed this pattern by explaining that they avoided steep slopes because they were harder to farm, had more erosion, and attracted less sunlight.

Second, soil erosion had indeed occurred at high levels on the steepest land, but less seriously on the land most used for agriculture. The cesium-137 measurements of erosion showed that erosion averaged 24 tonnes per hectare per year between 1963 and 1991 for the "least" eroded land, but this rose to 64 tonnes per hectare per year on the "most" eroded category. However, the physical area for this higher rate of erosion totaled only about 5 percent of the total research area, and most rates associated with agricultural land were well below this upper limit. These findings indicate that erosion in some locations was indeed at rates considered high in Thailand, but that most agricultural land did not experience the highest rates.[6]

Third, information collected suggested that natural processes account for much local erosion and sedimentation. GIS data of slope steepness indi-

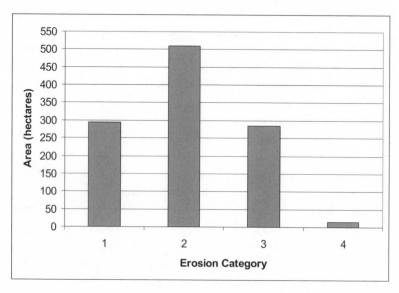

FIG. 6.3 *Categories of soil erosion in Pha Dua study area*

cated a marked absence of relatively gentle slopes of between 10 and 20 percent (figure 6.4). The absence of these slopes is obvious to any observer because the landscape is characterized by hummocky, rounded land with convex slopes (slope gradients are gentle at ridges, but become gradually steeper downslope; figure 6.5 pictures this type of landscape). Gullies of up to 1 or 2 meters in depth often exist at the bottom of slopes. This has been described as an "all-slopes-topography," which is found on granite land in other locations (such as Brazil and South Africa, see Twidale 1982:177), or as similar to the so-called *pahiros* of Nepal mentioned above. Importantly, villagers explained that these gullies existed before the establishment of the village in 1947 and that they occurred on both forested and agricultural land. Such deep gullies may therefore be sources of erosion and sedimentation that predate agriculture. Indeed, villager actions may even reduce their impact on soil movement. Some farmers preferred to cultivate vegetation and banana trees in these gullies and surrounding slopes because these were considered valuable sources for bamboo and banana trunks that were fed to pigs. One villager claimed pigs preferred banana trunks grown in gullies to those planted on farmland.

Finally, contrary to the findings of other research about farmer attitudes, farmers in Pha Dua did perceive erosion to be a problem, and they took steps to avoid it. Interestingly, there were problems in discussing "ero-

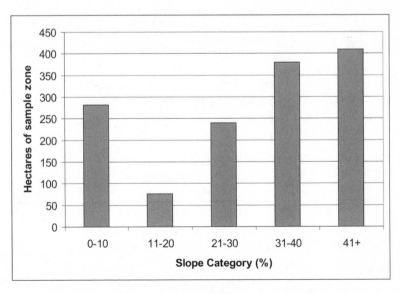

FIG. 6.4 *Categories of slope steepness in Pha Dua study area*

FIG. 6.5 *Hummocky slopes and vegetated gullies*

sion" as a concept known to both researcher and farmers. Using the Thai language, the most obvious term for erosion is *kaan phangthalai khong din* or, literally, "the falling down of soil." Sometimes, farmers interpreted this phrase to mean "landslides," which had not been experienced often, and hence farmers were quick to deny this as a problem.[7] Such communication problems may account for survey results that have led others to conclude that there is a lack of awareness of erosion among upland farmers. But, in Pha Dua, when the topic of soil in general was discussed, farmers very clearly described poor soil fertility, soil moving down slopes after rain, or the rapid loss of agricultural productivity following cultivation on steeper slopes. Farmers explained they were happier to cultivate flatter land more frequently than to increase cultivation on steeper slopes, even though they acknowledged this strategy would mean shorter fallow periods on flatter land. Detailed discussions also revealed that farmers had adopted a new system of local land tenure during the early 1970s (after some twenty-five years of settlement), which allocated land to specific households and families (before, it had been an open-access system). This new system of land tenure encouraged farmers to cultivate land continuously in order to demonstrate that they intended to keep the land, an innovation they hoped would enhance their formal tenure security (a pattern observed elsewhere in northern Thailand, see Turkelboom et al. 1999).

These various findings contradict important aspects of popular narratives about erosion, but they do not dismiss the problem of erosion, or agriculture's role in enhancing it. Population growth has increased some cultivation on steep slopes, but most cultivation still occurs on the flatter slopes. This trend may therefore mean that the biggest threat to soil fertility comes from the exhaustion of soil nutrients by repeated cultivation, rather than simply the removal of nutrients by erosion (this issue, and the effectiveness of fertilizer as a remedy, is discussed further in chapter 7). Moreover, agriculture may not be the only cause of downstream sedimentation because the region is geologically eroding through naturally occurring deep gullies. Farmers are aware of the risks of erosion, and take steps to avoid it, but for a range of social, economic, and political reasons, they feel compelled to cultivate land frequently.

The Akha in Chiang Rai. Turkelboom (1999) conducted an in-depth study of farmers' responses to soil erosion in the Akha village of Pakha in Chiang Rai province. This village, which is between 700 and 900 meters above sea level, was established in 1976 on sandy-clay soils underlain by granite, shale, and a slaty rock known as phyllite. This study offers another chance to assess the impacts of land shortage and commercialization of crops. When the village was established, most farmers cultivated rice and maize, as well as raising cattle. Since the 1980s, farmers have supplemented these activities with the cultivation of cabbage, beans, and tree crops. The study used a combination of experimental plots, erosion surveys, and participatory discussions with farmers.

A number of important findings emerged from this research. First, there was little doubt that agriculture was enhancing erosion. Tillage erosion was apparent because farmers experienced declining soil fertility at the top of steep slopes, in locations where water erosion was less likely to occur because of the comparative lack of slope length. Gully erosion was also evident. This village also had deep, naturally occurring gullies between convex slopes. But there were also smaller gullies—some 10 to 15 centimeters in depth—on agricultural land that did not occur under forest cover. These gullies apparently resulted from overland flow being generated during rainfall on steep slopes or from water running onto slopes from other sources, such as from roads. Sometimes landslips occurred when streams or paths undercut slopes. The erosion on slopes, however, was also found to increase soil fertility when soil was deposited on lower slopes, around lines of crops, or on leveled land.

Second, however, farmers were aware of these problems and adopted various methods of soil conservation. Mulching reduced the impacts of erosion during the early weeks of cultivation of some crops such as ginger. Diversion channels—or small trenches 10 to 20 centimeters deep— were drawn across fields to reduce waterflow and to demarcate field ownership. The use of tree crops on slopes was also increasing, partly because some farmers saw them as a more reliable source of income. Yet, the overall perception was that soil fertility was declining. Various methods were used to express this. Some elders liked to tell the mythological story of a giant, underground snake or piglike monster (*pjengcha*) that caused landslips and political havoc every thirteen years. Others reported that "you can see the bones through the soil now" or that "the land is becoming like old people—they are not strong enough to hold anything anymore" (Turkelboom 1999:172, 190). Here, again, there are indications that farmers are very capable of describing soil problems in terms that are meaningful to them. In a formal survey, they may not identify "erosion" (however it may be translated) as a high priority problem but, given the opportunity, they can describe the challenges of soil management in various locally appropriate ways.

Third, upland soil erosion was not likely to result in downstream sedimentation in rivers. Contrary to many popular narratives of soil erosion in northern Thailand, Turkelboom found that much eroded soil was deposited near the source of erosion, rather than transported long distances to lowland river systems. He found that colluvial (that is, gravity-carried) soil deposition took place on some extremely steep slopes of up to 60 percent.[8] Furthermore, Turkelboom's study found that only a third of agricultural fields bordered streams, meaning most sedimentation took place well away from the stream network. Turkelboom (1999:169) commented that "eroded sediments of 67 percent of the fields are translocated inside the catchment and may take years, or even centuries to reach the hydrological network."

And fourth, the erosion risk of new commercial crops was not as bad as suggested by popular narratives. Turkelboom compared the generation of erosion from different crops and cropping systems. In fact, he found that upland rice (the most "traditional" Akha crop) had the highest rates of 60 tons per hectare per crop cycle. Maize and beans were classified as the least erosive cropping systems, with median soil losses of respectively 19 and 10 tons per hectare per crop cycle. Erosion in cabbage fields lay in between these two extremes. Importantly, he found that the variation in erosion was related to cropping systems (the timing and manner of cultivation) rather than the crops alone. He noted that "the contradictions between the literature and the observed data . . . indicate that erosion susceptibility does not only depend on crop morphology and crop growth, but is also subject to a whole set of local-specific cultivation practices. . . . Therefore, it is difficult, if not impossible, to generalize about the effects of crops on erosion. The consequence is that cropping systems should be compared, rather than crops" (Turkelboom 1999:134).

The impacts of cabbage on erosion are particularly interesting. Turkelboom observed that the main risks from cabbage arose from the relatively small surface area of cabbage, which usually increases the area of soil exposed to rainfall. Moreover, cabbage was often cultivated on banks of soil that had been raised some 5 or 10 centimeters above surrounding soil, with trenches in between. These soil banks were occasionally susceptible to the formation of rills, and the trenches could enhance runoff onto surrounding land. But against these risks, cabbage was often cultivated during the dry season (with irrigation), and was therefore much less exposed to erosive rainfall events. Moreover, if the price of cabbage fell, the Akha farmers would abandon cabbage fields, which would then become covered with grass and other invasive plants, reducing the risk of any further erosion.[9]

Turkelboom's study provides two main lessons for erosion research. First, it is difficult to generalize about erosion. Erosion is not only the effect of stable factors such as slope length, but also results from dynamic influences such as the cropping system, timing of cultivation, and the short-term trends in crop prices. Second, it is important not to generalize about farmers. Turkelboom (1999:208–11) identified five levels of entrepreneurialism or concern for soil conservation: secure investors (who owned paddy fields and fruit plantations); profit maximizers (adopting high-risk crops such as cabbage); diversifiers (farmers who mix rice cultivation with limited cash crops); survivors (those who cultivated only rice on a short-term basis); and dropouts (who relied solely on wage labor and petty business). The survivors accounted for some 30 percent of the village. The point of this classification is to acknowledge that soil and crop management does not take place uniformly across single ethnic groups, but that there is great diversity between and within households.

This important work clearly suggests that more attention should be given to where and how erosion is caused, rather than in adopting universal assumptions about the impacts of upland agriculture on erosion and sedimentation. Turkelboom's study indicates that much concern about the downstream impacts of erosion in Chiang Rai is misplaced, but that there are strong grounds for concern about declining soil fertility. New commercial crops do not necessarily add to erosion risks, but poor farmers who continue to cultivate upland rice as their main livelihood strategy are experiencing a decline in productivity (a similar finding to that reported in chapter 5 from Mae Uam). This trend highlights the need for development assistance focusing on livelihood sustainability, rather than on controlling upland agriculture because of its alleged impacts on lowland sedimentation.

The Lahu in Chiang Mai. Jones (1997) studied a Lahu village in Chiang Dao district, in the north of Chiang Mai province, on land between 630 and 700 meters above sea level, on silty-clay loam soils covering limestone and shale. Farmers cultivated a combination of rice, maize, pumpkins, and potatoes as main crops.

The study aimed to explore the likelihood that the Lahu would adopt soil conservation measures being promoted by the Land Development Department by examining, among other things, the way farmers viewed erosion. Previous research on experimental plots had enabled the selection of a vegetative soil conservation measure (alley cropping with leucaena and pigeon pea), which had been found to significantly reduce soil erosion rates relative to the farmers' current practices. The Land Development Department had assumed that if erosion were a primary concern for farmers then such technology would undoubtedly be adopted.

In-depth interviews were conducted with farmers about their experience of erosion and how they responded. Once again, Jones found that speaking with hill farmers about "erosion" was problematic, because most of them already avoided the steepest slopes where erosion occurs most. In this village, farmers did not mention erosion as a problem when asked about problems for food production (although they agreed, when asked directly, that erosion did affect yields). However, all described problems of declining soil fertility, including the labor demands of weeding and the increased need to use weed killer. Consequently, most farmers discussed problems of land shortage, or a lack of agricultural productivity, rather than erosion explicitly.

Jones (1997:264) argues that research on erosion needs to avoid "unconsciously held assumptions about what constitutes sustainable land management." The Lahu farmers may not perceive outsiders' definitions of erosion, but this may be for very good reasons: "Local knowledge is oriented towards problem solving. . . . . [The Lahu] do not consider the changing status of soils to be a problem (rather weeds are the reason they migrate). It is more important that they find fertile ground to move to, and hence have accumulated a greater knowledge of indicator species" (Jones 1997:264). In fact, the Lahu are well known for their knowledge of soil fertility: one upland researcher found that Lahu use at least sixty-one species as indicators of the suitability of soil for cultivation (A. R. Walker, cited in Jones 1997:253).

This study highlights the differences between farmers' and development workers' perceptions of soil degradation. In the past, when these Lahu farmers were pioneer shifting cultivators, they tended not to invest in enhancing the long-term productivity of soils and had little knowledge of soil conservation measures (albeit according to Western definitions). However, as farmers found that there was no longer new land available for them to cultivate, and they intended to remain in the one area, they could be expected to adopt soil conservation technologies that enhanced or maintained yields over the long term, without requiring additional labor or capital inputs. However, Jones found little evidence from the Land Development Department's data that the proposed soil conservation measures resulted in higher yields over a five-year period. Farmers were therefore unlikely to adopt these measures unless they were seen as more productive than their own practices in the longer term, or as a rapid means of controlling weed growth or enhancing soil fertility in the short term. This study therefore showed that soil conservation efforts might be more effective if they match farmers' concerns more directly rather than focus on outsiders' preoccupation with erosion.

It should be clear that these three case studies do not suggest that upland erosion is unproblematic. But they do show that local farmers have good reason not to regard it as universally degrading. These different perspectives suggest that it may be unwise to give too much attention to erosion as the sole, or even primary, cause of upland soil degradation. Declining soil fertility may be caused by long-term cultivation of crops, with or without the removal of nutrients by erosion. Similarly, cultivation may encourage invasive grass species, other plants that are considered weeds by local farmers, or soil-borne crop diseases requiring greater expenditure of time and labor in preparing sites for cultivation. From the point of view of the upland farmer, erosion is undoubtedly something that affects agricultural productivity, but it may not be an overriding problem. Assessing soil degradation using standardized erosion models such as the USLE ignores the diverse challenges that farmers face in managing their soils. Finally, the case studies also add support to the view that soils eroded from agricultural fields in the uplands may not be directly linked to low-land sedimentation.

ROADS, PLANTATION FORESTRY, AND GRASS STRIPS

So, what are the sources of lowland sedimentation other than upland agriculture? And are there other factors that may contribute to erosion? The narrative of erosion in northern Thailand usually focuses on the alleged negative impacts of cultivation by upland farmers. But some state-led activities may also contribute.

Do Roads Cause Erosion?

Since the late 1960s, the Thai government has embarked on an extensive road-building program in the northern uplands in order to enhance national security and promote local development. In 1969, one such road was built in the far north of Chiang Rai province, with the assistance of U.S. Navy engineers (the so-called Seabees). This road was to gain notoriety as a route by which opium caravans traveled south (McCoy 1972:353). The anthropologists Jane and Lucien Hanks witnessed the road being built. Their observations are sobering: "Sadly, when the Seabees departed, the road almost disappeared after a year or two of rains because no provision had been made for its maintenance. However, it did survive, though cut by deep washes and mud slides at many points" (Hanks and Hanks 2001:200).[10]

Various studies in different countries have proposed that roads contribute more to soil erosion than suggested by the roads' modest surface area. In Indonesia, one inquiry observed that rural roads covered just 3 percent of the study area, but contributed 24 percent to the total basin sediment yield (Rijsdijk and Bruijnzeel 1991). Similar results have also been found in Africa (Dunne and Dietrich 1982) and South America (Harden 1992). In northern Thailand, Sheng tentatively estimated that 30 percent of erosion and sedimentation results from road construction, although it is not clear how this figure was reached (cited in McKinnon 1986:22).

Ziegler and colleagues (Ziegler and Giambelluca 1997; Ziegler,

Giambelluca et al. 2000) analyzed the impact of roads on water delivery and erosion in northern Thailand using a rainfall simulator and a computer model. As a case study, they used a remote and mountainous area of Chiang Mai province, with altitudes ranging between 750 and 1,850 meters. In this area, roads account for only 0.25 percent of the landscape, but the study results showed that hydrological and erosional impacts of roads are substantially greater than those from agricultural lands during storms of normal magnitude. The usual pattern observed involved two stages of erosion. First, the early rains of the wet season washed away the dry, fine sediment that had accumulated on roads during the dry season. Second, storms that were more intense then created deep ruts and gullies, accelerating sediment transport. The authors concluded that the ability of soil to absorb water was one order of magnitude less on (unpaved) road surfaces than on any other land surface. Consequently, the construction of roads affects the ability of land to hold water and increases the generation of erosive overland flow. A simulation of sediment yield in a case-study subcatchment suggested that it was negligible with 25 percent of the catchment converted to various stages of upland agriculture. However, the addition of a road through a small lowland portion of the catchment generated substantial sediment delivery during larger storm events. Their overall conclusion is crucially important:

> The results emphasize that basin sediment yield is not a reliable indicator of the existence of severe erosion within a watershed. Rather, sediment budgeting approaches are needed to uncover important sediment sources that occupy small percentages of the total basin area (e.g., roads). Finally, the trend of focusing solely on erosional impacts of agricultural practices, ignoring impacts associated with unpaved roads, is not a sustainable conservation strategy for managing upland watersheds in SE Asia. (Ziegler, Giambelluca et al. 2000:1)

A similar argument was put by Chamnonk (1983) for the Mae Taeng watershed in Chiang Mai province. Chamnonk argued that road length was the single-most important variable in explaining amounts of runoff and suspended sediment in this watershed.

Accordingly, it seems difficult to ignore the significance of roads as contributors to soil erosion. Roads add to sediment sources when they are first constructed, and steep road cuttings in mountain areas are a common source of readily mobilized soil. Roads have compacted surfaces that increase and concentrate overland flow, causing both sheet erosion and gullying. Roads are also often well connected to the stream network and can readily deliver mobilized sediment to streams. Further discussions of erosion need to acknowledge these various factors and seek better planning, routing, and maintenance of upland roads.

Does Plantation Forestry Reduce Erosion?

Widespread upland tree planting has been a key government strategy in the fight against erosion since at least the early 1970s. Land classification policies in the uplands advocate the restoration of tree cover on large swaths of land considered inappropriate for agriculture, and the Royal Forest Department has often promoted teak and pine plantations as chief forms of reforestation. This advocacy of reforestation is based on the popular view that tree cover reduces erosion by reducing the splash effect of rainfall and by maintaining a surface litter layer that can absorb water and reduce the generation of overland flow (Sadoff 1991). Tree roots are also said to bind soil and to prevent large-scale movement of soil when it is wet. These claims are sometimes backed by measurements from experimental plots that suggest that sheet erosion under forest cover is far lower than sheet erosion on cultivated land (Nipon 1991).

On hydrological grounds, some caution should be exercised about widespread tree planting, given that trees are high users of water (see discussion in chapter 4). There may also be grounds for questioning the widely held view that tree planting inevitably reduces erosion. A number of research findings suggest that plantation forestry may not necessarily reduce levels of erosion, and at times may even exacerbate soil management problems.

First, the claim that erosion is minimal or nonexistent under forest cover is misleading. As discussed in the case study of the Mien village above, overland flow can occur under forest cover and this can lead to gullying. In particular, it is increasingly clear that forests have a limited impact on modifying overland flow in heavy storm events, and there is growing evidence that such peak events make a disproportionately high—and perhaps even dominant—contribution to erosion and sedimentation (I. Douglas 1999:1728; Pongboun et al. 2000). Moreover, while plot-level studies of erosion may highlight significant difference between forest cover and cultivated landscapes, such studies are not designed to measure all sources of erosion and generally do not include the deeper forms of gully erosion (Morgan 1986; Bocco 1991). As noted in relation to Forsyth's research in Chiang Rai province, gully erosion can take place on both cultivated and forested land and is not necessarily caused by forest clearing for agricultural purposes.

Second, international research suggests that some forms of plantation forestry might actually increase erosion. Observations from Costa Rica and India have shown that monoculture forests (those with a predominance of one species, such as with teak or pine plantations) may remove the dissipating effect of the tree canopy on the erosive effects of rainfall (Calder 1999:16–19; Hamilton 1987:258). For storms with small raindrop sizes, individual drops tend to amalgamate on the surface of leaves until a large drop is formed, which then falls to the ground. If trees are tall, then the kinetic energy of this process may even exceed natural rainfall.[11] This effect can be particularly marked for tree species with large leaves, such as teak. Teak plantations—which are common in northern Thailand—may therefore increase the erosiveness of rainfall (Calder 1999:18). This problem was also noted by the Food and Agriculture Organization of the United Nations (FAO) in Phetchabun province, along with the additional problem that some plantations run up and down slopes and therefore can concentrate overland flow (Marghescu 2001). This erosive effect can be compounded when the leaf litter on the forest floor is reduced, which happens regularly in plantation forests as a result of controlled burning activities. In Lampang province, Sutthathorn (1999) found that regular fires in forest plantations, often started by plantation mangers to control weeds, had decreased soil organic material, increased soil acidity and, ultimately, increased erosion.[12] As Chomitz and Kumari (1998:16) point out, "ground cover, rather than canopy, is the chief determinant of erosion," and if plantations are managed in a way that reduces or eliminates ground cover their benefits in terms of preventing erosion are likely to be illusory.

Third, it is necessary to consider what types of land cover plantation forests are replacing. Comparisons of erosion rates between bare soil and forest cover do not necessarily reflect real-world conditions. Most plantations are established on grassland, shrubland, or in various types of secondary forest, often including the fallowed fields of upland farmers. Many of these areas already have substantial ground cover and numerous "filter strips" of different vegetations types, both of which mitigate erosion. Nipon (1972) found that erosion on *Imperata* grassland was less than that in evergreen forests—a key point that contradicts statements by some conservationist NGOs that altering evergreen forests will necessarily result in erosion and "environmental disaster" (Svasti 1998; see also Gibson 1983:379).

Are Grass Strips the Solution?

And finally, some analysts have proposed using grass strips as a practical way to prevent erosion on agricultural slopes. This method involves planting hardy species of grass, such as vetiver, at regular intervals along slope contours. The aim of the strips is to reduce the effective length of the slope, which is an important determinant of erosion, and to trap soil before it moves downslope. The strips also help to prevent the formation of overland waterflow. They are widely regarded as a highly effective means of erosion control and have been promoted in many areas of upland northern Thailand since at least the late 1980s. One royal foundation even allocates the King of Thailand Vetiver Awards for outstanding scientific or extension work relating to vetiver grass (Vetiver Network 2005).

Clearly, preventing erosion on steep slopes is an important way to prevent declining soil fertility and can help to reduce the contribution of upland slopes—even if small—to lowland sedimentation. But some analysts have argued that grass strips overlook the more important physical causes of declining soil fertility and may introduce new problems of their own. Soil scientists have suggested that there should be a greater emphasis on restoring soil nutrients by planting crops that fix nitrogen or other nutrients in soils. And others have pointed to the tendency for grass strips to get out of control and actually add to farmers' weeding work in the hills: "The worst scenario is when vegetative buffer strips become a weed problem themselves. This was reported for several grass species that were introduced for soil conservation purposes and later became serious weeds, not only in the fields where they were planted but all over the region" (Van Keer and Turkelboom 1995:14). And it is often reported that farmers in some areas only adopt grass strips because development agencies pay them small amounts of money as incentives or because they think it may enhance their tenure security (Forsyth and A. Walker, personal observations and conversations with farmers in Chiang Rai and Chiang Mai provinces).

The Thai-Belgian Soil Fertility Conservation project, active in northern Thailand during the 1980s and 1990s, reflected these various forms of skepticism about grass strips (Van Keer et al. 1998). The project noted that the most effective solutions to soil degradation lay in a more holistic understanding of the diversity of problems faced by farmers, including availability of labor and the time expended in preparing fields for cultivation. Grass strips may therefore focus too closely on managing the biophysical process of erosion alone, rather than on acknowledging how soils are considered problematic by the farmers working them. Soil fertility work should seek to reduce the impact of weeds, maintain high levels of soil nutrients, and acknowledge farmers' own descriptions of farming problems, rather than assume that controlling erosion alone is always the most effective solution. This may not preclude the use of grass strips with other forms of soil management (Salzer 1987). But it might mean that other methods are considered preferable. For example, Turkelboom (1999:141) concluded that diversion ditches dug by Akha farmers did not compete with crops and were easy to adopt, and had benefits for limiting erosion on some steep slopes.

CONCLUSION

Scientists must be more precise in their language when discussing erosion and sedimentation from shifting agriculture. Even under the unstable form of shifting agriculture, erosion consequences may be somewhat overrated, or at least may be distorted by erosion resulting from road construction, urban development, drainage outlets, and other civil engineering rather than agronomic activities. (Hamilton 1985:686)

Is erosion an important problem in northern Thailand? Undoubtedly yes. But popular accounts of erosion exaggerate its importance in various ways, simplify its nature, and blur the different components of declining soil fertility and lowland sedimentation. The result of these simplifying misrepresentations is to support a variety of interventions that may not address underlying problems and that avoid alternative, more successful, steps. Once again, it is evident that generalized narratives of environmental crisis tend to displace local variation and nuance. This key point is made simply by Van Keer and others (1998:72), who worked with the Thai-Belgian Soil Fertility Conservation Project: "It cannot be emphasized strongly enough that erosion is a very site-specific problem. In some areas/fields erosion may be of major concern, whereas in other areas/fields it may be of no concern at all."

So, what does this situation tell us about social and political influences on environmental knowledge? To begin with, there is the problem of identifying precisely what the problem is. Erosion occurs in most locations of northern Thailand, and indeed in most regions of the world where there is rainfall and sloping land. Yet, the distribution of "problems" resulting from erosion is less uniform. There is a tendency for popular discussions of erosion to assume that any form of erosion must necessarily be problematic and that erosion must be stopped. But the rates and impacts of erosion vary considerably. Some forms of erosion do not present problems to land users, although this may change when land uses change. "Erosion" is also often used as an umbrella term for various other environmental processes such as declining soil fertility, sedimentation, gullying, and the normal geomorphological movement of soils over time. But these processes do not always occur simultaneously, nor do they arise from the same causes. Consequently, grouping them all together and labeling them negatively can be highly misleading. And trying to solve all by the same approach is likely to fail. There is a need to disaggregate the diverse processes involved in soil erosion and deposition to see where problems are caused and how they may best be addressed. Lowland sedimentation may actually be triggered by water extraction rather than erosion on upland slopes. Roads or naturally occurring gullies, rather than erosion from upland agriculture, may dominate much lowland sediment delivery.

There is also the problem of using scientific models and statistics out of context. The Universal Soil Loss Equation (USLE) has been used to predict erosion across Thailand, yet has been criticized for overlooking significant differences in how erosion is generated in different parts of the world. Data from experimental soil erosion plots are used to justify tree planting as a solution to erosion, yet these data overlook how gully erosion may occur under forest cover, or the empirical evidence that shows that some plantations may actually increase erosion. At present, data from the USLE and experimental plots are used to describe soil processes and to support land-use policies in northern Thailand that cannot be justified using alternative, and more locally specific, information.

A further significant point is that there has been an unwillingness to allow local people in the uplands to define environmental problems in their own terms. Some analysts have claimed that upland farmers rarely perceive erosion to be a problem, and consequently are irresponsible and in need of education. But, in fact, more locally grounded studies have shown that farmers perceive the effects of erosion and use their own terms to describe its various processes. This situation presents an example of different "problem closures," whereby different actors define environmental problems in varying ways, resulting in the different accumulation of information and explanation. In northern Thailand, it would seem that the dominant belief among government agencies and some agricultural researchers that various forms of upland cultivation are necessarily degrading—and that upland erosion must necessarily cause lowland sedimentation—has led these actors to try and solve all problems through rather simplistic approaches such as plantation forestry or the encouragement of grass strips. Yet, diversifying the erosion problem into the different components and causes of on-site soil fertility decline and off-site sedimentation may allow the adoption of more flexible solutions that more closely match the concerns of upland, and lowland, farmers. What is needed is a new approach to soil science that focuses on the holistic experience of soil degradation by land users, rather than the adoption of universalistic approaches to the cause, effect, and solution to erosion implied in techniques such as the Universal Soil Loss Equation or in convenient narratives about the degrading impacts of upland agriculture.

7 Agrochemicals

THE SPECTER OF CHEMICAL CONTAMINATION has played an important role in justifying regulatory intervention in the uplands. Agrochemical
use is widely believed to bring considerable risks to ecosystems and to
human health. Discussions of upland chemical use regularly feature familiar concerns about environmental fragility and environmental crisis
brought about by irresponsible agricultural production and commercialization. In addition, this narrative of environmental crisis conveniently
places a selective focus on the activities of particular groups of upland
farmers, despite the widespread use of chemicals in both upland and lowland farming systems.

In June 2003, for example, the Thai Ministry of Natural Resources
and Environment announced that it was to conduct "a study on the use
of pesticide in ecological-sensitive watershed areas to limit their use and
promote environment-friendly farming practices" (Anchalee 2003).
This study chose two case-study sites, one in Nan province and the
other in Chiang Mai province "because they were located in Watershed
Class 1A, very ecological sensitive areas and where all man made constructions are prohibited." A ministry spokesperson commented that the
"problem of agriculture in highland [areas] is rather sensitive since you
deal with tribal people that have their own culture." In an earlier visit
to one of the study areas he found that the local villages—"ethnic Lesaw
[Lisu] people, once a nomad hill tribe from China's Yunnan province"—
had been involved in "self-sufficient and organic farming for decades"
but that they had "turned to using pesticides after the state and com-

panies promoted mono-crop farming such as barley, lychee, persimmon and cabbages."

This brief report encapsulates many of the perceptions surrounding agricultural chemical use in Thailand's northern watersheds. The underlying narrative is the familiar account of preexisting sustainability disrupted by the external intrusion of both state and market. The social focus is narrow, with public concerns focusing on minority tribal groups whose presence in Thailand is both recent and, quite possibly, illegitimate. And a specific environmental focus is placed on sensitive Class 1A areas, with the *Bangkok Post* headline—"Contamination"—reflecting widely held anxiety that these nationally significant upland water sources have been sullied by the promotion of "mono-crop farming and the use of pesticides since 1990" (Anchalee 2003).

These idealized characterizations of both landscapes and people previously untarnished by modernization have influenced how agrochemicals are represented in public discussion. In this simplified narrative, chemically supported agriculture is framed as an inappropriate presence in fragile upland ecosystems, underlining the importance of watershed classification and land-use regulation. There is no room for alternative valuations of agrochemicals, such as their role in supporting poor farming livelihoods, nor is there room for consideration of the ways in which idealized images of pristine watershed forest and ethnic traditions might give an inaccurate picture of environmental and social processes in the uplands.

These key perceptions about agrochemical use in Thailand's northern uplands have emerged over time and in specific circumstances. Agrochemicals have played a central role in the recent transformation of upland agriculture, and there has been a subsequent backlash against upland chemical use among government agencies, media, and NGOs. This backlash has spawned a range of alternative "chemical-free" approaches to upland agriculture. Critics of agrochemical use have used scientific and other knowledge claims to create the appearance of known risks and certain impacts, despite the persistence of very significant uncertainty. This "stabilization" of uncertain knowledge indicates that dominant perceptions about agrochemicals in northern Thailand are shaped more by political concerns about "appropriate" upland livelihoods than by a clear understanding of the risks and benefits of chemical use.

THE CHEMICAL REVOLUTION IN THE UPLANDS

If you don't use chemical fertilizers, you don't eat.

—*Mien woman in Chiang Rai province (Forsyth fieldwork 2004)*

A cursory examination of the ethnographic record suggests that up until around the 1960s chemical use in the agricultural systems of Thailand's northern catchments was minimal. By and large, while concerns about declining soil fertility and pest infestation were relatively common, farmers—most of whom had minimal cash income to spend on external inputs—relied on fallow and manure to maintain soil fertility and on crop diversity to reduce risks of pest infestation and disease. "The fallow is the single most important factor in the system's maintenance, restoring soil fertility and controlling pests, diseases and weeds" (Kanok et al. 1994:11). In

---

AGROCHEMICAL USE BEFORE THE 1970S

Moerman's classic account of the paddy farmers of Chiang Kham district in the 1950s provides a good indication of the prechemical farming system and some of the factors driving adoption of chemicals. Despite farmer concerns about declining yields on "tired" land, fertilizer use was not considered:

> New land, increased herds, and tractor rental—not commercial fertilizer—are their answers to declining yields. Some of them theorize that fertilizer is unnecessary because Ban Ping's fields are close to the mountains and thus get the freshest water with the most plentiful nutrients. . . . Fertilizer is seen as a costly substance used by a few Chinese market gardeners and by large-scale citrus growers. To the villager, fertilizer is a symbol of the townsman: largely irrelevant to village farming, but pertinent to the villager's image of himself. As he carts it to the fields, a village lad calls manure "the fertilizer of the hicks," and so shows that he has begun to make the invidious comparisons used by townsmen. (Moerman 1968:49–50)

This account is worth quoting further, as it provides some important insights into the ways in which new chemical technology made its way into farmer's consciousness and, eventually, practice:

many upland farming systems, weed infestation was a formidable barrier but it was dealt with by hand weeding—a major labor input that limited the area that could be cultivated (Hinton 1978:196)—rather than by the use of herbicide. On the supply side, rudimentary transport infrastructure meant that the distribution of agricultural chemicals, especially relatively bulky fertilizers, was virtually nonexistent in most upland areas.

The adoption of inorganic agrochemicals in the uplands was a complex process. As shown by Moerman's study of paddy farmers in Chiang Kham (see "Agrochemical Use before the 1970s," opposite), adopting agrochemicals often involved locally specific combinations of biophysical, economic, and cultural factors. However, within this complexity there are a number of key supply and demand factors. First, supply has been helped by dramatic improvements in transport and marketing infrastructure that have permitted the distribution of agricultural chemicals by an array of private, government and nongovernment agents. Second, many of the major upland development programs have promoted agrochemical use

The young people frequent the town more than their elders do; they have seen fertilizer in the shops and talk about it in Ban Ping. This familiarity has begun to invert the traditional hierarchy of farming knowledge, in which old people had been thought to know more than the young. . . . Villagers know about fertilizer only when, like the headman, they have special access to the town and its officials and merchants. Sometimes the district officer, as he tells headmen about progress, mentions fertilizer along with toilets and eating eggs. (Moerman 1968:50)

When Moerman returned to the village just four years later he found that these urban experiences had begun to transform farming practices:

Another material change in farming is that many villagers are now willing to use chemical fertilizer on failing seedbed patches; some use it on the entire seedbed, even when the rice is coming up well. It would seem that only members of this latter category have begun to think differently about farming; at least one of them claims to calculate (however imperfectly) whether or not the net gain from using fertilizer is substantially greater than its cost. (Moerman 1968:187–88) as a key component of upland opium replacement, crop intensification, and commercialization. Adoption has been encouraged both by direct provision of agricultural inputs and by various demonstration schemes that communicate improved yields to farmers. Third, private agricultural middlemen and brokers have also been central in promoting chemical use by providing chemicals and instructions on their use. Many new contract-farming arrangements require that farmers follow these instructions and adhere closely to agrochemical application schedules. Fourth, prices of agrochemicals have remained relatively low because of tax concessions and an extensive and highly competitive agrochemical market (Witoon 1997:66). In fact, Ruhs and colleagues (1997:32) report that the real price of pesticides declined by almost 50 percent between 1986 and 1996. A nationwide preference for cheap agrochemicals has meant that there has been relatively high use of hazardous substances that are sold cheaply on the international market (Jungbluth 1996:11).

There are also a number of important demand factors. Crucially, as discussed in earlier chapters, population growth and state forest regulation has dramatically reduced the length of upland fallows, meaning that there is much less time available for natural processes of soil fertility restoration. Shortened fallow periods have also compromised naturally occurring processes of pest, weed, and disease control. Degraded swidden systems are vulnerable to invasion by *Imperata* grass and, as *Imperata* rhizomes are resistant to fire, some farmers have tended to use chemicals as the main means of control. Second, widespread increases in double and triple cropping[1]—often facilitated by improved irrigation infrastructure—have required supplementary nutrient sources and labor-saving methods of weed and pest control. The labor-saving contributions of agrochemicals have become particularly attractive as intensified agricultural production has come to compete with a wide range of off-farm labor opportunities and greatly increased school attendance. Third, there has been a widespread decline in livestock raising, meaning that natural manure is much less readily available than it used to be. Fourth, higher cash incomes and the extension of credit has meant that farmers are in a much better position to purchase agricultural inputs. Finally, and probably most importantly, the key driver of the agrochemical revolution in the uplands has been the relative decline in the cultivation of rice, maize, and opium and a dramatic increase in the production of vegetable and fruit crops. Jungbluth (1996:13) indicates that rice in all of Thailand occupies around 44 percent of agricultural land, but its share of the chemical market is about 20 percent. By contrast, vegetables and fruit account for 20 percent of agricultural area but consume about 30 percent of agricultural chemicals. Referring specifically to insecticides, Jungbluth (1996:14) reports that the average intensity of application on rice is about US$1.50 per hectare, while for vegetables it is over US$210 per hectare. Fruit orchards have a particularly poor reputation for excessive pesticide use, somewhat ironic given that these orchards are often promoted as an environmentally friendly alternative to annual cropping.

Cabbage Production by Karen Farmers in Mae Hong Son Province

For many observers, cabbage production in the uplands of northern Thailand is symbolic of destructive agricultural practice, and it is an image that underpins many of the region's environmental narratives. But what are the local circumstances of cabbage production? Some valuable insights are provided in a recent study of the Karen villages of Mae Chang and Don Luang in Mae Hong Son province (Samata 2003). Up until the 1960s this was an isolated area, though its remoteness was lessened somewhat by the construction of a nearby interprovincial road in the 1950s. As in many other Karen communities, upland cultivation of rice is an important component of the local agricultural system and, in the past, heavy reliance was placed on fallow periods to maintain fertility and limit weed infestation. However, this upland system has been undergoing long-term transformation. Hinton's study (1978) of Don Luang in the 1960s describes an agricultural system "under severe stress," with population pressure on land resulting in shorter fallow periods, lower yields, and regular subsistence shortfall.

Since the 1960s, there has been considerable population growth. Data compiled by Samata (2003:74) indicate that the combined population of Don Luang and Mae Chang has almost exactly doubled, from 402 to 803. This population increase has made resource pressures on land even more critical. Samata notes that in Don Luang it is now "nearly impossible" to fallow land, while in Mae Chang the fallow cycle is only four or five years (Samata 2003:128, 148). Across both villages over half of the households reported that in 2002 they did not produce enough rice to support themselves (Samata 2003:162). In response to these pressures, farmers in both villages have invested in the construction of irrigated paddy fields and now almost one-third of farmers combine upland and paddy farming. The good rice yields from paddy farming mean that these fields make a very important contribution to the food security of the households lucky enough to own them, and it enables them to allocate larger areas of their upland fields to nonrice crops, especially cabbage (Samata 2003:132–33, 156).

Samata found that cabbages are cultivated predominantly on upland fields during the wet season and, to a much smaller extent, on paddy fields in the dry season (with irrigation). How did this agricultural transformation—from rice to cabbage—occur? Samata identified two factors. First, two agricultural extension offices were established locally in the 1960s and 1970s, and these promoted commercial cultivation of coffee and cabbage (Samata 2003:87). Second, and more importantly, the Karen were also influenced by nearby Hmong farmers who hired Karen villagers as cabbage-field wage laborers during the years when cabbage was first introduced to the district. Drawing on their experience working for Hmong farmers, the Karen of Mae Chang took up cabbage cultivation on a more extensive basis in the late 1980s. There has been considerable fluctuation in the level of commitment to this crop—mainly due to substantial losses and crop failures experienced by some farmers—but in 2002 almost half of the households in Mae Chang and two-thirds of the households in Don Luang grew cabbages (Samata 2003:74, 90). The result was a significant transformation of the upland landscape, with about 20 percent of upland fields in Mae Chang devoted to cabbages and over 40 percent in Don Luang. In relation to Mae Chang, Samata suggests that the one-million-baht village fund—a nationwide government initiative in local-level credit provision—has contributed significantly to the current level of cabbage production. She notes that the "majority of them [farmers] had been looking for the chance to engage in cash cropping for a long time." What held them back was the lack of "investors to give them the opportunity to grow cabbage" (Samata 2003:90). The newly established village fund provided the capital and the nearby cabbage-marketing center of Mae Ho provided a relatively convenient market outlet. (Figure 7.1 pictures cabbage cultivation.)

Cabbage cultivation is characterized by a level of chemical input that appears to be unprecedented in the farming systems of Mae Chang and Don Luang:

> The typical work schedule for the cabbage cultivation starts around the end of May or June. They start to clear the land, and to grow a nursery of cabbage for about 35 days. In August, the seedlings from the nursery are trans-

FIG. 7.1 *Cabbage cultivation in Mae Chang*

planted in other plots at an interval of 30 cm. They start to weed often and continue this work until the harvest time. During this period, they put chemicals on the seedlings 10 days after transplanting. And then they apply three kinds of fertilizers (e.g., type 16–20–0 fertilizer to enrich the soil in the beginning, and type 21–0–0 fertilizer for making the cabbage a good-looking round shape three weeks after transplantation). If they find insects on the cabbage, they apply pesticide. It generally takes about three months before harvesting the cabbages. (Samata 2003:151)

Samata's account suggests that farmers use chemicals as a core means to reduce the risk of crop failure, and hence to avoid financial hardship. In "precabbage" farming systems, farmers tended to avoid risk by focusing primarily on crop diversity and fallow. But under new conditions of land scarcity and cash cropping of cabbages, an alternative approach is needed. Farmers report that they have always applied fertilizer to cabbages and amounts are "increasing year by year to maintain high yields" (Samata 2003:109). Moreover, if they "discontinue applying fertilizer, or if they keep applying the same amount of fertilizer as the previous year, the soil cannot maintain the same degree of fertility" (Samata

2003:109). And applying fertilizer to cabbage also increases the productivity of rice grown on the same land in later years. Accordingly, Samata notes that farmers have adjusted their choice of upland rice varieties in line with the chemically enhanced fertility of the soil. It is notable that, despite minimal fallow,[2] upland rice yields are substantially higher in Don Luang (3,348 kilograms per hectare) than they are in Mae Chang (2,040 kilograms per hectare), possibly as a result of the higher level—and greater regularity—of cabbage cultivation (Samata 2003:140, 143).

Strikingly similar observations have been made in relation to the Karen village of Mae Rid Pakae, also in Mae Hong Son province. Kanok and colleagues (1994:54) state that "access to productivity enhancing technology, i.e. fertilizer, irrigation, pesticides, is the key to the recent success of Mae Rid Pakae's agricultural system." Like in Mae Chang and Don Luang, this is an agricultural system that has evolved from a predominantly subsistence-oriented system to one that emphasizes commercial production of cabbages and bell peppers. Kanok and colleagues (1994:59) report that these crops are "heavily dosed" with both fertilizer and ammonium sulphate. Rice, by contrast, is never fertilized, despite the distribution of substantial amounts of fertilizer by a local development project for rice production. It seems that the distributed fertilizer has been used mainly to support cash cropping and the residual fertility benefits have made fertilizer application to rice crops unnecessary: "Obviously enough fertilizer is left over from the cabbages, so there is no need to give it again. . . . Evidence of extremely good growth and yields can be seen in the field during or even after harvest. All the farmers interviewed reported that rice yields following cabbage are now double or triple what they were before cabbages were introduced" (Kanok et al. 1994:53).

The use of fertilizer in these various villages can be understood in terms of the long-term dynamic of the upland farming system. When Hinton described Don Luang in the 1960s, he provided a "gloomy prognosis," suggesting that it was "difficult to see a way out of the impasse" of diminishing fallow and declining yields. He argued that fertilizer application "would undoubtedly improve yields" but that it could have a negative effect on soil structure and, echoing the popular narratives discussed in the previous chapter, "result in rapid erosion." He also claimed that cash cropping "does not seem practicable" because the farmers "certainly do not have enough land to grow rice and another crop" (Hinton 1978:197).

What Samata's recent study shows is that substantial numbers of farmers have attempted to address this resource impasse both by cash-crop cultivation and by fertilizer use. While, as Hinton notes, cabbage cultivation reduces the area available for subsistence production, the effect of residual fertilizer appears to have been a substantial increase in rice yields. Hinton's study (1978:194) found that average rice yields on upland fields were 1,404 kilograms per hectare, less than half that reported by Samata. This increase in yield has occurred despite further substantial reductions in fallow periods since Hinton made his gloomy predictions.

Diversification by Hmong Farmers in Chiang Mai Province

A broadly similar process of agricultural change has taken place in the Hmong village of Buak Jan, in Chiang Mai province, but here state intervention rather than population growth appears to have been the key driver of change.[3] Buak Jan is located about 30 kilometers to the west of Chiang Mai city. It is located at an elevation of about 1,300 meters and commands a magnificent view of the surrounding valleys. The village was first settled in 1964 when a group moved from a nearby village in search of more productive land. Between 1964 and 1974, it relied on growing opium, upland rice, and maize, a pattern common in Hmong villages throughout the region. According to the village headman, opium cultivation was stopped in 1974 as a result of direct intervention by the Thai government, with soldiers coming to destroy opium fields. This intervention marked the beginning of significant experimentation with vegetable crops, although rice remained an important subsistence crop during the 1970s and 1980s. One of the early crops attempted was potato, with some input support (fertilizer in particular) from United Nations agencies that were encouraging opium replacement. Traders came to the village to buy the crop but prices were unstable and unreliable. Eventually potatoes were abandoned, largely because of disease.

During the 1980s and 1990s a wide variety of opium-substitution crops were trialed and vegetables came to dominate the agricultural system. Survey data indicate that during the 1980s, vegetables covered around 60 percent of the cultivated area, much greater than rice (about 20 percent) and maize (about 10 percent). Vegetable crops included cabbage, carrot, sweet corn, kidney bean, and sugar beet. In the mid-1990s the Royal Project Foundation introduced gerbera (*Gerbera jamesonii*), a flower that provides colorful daisylike blooms (figure 7.2). This has been adopted by a large number of farmers given its relatively reliable income (in comparison with vegetable crops). Flowers are sold to traders who,

FIG. 7.2 *Flower cultivation in Buak Jan*

in turn, sell in the large flower market in Chiang Mai. Gerbera cultivation has become a distinctive feature of the landscape, covering almost one-quarter of the cultivated area. The transformation brought about as a result of vegetable and cut-flower production has been dramatic, with rice now grown on only a few scattered plots and opium production almost completely abandoned. Another important trend over the past two decades has been the increase in the area of fruit trees (such as lychee), partly as a result of encouragement from Royal Forest Department staff who see fruit trees as an environmentally benign form of cultivation. During the 1980s these covered about 10 percent of the cultivated area, while in the 1990s this increased to over 40 percent.

The hillslopes of Buak Jan are now intensively cropped, and many farmers grow two or three crops per year. Government regulation means that there is relatively little opportunity to open up new fields and wholesale village relocation is now out of the question. Moreover, many farmers have made substantial investments in their land—in the form of water supply systems, greenhouses, and terracing—and hence are unwilling to abandon plots. In order to maintain soil fertility on these permanently cropped fields, farmers have adopted significant fertilizer inputs. A recent study undertaken by Schoenleber (2002) in Buak Jan and some nearby Hmong villages found that inorganic fertilizer use was widespread and had largely displaced various traditional forms of organic fertilizer. Overall, she found that most farmers were applying more nitrogen than was actually required by the crops (a common problem worldwide). But this was not a uniform picture, and one of the study's key findings is that there is great variation in the level of fertilizer use by different households. For example, in relation to carrot cultivation, nitrogen application ranged from about 60 to over 240 kilograms per hectare. For cabbages, the range was even greater, from 120 to almost 720 kilograms per hectare. And on the increasingly popular gerbera the range was astonishing, from 300 to almost 2400 kilograms per hectare.

There has also been a significant increase in herbicide and pesticide use to support these new forms of production. As noted above, national data indicate that chemical use is much higher on cash crops than on subsistence rice crops. In Buak Jan, farmers now use pesticides routinely. These Hmong farmers report that vegetable, flower, and fruit crops are vulnerable to insect attack and that pesticides help maintain overall yield and product quality. Herbicides are also employed to control weed infestation. This labor-saving technique is especially useful, as average family sizes have declined and many workers now pursue nonagricultural opportunities in Chiang Mai or even farther afield. There is some local concern about the impact of these chemicals on human health—one woman boasted that she had reached the age of 94 because she had never used chemicals—but this concern is accompanied by the view that agrochemicals are now a necessary part of an intensified agricultural cycle.

THE BACKLASH AGAINST AGROCHEMICALS

A 12–member Senate special committee on toxicity and hazardous waste visited Phop Phra and Mae Sot districts in Tak on Sunday and found rampant use of dangerous pesticides and weed killers on farms in the area. Panel chairman Malinee Sukavejworakit said their visit followed complaints about the widespread use of toxins. She said a study found thousands of tonnes of chemical fertilizer, pesticide and weedkiller were used annually in border districts, especially Phop Phra and Mae Sot, as well as in catchment areas of the Moei river. "We are concerned that over 100,000 tonnes of produce is supplied daily to Bangkok and other provinces. Supplies may be distributed to nearly the whole country, yet most of it has not been checked. We are concerned about consumers' safety," she said. (Supamart 2003)

The case studies discussed in the previous section show that fertilizers, pesticides, and herbicides have been important components of the agricultural transition that has taken place in the uplands of northern Thailand. Agrochemicals have played a role in supporting vulnerable livelihoods, encouraging the transition away from opium production, and reducing pressures to clear forested areas for cultivation. But the subtleties of these localized processes of agricultural intensification tend to get lost in a climate of concern about upland degradation. Clearly, there are reasons to be concerned about the potential impacts of agrochemicals on both ecosystems and human health. But a simplified narrative of environmental crisis has developed to describe the impacts of chemical fertilizers in terms that are somewhat simplistic and that help legitimize a range of regulatory interventions in the lives of upland farmers. Some of these interventions are violent, others are more bureaucratic, while others again are based on education and promotion of the farmers' own local ecological knowledge. But all are based on the underlying premise that agrochemicals are "matter out of place" (M. Douglas 1966:160) in the wild(er)ness of the uplands.

The well-known dispute in Chom Thong provides some examples of how chemical use has been represented in Thai public discourse.[4] These reports are usually framed in terms of the greed, irresponsibility, and inappropriateness of the Hmong, and support persistent arguments about the need to resettle villages and control upland agriculture. In 1990, for example, one newspaper article argued that the use of agrochemicals at Chom Thong was "a question of resettlement" (Nantiya 1990). In 1997, a further article was provocatively titled "The source of life is poisoned" (Supradit 1997b). This article openly dismissed the claims of the Hmong headman of Pa Kluay village that farmers there used no more pesticides and fertilizers than anyone else, alleging that "his statements may be taken with a grain or two of salt." Just how much skeptical salt was made clear by the following subheading: "unfit for pigs." The article then went on to cite the views of an academic from Chiang Mai that the "highland farmers use so much pesticide that they dare not even consume their own farm products. They use a one-litre bottle of pesticide with 200 litres of water to sprinkle their cabbages. They don't even dare feed their pigs with the cabbages they grow." The article closed with the observation (or, perhaps, threat) that a "minor agricultural war seems to be imminent in the north."

One important characteristic of both these reports is the certainty with which they cite claims that agrochemicals were polluting downstream water supplies, and that these chemicals were at unacceptable levels. The 1990 article cited Phra Phongsak—the monk most associated with lowland protests against the Hmong—as saying that villagers had become ill from drinking water. And the 1997 article quoted a representative of the Royal Forest Department as saying that "an authoritative report by Chiangmai University has claimed that some pesticide residues found in the water exceed safety standards." These statements highlight the way in which much discussion of agrochemicals is conducted as though there are no doubts about their impacts on soil and water, as though their routes of transmission are known, and as though these processes do not vary. To be clear, there are good reasons to suspect that upland chemical use may sometimes have adverse downstream effects. But there has, in fact, been little concerted research on any of these matters, and it would seem that different activists use contrasting evidence selectively to either condemn chemical use or support upland farmers by denying that risks exist.

In 2000 there was another, more violent episode in Pua district of Nan province.[5] Lowland *khon muang* farmers—assisted by activists from Chom Thong—accused the Hmong of contaminating water supplies by using pesticides on fruit trees, as well as destroying forest and causing water shortages. As a result, the lowland farmers eventually deliberately set fire to the Hmong orchards. There had been tensions between the two groups for some time. The Hmong had lived on higher land in a neighboring district but, given communist influence in the area, were thought to be a security threat. A considerable number of Hmong farmers were forcibly resettled in the late 1960s (along with some Mien) to a military airfield very close to a long-established *khon muang* village. In the 1990s, given agricultural difficulties and population growth in the resettlement site, some Hmong farmers started to plant fruit trees on the land they used to inhabit in the uplands. Gradually, upland areas were acquired from villagers living nearby and the orchards expanded. Irrigation water for the fruit trees was drawn from nearby streams. Officials and lowland villagers accused Hmong farmers of clearing trees on land that had been declared as national park. A further factor contributing to the tension was that here, as elsewhere, discourses of environmental contamination were linked with charges leveled against the Hmong of drug production and distribution, in this case amphetamines. This narrative linkage is not unusual, often facilitated by the fact that one Thai word (*yaa*) can be used to refer to both chemicals and drugs.

In the buildup to the confrontation, NGOs sympathetic to the Hmong orchardists responded to charges of downstream chemical contamination by testing water samples. They asserted that the samples were not contaminated, though it is not known if these tests were any more accurate or authoritative than those used by conservationists to attack the Hmong. In May 2000, lowland villagers were reported to have "issued an ultimatum, demanding the Hmong . . . to immediately abandon their lychee orchards which they claimed are watershed area" (Jarat 2000). Eventually this led to conflict. In June and August 2000, many thousands of lychee trees were destroyed, and some houses burnt, in raids staged by lowland villagers. "Witnesses reported that the demonstrators were also guarded by over 200 border patrol policeman, who were fully armed with machine guns. All of the demonstrators were provided with machine saws, fuel and food" (Jarat 2000). Allegations have been made that the raids were actively supported by the Royal Forest Department. A representative of the Hmong farmers reported,

> The lowland people also accused us of destroying the upland watershed areas and causing water shortage in the lowlands as well as polluting the water resources by overuse of chemicals. We are very confused and cannot understand why this is happening to us. We have been living and using the area for a long time. Why did they wait until our fruit trees had matured and [were] giving fruit, and then now want us to leave our farmlands? (Suradej 2000:44)

Of course, many NGOs sympathetic to the cause of upland farmers have been vocal in their condemnation of these violent acts. But NGO representations themselves are often ambivalent about Hmong farming practices, particularly when they involve what is stereotypically described as the "monocropping" of cash crops.[6] This ambivalence is particularly marked in relation to the downstream impacts of upland chemical use. The Northern Development Foundation—one of the most active advocacy NGOs in Chiang Mai—illustrates this stance in their account of the impact of Hmong cultivation on the Karen villagers of Mae Kha Pu in Chiang Mai province. The report notes that most of the resource management problems in Mae Kha Pu are the result of external factors, especially the fact that Hmong farmers "cultivate in the watershed area and have a strong impact on the internal ecological system due to their high use of chemicals" (NDF 1999:127). Some of the details of the dispute with the Hmong are discussed:

After the Hmong stopped growing opium in 1991 they began to grow cash crops, for example, cabbage and other cool-season plants instead. They grew them near Ihuak Stream, Peung Stream, Nam Jahng Stream, all of which were water sources in evergreen forest. The Mae Kha Pu villagers used the water for consumption and agriculture. In 1992 the Mae Kha Pu villagers spoke to the Hmong to ask that they stop growing cabbage and stop using pesticide and weed killer in that area. But they were unable to agree. (NDF 1999:111–12)

As the conflict escalated, the Karen villagers destroyed some of the Hmong farmers' irrigation infrastructure and in subsequent negotiations managed to limit the area of watershed "damaged" by the Hmong farming practices. There have been no reports of NGO condemnation of this Karen aggression.

Rediscovering Organic Agriculture

The widespread concerns about agrochemical use in the uplands have prompted an array of alternative approaches from various environmental organizations and agencies in Thailand. Official recognition of alternative agricultural approaches is reflected in the commitment of the Eighth National Economic and Social Development Plan to achieve over four million hectares of "sustainable agriculture." According to one commentator this official commitment to sustainability involves a move away from the promotion of monocropping, a reconsideration of government subsidies for agrochemicals, and greater collaboration with NGOs to pursue agricultural alternatives (Pitipong 1997:2–3). The Department of Agriculture Extension sets out a six-stage path to organically based sustainability with the final objective, stage six, described as "rotational cropping with the use of organic fertilizer and herbal pesticide. Chemical residues in the soil will return to a safe level and the soil will become increasingly fertile" (Department of Agricultural Extension 2004). Over the past few years there has also been a more concerted focus on "food safety," a product both of consumer anxiety and of concerns from trading partners about contaminated imports. In 1999 the government "declared an organic agriculture policy to make Thailand a centre for organic agricultural produce," and 2004 was declared to be National Food Safety Year complete with an inspirational slogan: "building security for producers, building quality of life for consumers—the vegetable production campaign project makes us safe from pollutants" (Department of Agricultural Extension 2004).

Integrated pest management (IPM) is one specific initiative promoted by the government in collaboration with international agencies. In 2001 the Danish development agency DANIDA launched a major IPM initiative in Thailand, with the "highland area near Chiang Mai" selected as one of the priority areas for its operation. In these areas DANIDA is working in partnership with the government upland development agencies and the Royal Project Foundation. The project promotes a wide range of alternative methods, based on four key IPM principles (DANIDA 2004). First, farmers are encouraged to "grow a healthy crop" ("healthy plants are stronger and thus better equipped to withstand attacks by pests and diseases"). Second, they should "understand and conserve defenders" ("biological control agents are the defenders of the crop because they are natural enemies of the pests"). Third, farmers should "visit fields regularly" ("by knowing what is going on in the field, the farmer can take the correct decisions and take swift action when needed"). The final result is that "farmers become expert in crop management" ("they continue to improve their crop management by experimenting in their own field and share their knowledge with other farmers"). Intensive training programs are undertaken for key farmers at some of the Royal Project Foundation's major upland field stations. Overall, the IPM program seeks to draw on and promote farmers' local knowledge, rather than encouraging dependency on external agricultural inputs. But its regulatory role in promoting "appropriate" farmer behavior is clear.

There are now numerous small projects operating in the uplands and promoting various forms of organic agriculture, often motivated by a desire to move agricultural production in more self-sufficient directions. One such project is located in the grounds of a meditation temple on the mountain slopes overlooking the district town of Fang. In the grounds of the temple there is a large demonstration garden that promotes the benefits of chemically free cultivation. The project is supported by the Ministry of Education as part of its commitment to implement the theories of the king in relation to self-sufficiency in agricultural production.

The narrative of environmental crisis that motivates the project is vividly summed up in a series of three posters displayed in a shelter at the center of the garden (figures 7.3A–C). The first poster displays the "natural ecological system" in which living things—people, animals, plants, and soil—depend on each other, producing a fertile system. Bold

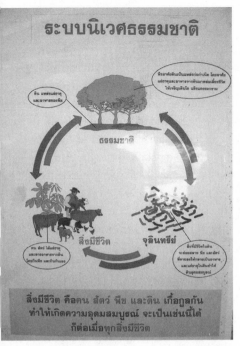

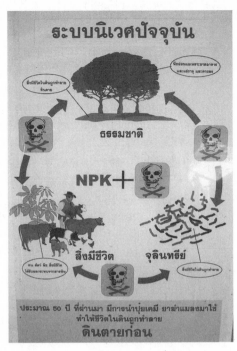

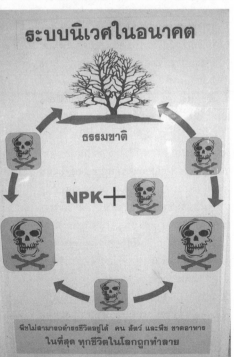

FIG. 7.3A-C *The chemically induced environmental crisis*

double arrows link the key elements of the system into a cycle of inter-dependence. Crucial in the system are the "microbes"—the living things in the soil—that break down dead plants and animals into food and elements that make the soil fertile. As a result, plants, animals, and people derive elements and nutrients from the soil, and nature is "strong and beautiful." But in the current ecological system—with the second poster's color scheme turning from green to red—these living things within the soil have been destroyed as a result of "approximately 50 years of chemical fertilizer and insecticide." Plants, animals, and people suffer the effects of "poison" and plants are weak because they lack the crucial nutrients and elements that the soil can no longer provide. Ominously, at the bottom of the poster is the warning that "the soil dies first." The third poster, illustrating the "ecological system in the future" is apocalyptic. All the various components of the life cycle—save for a single dead tree—have been replaced by the gruesome skull and crossbones of death. "Plants cannot live" the poster declares. "People, animals and plants lack food and, in the end, all life on earth is destroyed."

In order to redress this balance the project promotes a product called EM (Effective Microorganisms). The product has been developed as part of the Japanese "Kyusei nature farming" system, which aims to "save the world and mankind through natural farming methods" (Sununtar and Gilman 2004). According to information from the international EM Trading Web site (Simpson 2004), "Effective Microorganisms . . . are a group of beneficial microorganisms that jump start healthy microbial processes in the soil-plant ecosystem. The use of the EM culture allows gardeners and farmers to concentrate on building and feeding a healthy micro flora in soil."

At the meditation temple in Fang, considerable emphasis is placed on the safety of EM, with visitors to the demonstration garden urged to drink a glassful. Posters on display at the project state that EM can be directly applied to plants or can be used in the production of microbial-based fertilizer. It can also be fed to animals to promote strength and restore health. Various "environmental" uses are also promoted, including bathroom and kitchen cleaning and treatment of wastewater. The effectiveness of the EM product is demonstrated in a series of gardens in which various vegetables, herbs, and flowers are grown. The project has also undertaken some modest extension, primarily through farmers who are "students" at the temple. One farmer was using EM in the contract production of herbs that were to be sold to a Japanese company for use in alternative medicines.

Despite the strictly organic prescriptions of the company, he took a pragmatic approach to organic agriculture and was intercropping the herbs with garlic that was still receiving the standard chemical treatment. The degree of his organic pragmatism was highlighted by the fact that much of this land was located on a recently cleared area of upland forest.

PRIVATE ENTERPRISE AND ORGANIC AGRICULTURE

Private companies have wasted no time in cashing in on interest in organic agriculture. Agricultural supply stores in rural areas now feature a range of organic alternatives, and traveling salesmen promote a range of environmentally friendly remedies. One company promotes a "hormone fertilizer" that is described as "fertilizer with life, which is not a poison for users. It is safe for consumers and keeps nature in balance." It is the product of "combined research from important national-level research organizations in China." The company's promotional material suggests that this "biological fertilizer is appropriate for all types of crops because it has nutrients that are beneficial for almost 100 percent of plants. If used regularly a farmer's fields will improve and the use of fertilizers will also decrease. It should be used alongside our biological water fertilizer that will make a farmer's plants and soil the most fertile." The company produces a "strawberry fertilizer" that is widely promoted in Samoeng district of Chiang Mai province, Thailand's largest strawberry-producing area. This marketing is a direct response to concerns about the level of chemical use in strawberry production. The company salesman has distributed a list of "chemicals banned for crops exported to China," playing on farmer anxiety about the marketability of their crops.

Sources: Company promotional material and A. Walker fieldwork 2003.

REDISCOVERING UNCERTAINTY

Common claims about chemical use and environmental crisis are based on the elimination of uncertainty. Particular activities (especially the commercial cultivation of vegetable crops) are confidently and colorfully linked to particular negative outcomes (soil, water, and human contamination).

Plus, while it is generally acknowledged that chemicals are widely adopted, some specific social groups (especially the Hmong) are portrayed as playing a lead role in environmental contamination. Proposals for alternative agriculture seek to convert upland farmers to more organic and apparently self-sufficient forms of cultivation, away from the certain fate that will follow from ongoing chemical use. But how far is the apparent certainty of this narrative based on scientific evidence? Or are scientific uncertainties hidden in this narrative? It is worth looking more critically at some of the narrative's claims about water contamination, soil degradation, and impacts on human health. In each case there appears to be room for greater uncertainty, ongoing inquiry, and a more sensitive engagement with the constraints and risks faced by upland farmers.

Negative Impact on Water Quality

> Cabbage is a crop that needs a lot of water, or, in the absence of water, a lot of pesticides. Therefore, during the dry season Hmong often use large amounts of pesticides, a problem to the people downstream who use the stream water to wash clothes and for bathing. However, because cabbage is a heavy and bulky product, the Hmong would not be involved as much in cabbage production had the government not built the roads and encouraged cash crops as alternatives to opium. (Delang 2002:496)

One of the most common claims is that upland chemical use, especially by Hmong farmers, has a negative impact on downstream water quality. This claim has become one of the main elements in the condemnation of intensive upland agriculture. But the claim appears to have developed in the absence of good scientific studies on the impacts of upland chemical use on water quality (Waranoot and Dearden 2002:2013). It is striking how little material is to be found in the scientific literature, despite the "scientific" aura that surrounds a great deal of the discussion. In the mid-1990s, Kanok and colleagues (1994:xxv) noted that "definitive data on the evidence of pesticide pollution of water and soils are non-existent." Similarly, a nationwide review of "agricultural diffuse pollution" undertaken by the Land Development Department (Tonmanee and Kanchanakool 1999) noted that "research studies on agricultural diffuse pollution in water resources in Thailand show that nutrient loads and pesticide residues still do not exceed the standard level." And, as

"When lowland Thai villagers in one subcatchment of the Mae Chaem watershed first observed signs of deteriorating water quality, they were convinced that pesticides used by the ethnic minority Hmong village on the upper slopes must be the cause. However, monitoring just downstream from the Hmong village indicated that the water was still of good quality at this point. Water samples were then taken at a series of points along the stream to identify the source of the pollution. As a result of this exercise the [lowland] Thai villagers realised that the problem occurred during periods of heavy rainfall, when the stream overflowed its banks and ran through their own rice paddies, where it became contaminated with agricultural chemicals. The monitoring exercise helped reduce tensions between the two villages and also alerted the Hmong village to the fact that downstream water quality was being monitored."

Source: ASB 2004

recently as 2002, Mingtipol and colleagues (2002:34) concluded that "investigations on the effect of land use changes on water quality are quite new and very few have been carried out in Thailand."

However, Mingtipol and colleagues (2002:34) do report some research findings. First, a study published in 1988 found that levels of eutrophication-causing plant nutrients (N, P, K) in the main northern rivers (Ping, Wang, Yom, and Nan) were "lower than the standard set by [the World Health Organization]." Second, heavy-metal concentrations in these rivers "were close to natural levels," though relatively higher in the rainy season. Third, in a study undertaken in the mid-1980s, organochlorine insecticides (in the form of dieldrin and DDT) were detected in these northern rivers. Concentrations were found to be evenly spread in both upland and lowland areas, but they "had not yet reached hazardous levels of drinking," though there were concerns about the impact on aquatic life (Mingtipol et al. 2002). The possibility that the source of such DDT contamination lies not in agricultural use but in antimalarial campaigns conducted by public health agencies was not considered (Stuetz et al. 2001).[7]

So, while international experience suggests that there are likely to be problems with downstream contamination in some areas, the fragmentary evidence from northern Thailand clearly does not match the certainty expressed in the dominant narrative. Further research may contribute to greater nuance in relation to this aspect of environmental knowledge—and a greater appreciation of the relative contributions of upland and lowland agriculture to water-quality problems (see "Participatory Monitoring," p. 191). But real progress will also depend on a willingness to move outside the comfortable narrative that narrowly focuses environmental blame on specific social groups, and that relies on confident and simplified biophysical explanations of risk.

Soil Degradation

What then of the argument that chemical use results in soil degradation? In much recent discussion there seems to be a widespread feeling that the increases in yield experienced by farmers using agrochemicals are short-term gains only and that longer-term trends will be toward soil degradation. The gains of upland modernity are seen as being unsustainable. These concerns focus on a number of different factors. Use of chemical fertilizers—rather than fallow or manure—is said to have reduced the level of natural organic matter in the soil, negatively altered the structure of the soil, and to have created an unfavorable chemical environment for beneficial soil microbes. In turn, these on-site problems are said to cause a range of other environmental problems. The loss of organic matter and soil structure results in soil compaction, reduced infiltration, and increased runoff (itself contaminated), contributing to the hydrological problems of wet-season flooding and dry-season water shortage discussed in chapter 4. Similarly, while fertilizer application may maintain fertility in the short term, long-term chemical treatment ultimately results in sterile soil, prompting abandonment and further forest clearing in search of new areas of cultivation. As intensive agriculture is pushed onto increasingly marginal and fragile land—where soil fertility challenges are even greater—the land-degrading cycle of chemical treatment, degradation, and abandonment continues.

Again, it is surprising how little detailed research has been undertaken on the contribution of agrochemicals to soil degradation in upland areas. As with water quality, the level of popular concern does not appear to be matched by investment in detailed local research. In fact, even basic data on soils in most upland areas are lacking, with the Land Development Department's soil classification maps categorizing the vast swaths of northern Thailand in the single category of "slope complex." This fundamental lack of data underlines the cultural and political basis on which confident narratives of soil degradation are constructed. There are two particular areas in which a much greater degree of uncertainty and inquiry appears warranted.

First, there is little doubt that forest clearing and cultivation—especially in the absence of fallow periods—results in a decline in soil organic matter, with a negative effect on the availability of soil nitrogen, a crucially important plant nutrient. As Lindert (2000:239) states in his detailed analysis of soil quality in China and Indonesia, "total nitrogen and organic matter surely decline when previous forest or grasslands are first cleared and cultivated. The decline may even continue thereafter, as cultivation intensifies." Local studies undertaken in upland northern Thailand illustrate this trend. For example a study undertaken by Möller and colleagues (2002:981) indicates that an area of cabbage cultivation had 40 percent lower organic carbon and 25 percent lower organic nitrogen compared to the soil from an area of primary forest (but note that this was after fifteen years of cultivation). Similarly, Elliott and colleagues (2003:179) found that soil organic matter on abandoned upland fields was almost 30 percent lower than in nearby undisturbed forest.[8]

Such results rightly motivate the common advice to upland farmers to maintain and even increase the return of organic matter (plant residues, manure, and compost) to cultivated soils. But the key issue is the effect of organic matter decline on the long-term sustainability of agricultural yield. Van Keer and colleagues (1998:62), who have undertaken extensive research on soil management in highland areas of Thailand, have a relatively optimistic perspective that sits uneasily with the popular narratives of degradation: "As long as the soil organic matter stays above a certain 'critical' level, there is no reason to worry. These critical levels are difficult to define (they are soil and climate specific). But as soil organic matter levels in the highlands are fairly high, soil organic matter decline does not seem an issue of capital concern."

One of the reasons organic matter decline may not be a "capital concern" is that, despite the stigma they carry, artificial fertilizers appear to provide a yield-sustaining alternative to naturally occurring soil nitrogen. Indeed, as noted earlier, some farmers find that dry-season fertilizer application has a positive effect on wet-season rice yields. Again, Lindert's analysis (2000:225) of soil condition in China and Indonesia suggests that "substituting quick-release nitrogen fertilizer can eclipse the role of soil organic matter and nitrogen in agricultural productivity." Van Keer and colleagues' approach (1998:100) in northern Thailand is somewhat more cautious, encouraging the maximum use of organic fertilizer but suggesting that chemical fertilizers are "in many cases a necessary input to boost the development of more sustainable cropping systems. Their use may allow many nutrient-poor soils to become productive while at the same time enabling farmers to withdraw lands of low quality . . . from cultivation." Interestingly, they also report on international research that has indicated that artificial fertilizer can enhance soil organic matter by encouraging the production of roots "that remain in the soil after harvest . . . and contribute thereby significantly to the soil organic matter pool" (1998:101).

A second, and related, issue is that of soil compaction and the commonly held view that chemical treatments have resulted in "hard" or "concretelike" soils. Fieldwork in 2004 by Forsyth in an upland village in Chiang Rai province found some farmers claiming that herbicides made soil "hard and granular." Such anecdotal evidence, however, is not matched by local studies that can assess whether such findings are the result of the chemicals alone, the method and amount of application, or the specific circumstances of soil and landscape. Van Keer and colleagues (1998:101) argue that there is no evidence that the application of chemical fertilizer is, in itself, a cause of soil compaction. Rather they suggest that where it does occur it is a result of overall bad soil management— "over dosage of fertilisers, removal of plant residues, use of heavy machinery, too frequent tillage, lack of erosion control." The key, it seems, is to ensure that agrochemical use is combined with reasonable soil management practices. Again, the narrow conservationist focus encouraged by the degradation narrative may be more productively directed to a more holistic understanding of the ways that farmers manage upland soils rather than a specific, and alarmist, focus on the negative impacts of agrochemical use alone. It is relevant to recall the findings of some researchers, discussed in chapter 4, that actively cultivated soils in the highlands of northern Thailand have relatively high rates of infiltration when compared with other land covers.

In brief, there appears to be considerable uncertainly about the relationship between agrochemical use and soil degradation. This is even more so the case in relation to the impacts of agrochemical use on soil organisms. Here the certainty of popular accounts about lifeless and sterile soils contrasts with an apparent total absence of publicly available research.

This microlevel biodiversity has received much less attention than more charismatic plant and animal species.

Negative Impact on Health

> Over a period of more than ten years, he was heavily involved in farming for the market. This had an effect on his wife, who was in and out of hospital because of pesticide inhalation. The consequences for the environment and soil meant that he had to invest more in fertilizer and chemicals. They became increasingly sick and their income did not cover their investment. The family kept on thinking about how to find a way out of their problems until they became aware of a community organization development project. He made the decision to follow a new path to make his family free from pollutants in their bodies . . . by planting chemical-free crops and farming mixed fields to produce food safe for the consumer and the environment. (Paanee 1996:111)

There is also increasing alarm in Thailand about the impact of agrochemical use on health. Currently a great deal of the public attention focuses on the health risks to consumers of eating contaminated vegetables. Vegetables grown by Hmong farmers are particularly stigmatized as posing a threat to urban consumers. High-profile public relations campaigns reinforce this charged rhetoric. Yet again, this powerful narrative appears to have developed with very little available research on this important issue. It would seem the narrative derives its force not from scientific data but from its resonance with the broader cultural perspective that agricultural commercialization poses a threat to both the wild(er)ness of the forested uplands and to the benign flow of resources (such as clean water and clean food) from the uplands into the lowland cities.

The public health narrative promoted by state agencies, conservationists, and NGOs is also selective because it draws attention away from the more immediate risks to farmers who actually apply chemicals in agricultural zones. Research undertaken in central Thailand suggests that farmers' primary concern about agricultural chemical use is the immediate impact on their health (MAMAS 2004; Grandstaff and Waraporn 2004). Evidence from northern Thailand suggests that they may have good reason to be concerned. First, a study undertaken by Stuetz and colleagues (2001) of organochlorine pesticide residues in human milk among

Hmong villagers in Chiang Mai province found high levels of DDT, largely as a result of the use of DDT in antimalarial campaigns and its occasional illegal use in agricultural activities. Average estimated daily intakes by infants were 2.5 times the acceptable daily intake, with the estimated maximum intake in the sample group over 13 times the recommended level. While DDT spraying for malaria control has been largely phased out and organochlorine use in agriculture has also been "gradually banned," the residual effect is relatively long lasting and the study authors conclude that a "period of at least 10–20 years will probably be required before low levels of OCP [organochlorine pesticide] residues such as those reported from Germany and other industrial countries at the end of the 1990s can be reached" (Stuetz et al. 2001:54, 59). But the probable source of most organochlorine contamination is mosquito spraying rather than agricultural use.

However, there are other data that suggest a clearer link with agricultural activity. Between 1991 and 2001 Kunstadter and colleagues took blood samples from Hmong farmers in three highland villages (reported in *AgHealthNews* 2002). Chemical use in the sample group was relatively high, with farmers reporting that they used over 120 different varieties of agricultural chemicals. Qualitative research showed that many farmers, while aware of health risks, did not take appropriate protective measures. The blood screening "showed 20–69% of 582 Hmong adults with risky or unsafe levels of cholinesterase inhibition, an indicator of exposure to organophosphate and carbamate pesticides." Interestingly, the study found that exposure rates "are as high among those who do not actually apply pesticides as among those who do, suggesting exposure by routes in addition to direct contact associated with application." Whether this is from consumption of vegetable crops or other forms of indirect exposure (such as children playing with discarded bottles) is not yet clear (Kunstadter et al. 2001). A second phase of the study, which got underway in 2002, commenced longitudinal screening of over 200 residents in one of the villages previously sampled (Kunstadter et al. 2003). The initial screening found cholinesterase inhibition rates at "risky" or "dangerous" levels in 75 percent of cases. Disturbingly, children aged between one and nine were found to have the highest rates of "dangerous" cholinesterase inhibition. The study also found that many farmers reported symptoms such as headaches, dizziness, blurred vision, numbness, and itchiness after application of pesticides. These important studies add weight, and important local insight, to data from the mid 1990s that indicated that there were around 7,000 cases of pesticide poisoning reported to public hospitals throughout Thailand. Half of these were related to occupational use while the other half were suicidal (Girard 1997).

These findings are crucially important. They suggest that the main impacts of chemical use may fall on the farming communities themselves. This problem appears to be significantly more important, and urgent, than the off-site environmental impacts that receive so much attention in Thai environmental narratives.

CONCLUSION

Fears about chemical contamination have become a central component of the narrative of environmental crisis in upland Thailand. As in other aspects of this narrative, there is a strong tendency for the focus of alarm to fall on particular groups, ignoring the extent to which cultivators throughout Thailand have come to rely heavily on a wide range of chemical inputs. In the environmental politics of the uplands, Hmong farmers, in particular, have come to be associated with excessive chemical use, and they are widely stereotyped as being responsible for the production of vegetable crops that are so "chemically soaked" that the growers themselves would not eat them. Popular stereotypes hold that chemical use in upper watershed areas is damaging soil, contaminating water supplies, and threatening the health of consumers in urban centers. The atmosphere of environmental crisis contributes to the circulation of rumors that, in the interests of conservation and public health, some sensitive upper catchment areas will be declared chemical-free. Once again, fears about environmental hazard—interspersed with simplified visions of biophysical processes and stereotypical beliefs about different social groups— play an important part in ongoing attempts to regulate, and restrict, the activities of upland farmers.

The simplified narrative of chemical contamination gives the appearance of great certainty about complex environmental processes and agricultural transformations that are actually highly uncertain and varied. In particular, the narrative overlooks the role that agrochemical use has played in localized processes of agricultural intensification in the uplands. As the case studies in this chapter show, agrochemical use has played an important role in supporting the agricultural changes necessitated by population growth, land-use regulation, and opium eradication. This is not to deny that, in some cases, use of particular chemicals may be excessive. But the case studies clearly show that agrochemical use can play a role in maintaining, and perhaps even enhancing, agricultural productivity in the face of ongoing resource pressures. Given the policy goals of eradicating opium, reducing shifting cultivation, and conserving remaining forest cover, it seems unrealistic to expect that upland farmers will not pursue strategies of chemically supported agricultural intensification that are similar to those pursued by farmers throughout Thailand.

But the picture is not completely uniform. What the case studies also suggest is that there is likely to be substantial variation in chemical use, brought about by differences in experience, knowledge, perception, motivation, and ability. While the trend toward increasing use is unmistakable, this overall trend should not be allowed to conceal the extent of household- and village-level variation. A greater understanding of this variation, rather than generalized stereotypes, may hold the key to more effective management of chemical use.

Organic alternatives may be an important part of this management strategy. It is clear that some of the organic alternatives are attracting the interest of farmers (and consumers). For example, during fieldwork undertaken by A. Walker in Chiang Mai (2003–07), it became evident that many cash-cropping farmers are experimenting with various aspects of organic agriculture, partly motivated by concerns about the environmental impacts of chemical use and partly motivated by growing market expectations. Farmers undertaking contract cultivation for companies hoping to sell in "organic" markets are increasingly facing restrictions on the timing, types, and quantities of chemical input. But, at the same time, there is a need for a more realistic appraisal of the logistics of some proposed organic alternatives. The clear impression gained is that some of the antichemical advocates fail to make the fundamental distinction between gardening and farming. There is no doubt that impressively lush demonstration plots of organic vegetables can be established, and these provide impressive backdrops against which visiting dignitaries lament the ignorance and short-sightedness of local farmers. But the practicalities of adopting labor-intensive organic methods often pass without comment, as do the differential costs of organic versus nonorganic inputs. Until these practical issues are more realistically addressed, adoption of organic alternatives will remain sporadic. Simplifying narratives of chemical crisis are unlikely to do much to encourage adoption of alternatives by farmers who confront the day-to-day constraints of agricultural production.

A more realistic and engaged perspective on chemical use would benefit from a greater appreciation of uncertainty and local variation, and of the diverse levels of risk faced by different chemical users. While the studies on the impacts of agrochemical use are limited and fragmentary, they do suggest that some softening of the narrative of environmental crisis is warranted. At present there appears to be little evidence of severe or widespread impact on water quality. Yet, many observers claim that the links between upland agriculture and water contamination are certain and factual. This is another good example of different actors using sporadic evidence and overconfident assertions to create an impression of scientific certainty in order to legitimize political objectives. Problems with water contamination certainly will occur, but these are probably best dealt with through localized negotiation and participatory water-quality monitoring: the rhetoric of generalized crisis is of little practical use. Similarly, widespread concerns about the impact of chemical use on soil quality have, as yet, little support in the research literature. While there do not appear to be any good long-term studies, there are growing indications that appropriate chemical application can support long-term cultivation of cash crops and, in some cases, fertilizer residues can have very beneficial effects on subsistence rice yields. Again, no doubt, there are problems in particular areas—and there is considerable uncertainty about the impact of excessive pesticide and herbicide use on soil organisms—but these problems need to be addressed in terms of farmers' overall, and locally specific, strategies of soil management.

But there is growing evidence that health problems associated with chemical use need to be taken very seriously. In particular, the studies cited above indicate that the main threat from agrochemical use falls on the cultivators who apply them. Addressing this issue will require a concerted and ongoing public education campaign, probably combined with regulatory initiatives in relation to product availability, marketing, and labeling. Practical initiatives in mitigating this problem are clearly urgent. Such initiatives are unlikely to be helped by the emotive language of condemnation and ethnic stereotyping. Upland farmers are facing new and changing challenges and clearly require assistance in dealing with these tasks appropriately.

A key challenge arises from the fact that, increasingly, the work of applying chemicals is allocated to low-wage, vulnerable sections of the workforce, especially Shan and Karen refugees from the turmoil in Burma. Some impoverished upland villagers are also being drawn into dangerous chemical-spraying jobs in orchards and highly intensive vegetable and cut-flower enterprises. A study highlighting the health risks for these workers was undertaken by public health officials in border districts of Tak province. Results of blood tests taken from Burmese and Karen agricultural laborers found that up to one-third had blood toxin levels at "dangerous or nearly-dangerous levels" (Supamart 2003). Finding ways to improve the working conditions of these most vulnerable workers is one of the main challenges for environmental management in the uplands. Popular environmental narratives tend to emphasize the off-site impacts of agrochemical use, but the real impacts may be falling on those most directly involved in their application.

8 Biodiversity

BIODIVERSITY PLAYS AN IMPORTANT and growing role in the development and maintenance of Thailand's selective narrative of environmental crisis. Much information about biodiversity in Thailand emphasizes the numbers and distinctiveness of species to be conserved. According to the NGO Conservation International (2004), Thailand contains part of the Indo-Burma biodiversity "hotspot" in which there are said to be over 13,000 plant species and 2,185 terrestrial vertebrate species. One leading national environmental agency claims that plants found in Thailand alone account for an estimated 8 percent of the world's plant species. And Thailand's faunal diversity is said to be equally impressive: "at least 292 species of mammal . . . at least 938 avifauna species, 318 reptile species . . . 122 amphibian species [and] 606 freshwater fish species" (Office of Natural Resources and Environmental Policy and Planning 2004). An educational CD-ROM on biodiversity in Thailand claims that the country has some 12 percent of the world's fish species, 11 percent of the birds, 10 percent of the turtles, and 7 percent of the mammals. And the list of Thailand's biodiversity is likely to increase as scientific research progresses. For example, the CD-ROM advises that an estimated 2,000 species of plankton are still waiting to be discovered (Learn Online 2002).

There is considerable anxiety that this internationally significant biodiversity is under threat, and this concern has a profound influence on the generation and use of environmental knowledge. The Buddhist philosopher and social critic Sulak (2004) taps into a popular antimodernist sentiment with his emotive claim that Thailand's obsession with the free market has led to environmental destruction whereby "biological diversity and natural beauty are . . . lost under the onslaught of logging, hydro-dams and crop monoculture smothered in pesticides." The journalist Fahn (2003:112) laments the loss of Thailand's forests, "vast, living warehouses of biodiversity." Echoing widespread concern about the loss of this ecological richness, he writes that "some 40 percent of the kingdom's indigenous wildlife species are considered threatened, and at least half a dozen major animals have become extinct." Some of the victims of Thailand's "rapid and widespread extirpation of wildlife" are listed in Dearden's alarming account (1999:5): Schomburgk's deer is now extinct; the kouprey is probably extinct; and the brow-antlered deer, hog deer, Javan rhinoceros, Sumatran rhinoceros, long-billed vulture, estuarine crocodile, and false gharial are only found in captivity. According to Dearden (ibid.), "of the 282 species of mammals about 40 are classified as rare and endangered, and 190 of 916 bird species and 37 of 405 species of reptiles and amphibians are threatened with extinction."

These kinds of statements influence environmental policy and shape regulatory responses. The narrative of biodiversity crisis has played a key role in justifying ongoing state involvement in the management of natural resources. In particular, as the Royal Forest Department has moved from a forest exploitation agency to a forest protection agency, biodiversity protection has taken on considerable prominence, second only to the goal of protecting forest to secure lowland water supplies. The central regulatory approach under this strategy has been the establishment of protected areas. These now cover a significant percentage of the nation's total landmass, and the protected area system has been assessed as "one of the best in South East Asia" for the conservation of mammalian, bird, and plant species (ICEM 2003:63). According to the Wildlife Conservation Division of the Royal Forest Department (2004f), 53 wildlife sanctuaries were established by 2004 (with 6 more in process), plus 55 nonhunting areas and 19 wildlife conservation stations. The role of the environmental narrative in reinforcing state power is clearly demonstrated in the division's own statement that it had achieved its objectives of "resettl[ing] villages out of wildlife sanctuaries" (2004f) and, in the very next point, that it had accomplished "reintroduction and rehabilitation of some wildlife species such as pheasants and hoofed mammals." In other words, peasants out, pheasants in.

These regulatory interventions take place in a context of considerable uncertainty, given that scientific assessment of biodiversity is often very difficult. At the most general level, there is considerable uncertainty about the overall number of species and about which type of land use change may reduce, or enhance, diversity. In northern Thailand—despite considerable research on the abundance of biodiversity or the restoration of specific forest types—there are surprisingly few studies that measure overall biodiversity losses, or the relationship between biodiversity and land use. Much concern about biodiversity, instead, seems to be based on the transfer of generalized relationships between land-cover change and biodiversity observed elsewhere, combined with the "precautionary principle" (or the belief that it is better to protect environments now than wait to see if damage occurs). Consequently, it is difficult to critically explore the narrative of biodiversity crisis by drawing upon local empirical studies that confirm or refute claims of biodiversity decline. There is, quite simply, very little knowledge produced at this level of detail.

Instead, it is more useful to consider how the political debates about biodiversity in northern Thailand have led to the creation of an environmental narrative and the appearance of consensus about crisis. There are clearly good reasons for making biodiversity protection an element of environmental policy, but it is also important to consider the social and political factors that give rise to biodiversity narratives, and the livelihood-disrupting interventions that result.

As a starting point, debates about biodiversity protection in northern Thailand can be understood in terms of the broad environmental management divide discussed in chapter 1. On the one hand, there is the "conservationist" protected area perspective, informed by the "assumption that livelihood activities and nature are incompatible" (Vandergeest 1996b: 260). On the other hand, there is the "people-oriented" perspective, which argues that local knowledge, cultural diversity, and community-based management are the keys to holistic biodiversity protection. However, despite their important disagreements, both sides in this debate share the underlying view that upland biodiversity is in crisis and, moreover, both are inclined to point the finger of blame at upland commercialization and "monocropping," biodiversity's symbolic antithesis. The result is another "discourse coalition," where political actors may appear to be in disagreement with each other on policy issues, but end up reinforcing a common vision of biophysical reality that may not be as certain as claimed. In this case, there is vigorous political debate about the impact of local communities on biodiversity and their role in its management, but both sides use the symbols of biodiversity crisis—and the specter of monocropping— to add strength to their political claims.

In the 1950s, Bo Kaew [in Samoeng district of Chiang Mai province] was still deep in the forest. Tigers, wild boar, deer, other large animals and flocks of wild parakeets, pheasants, and many jungle fowl lived in the forests surrounding the village. As the local population grew . . . and as the Hmong cleared hill areas for opium cultivation, the wild animals began to disappear until now when there is little large game remaining. (Quoted in Dearden 1995:114)

International debates and researchers have played an important role in prompting awareness about biodiversity in Thailand. The Canadian bio-geographer Philip Dearden has been particularly influential, and has been a key advocate for state intervention in biodiversity management.[1] In a series of articles, Dearden has set out the case for a biodiversity crisis so severe that urgent remedial action is required. In one contribution from the mid-1990s, he states gloomily, "there has been a faunal collapse in Northern Thailand that has occurred swiftly and ubiquitously throughout the region" (Dearden 1995:111). He claims that upland modernization since the mid-1960s accompanied the region's decline from "being one of the richest areas on the planet in terms of diversity and abundance of species to being virtually a faunal desert" (ibid.). This faunal collapse has been driven both by the deforestation caused by agricultural expansion—"wildlife has simply been squeezed out" (Dearden 1995: 125)—and by unsustainable hunting practices. Adding his own characteristic color to widespread concerns about the directions of upland development, Dearden (1995:118) argues that the fundamental driver of this decline has been the "wave of change sweeping over the highlands and filling every valley with the probing tentacles of commercialisation." Moreover, commercialization was creating increasing social differentiation both within and between different upland groups, which "leads to a decline in the social cohesion and traditions of the societies, which in turn leads to over-exploitation of what were previously common resources" (Dearden 1995:123). The result is a classic tragedy of the commons—the collapse of biodiversity resulting from the increasingly commercial aspirations of the successful and the subsistence desperation of the poor (Dearden 1995:124). Ominously, Dearden argues that the faunal collapse should not just prompt conservationist concern, but that it will have fundamentally important implications for livelihood sustainability as key sources of supplementary nutrition become unavailable (Dearden 1995:125).[2]

A later paper, based on collaborative research with Thai foresters, highlights the impacts of ongoing settlement in Doi Inthanon National Park (Dearden et al. 1996). Here the language is rather more measured, but the overall message is similar. The authors explicitly critique the distinction sometimes made between "biosphere people" (who have "a major impact on global environmental processes") and "ecosystem people" ("who live within the constraints of the local ecosystem on a generally sustainable basis") (Dearden et al. 1996:126). Instead, they argue that so-called ecosystem people can have substantial local environmental impacts, and they present a range of international studies concerning the negative impacts of local hunting practices to support this view (Dearden et al. 1996:127). In Doi Inthanon National Park, pressures have arisen largely because of encroachment for agricultural land, with an estimated 41 percent of the park's area farmed in the mid-1980s by approximately 4,000 park residents. The authors claim that much of this encroachment has occurred since the park was declared—a phenomenon said to be relatively widespread in protected areas—a claim that seeks to undermine arguments by NGO advocates for upland farmers that protected areas have been imposed by arbitrary state action on long-resident communities. Apart from agriculture, pressures on the national park are also said to arise from hunting, gathering plants and plant products, cutting firewood and construction materials, and fire (both to clear agricultural fields and to stimulate mushroom growth). The finding that hunting is less prevalent within the park than in villages just outside is attributed to a "lack of suitable targets" (Dearden et al. 1996:135). Previous histories of hunting within the park are cited, again challenging common NGO claims that upland farmers have effective local systems of wildlife protection:

> Hunting is a favorite spare time activity of Karen men, who rarely fail to take their muzzle-loaders with them whenever they walk to a distant field or look after their water buffalo and cattle during the rainy season. Nowadays big game such as deer or wild pigs has become rare in the densely settled upper Mae Klang area, and thus the bag usually consists only of birds and rats. (Dearden et al. 1996:135)

Such views are reinforced in a further study of changing landscape structure and faunal diversity in two wildlife sanctuaries in Chiang Mai and

Tak provinces (Anak and Dearden 2002). The adjacent Om Koi and Mae Tuen sanctuaries make up almost 2,400 square kilometers of protected areas and are home to approximately 5,700 upland residents, predominantly Karen and Hmong (Anak and Dearden 2002:157). The study found that "the amount of montane evergreen forest has been severely degraded as a result of agricultural activities," with Om Koi losing 5 percent and Mae Tuen 50 percent between 1954 and 1996 (Anak and Dearden 2002:160). This agriculture had also resulted in forest fragmentation; the largest forest patch in Om Koi makes up about 17 percent of the landscape, and in Mae Tuen 4 percent, a decline from 23 percent in 1954 (Anak and Dearden 2002:158). The study argues that forest fragmentation had not affected overall bird species diversity (to statistically significant levels), but that it had substantially affected bird species composition in Mae Tuen. There was an increase in nectarivorous species but "the elimination of more sensitive forest obligates and large frugivores" (Anak and Dearden 2002:159, 161, 163).[3] Mammals were also affected, "with a marked decline in the numbers of species, particularly large species, and also a reduced abundance of more common species" (Anak and Dearden 2002:163). Larger mammals such as elephants, sambar, tigers, black bears, and leopards were not found at all in Mae Tuen (Anak and Dearden 2002:162). The study argues that hunting caused these declines in animal populations: "there has simply been too great a hunting pressure for wild populations to be sustained" (ibid.). The shooting of a forest guard in Mae Tuen had taken much of the enthusiasm out of sanctuary policing.

But despite these problems in guarding against hunting and agricultural encroachment, writers such as Dearden remain strong supporters of the protected area system. The common view is that the appropriate response to population and land use pressure within protected areas is to strengthen the systems of regulation and enforcement, rather than adopt alternative approaches (such as the proposed community forest legislation) that seek to enhance the tenure security of farmers in these areas. While acknowledging problems in local implementation, Dearden (1995:126) is sympathetic to the initiative in "designating Class 1 watershed areas as zones where habitation and commercial uses of the forest are not allowed."[4] Responding to a proposal that forms of private and communal title should be granted to farmers in such protected areas, Dearden and colleagues (1998:197) argue that "there should be some areas of the landscape where species other than humans are given priority for their livelihood requirements and where biodiversity values can be protected for this and future generations." This approach is sometimes also called "land-use zoning," or using "buffer zones" to isolate areas of human activity from areas where no activities are allowed. To achieve this, Dearden is open to the possibility of some village relocation where there are particularly negative impacts on biodiversity values. He argues that many farmers have settled in protected areas after they have been declared and that it is inaccurate and misleading to claim that this kind of action restricts longstanding residents from accessing their ancestral lands (Dearden et al. 1998:195). Echoing widely held perceptions about the differential ecological impacts of different ethnic groups—despite Dearden's earlier rejection of the distinction between ecosystem and biosphere people—this article proposes that ongoing occupancy by "some villages or ethnic groups" may be permitted while others are relocated, "depending on the relative effects of these groups on park ecosystems." The authors suggest that "different levels of sympathy" could be granted to long-established villages "with historical subsistence use rather than to villages which became established illegally after protected status had been granted and whose villagers grow cash crops" (ibid.).

The intermingling of environmental and social narratives is clearly evident in this argument. In the highly charged atmosphere of the uplands, it is hard not to read the statement about "different levels of sympathy" as an argument for the continued presence of Karen communities but the relocation of Hmong. One of the key messages to emerge out of the study of Om Koi and Mae Tuen is the much poorer biodiversity performance of Mae Tuen (Anak and Dearden 2002:160–61). One reason for this appears to be that a paved road runs through part of the Mae Tuen sanctuary, increasing access for commercial agricultural production, hunting, and new settlement. Of particular importance is that this access has encouraged commercial cultivation of cabbages on cleared lands, predominantly by Hmong farmers:

> MT [Mae Tuen] has become increasingly settled by the Hmong ethnic group, who are well known for their skill in cash crop cultivation. Large numbers of illegal and poorly paid immigrants from Burma can be witnessed during harvest time carrying the cabbages to the waiting trucks of the Hmong. In contrast, OK [Om Koi] is occupied dominantly by the more sedentary and longer established Karen ethnic group, who have shown less interest in clearing the forests they depend on to grow cash crops for distant markets. (Anak and Dearden 2002:161)

Similar arguments about the Hmong are presented by Savage (1994) in relation to the impacts of forest product collection and fire near the Hmong village of Pa Kluay (often vilified in the famous Chom Thong dispute). Savage's study—which was conducted in cooperation with the stridently conservationist Dhammanaat Foundation—involved survey-ing transects in forest zones to measure density of pine trees, saplings, and seedlings, as well as human damage to mature pine trees such as the removal of resin-imbued splinters for sale as fire starters. The study con-cluded that "damage to the pine stands from human activities appears to be severe, particularly in the youngest and oldest age classes" (Savage 1994:248). Regular burning in the forest had destroyed many seedlings and about 40 percent of the older trees were damaged by chopping. Sav-age (1994:250) suggests that agricultural development programs have "not only changed the agricultural base for villagers, but also their rela-tionship to an entire suite of natural resources." The result is "an unsta-ble [forest] structure . . . and ongoing drastic changes in the local forest landscape." Despite the fact that this area lies within national park, "scat-tered cattle wander through the forest grazing on grass and tree foliage, and the sound of wood chopping and gun shots are common."

These concerns within Thailand resonate with an emerging interna-tional view that stricter enforcement of protected areas is the key to achiev-ing successful conservation. Internationally, this "resurgent protectionist argument" (Wilshusen et al. 2002:18)—or "authoritarian protectionist approach" (Brechin et al. 2002:42)—asserts that conservation objectives have been lost in the trend to link conservation with sustainable devel-opment, typically in "integrated conservation and development projects" (ibid.). For example, Oates's account (1999) of "myth and reality" in the rainforests of West Africa argues that conservation and development pro-grams tend to be informed by relatively romantic views of local social orga-nization. In particular, Oates argues that assumptions of social solidarity and conservationist orientation are untenable given the realities of local power politics and the large influxes of migrant settlers into the very fron-tier regions that are often targeted for conservation initiatives (and that are made even more attractive by local development programs). Oates argues that donor resources allocated to costly conservation-development programs may have been better spent on relatively modest support for regulatory staff. These arguments gain support from studies, such as those undertaken by Bruner and colleagues (2001), that highlight the relative importance of enforcement in protected areas. Their study of 93 protected areas in 22 tropical countries (including three in Thailand) found that "park effectiveness correlated most strongly with density of guards. . . . The median density of guards in the 15 most effective parks was more than eight times higher than in the 15 least effective parks" (Bruner et al. 2001:126).[5] Significantly, and contrary to contemporary participatory orthodoxy, "local participation in management" was not found to correlate with park effectiveness. Overall, their conclusion endorses the effectiveness of "parks based" approaches to conservation: "Tropical parks have been surprisingly effective at protecting the ecosystems and species within their borders in the context of chronic under-funding and significant land-use pressure. They have been especially effective in preventing land clearing, arguably the most serious threat to biodiversity" (ibid.).

THE CASE FOR CULTURAL DIVERSITY, BIODIVERSITY, AND COMMUNITY MANAGEMENT

These protectionist approaches to biodiversity conservation have, of course, been challenged, sometimes in language that is equally strident. In many developing countries, there has been a strong reaction against the protected area paradigm and its assertion that livelihood activities and biodiversity conservation are incompatible. Instead, the common alternative viewpoint argues that human presence is desirable given the close relationship between cultural diversity and biodiversity. This view, which sometimes expresses somewhat romantic sentiments about the pivotal role of "local" people and "local" knowledge in biodiversity preservation, is internationally influential and has taken on particular nuances in the Thai context. Clearly there is much that separates this alternative approach from the preservationist approach, but the perspectives also share much in common and both often rely on a narrative of biodiversity crisis brought about by commercialization.

The view that local (especially "indigenous") groups can protect, restore, and even enhance biological diversity became especially popular during the early 1990s—before and after the 1992 Rio Earth Summit—but has remained influential since. In 1991, the Uruguay-based NGO World Rainforest Movement published an important statement that emphasized the biodiversity-conserving role of local knowledge. In the introduction to this book, the prominent Indian environmentalist and activist Vandana Shiva (1991b:7) attacked the "polarity and dualism" of mainstream conservation. She argued that conventional conservation approaches usurp the rights of "Third World peasants and forest dwellers" who are, in fact, active participants in the "biological renewal of life, through their cultures and lifestyles" (Shiva 1991b:10). The dualism that Shiva condemned is the distinction between "production" and "conservation." These are categories "which in industrial civilisation are separate and opposed" (ibid.), motivating the technocratic view that people and nature must be separated to achieve conservation outcomes. Shiva (1991a:44) then went on to argue that the result of this separation is a "schizophrenic" development strategy that promotes "uniformity"—principally through "monocultures"—in relation to production while promulgating "diversity" in relation to conservation. What is achieved, in the end, is the "destruction of diversity in spheres of production such as agriculture, forestry, animal husbandry and fisheries." Clearly, not all advocates of community management agree with Shiva, or use such strong language. But elements of this discourse still persist in debates in Thailand and elsewhere, and many studies draw attention to apparent spatial correlations between cultural diversity and biological diversity (see Terralingua 2004 for an explicit illustration of this).

In Thailand, versions of this argument have been voiced strongly by those who argue that the state's role in excluding local farmers from forest management has been counterproductive in terms of biodiversity conservation. In another essay from the World Rainforest Movement's book, Lohmann (1991:81) asked, "Who defends biological diversity?" and argued that the erosion of biological diversity in Thailand has been "economics-driven" and "has been greatly helped by the activities of the state and international agencies." He painted a vivid picture of an environmental crisis in which mainstream development approaches and state regulation have made it "increasingly difficult for the Akha, Hmong and other tribes to live in the customary ways which provided substantial protection for biological diversity" (Lohmann 1991:85). This perspective explicitly embeds discussion of biodiversity into wider struggles between local residents and powerful states. Lohmann (1991:96) argued that state-enforced protected areas are not an appropriate approach to biodiversity protection; rather "it is rural village groups and movements opposed to the schemes of governments, corporations and international agencies who are the powerful and committed defenders of biological diversity."

One notable feature of this debate in northern Thailand is the particular emphasis placed on Karen livelihood systems as a key component of upland biodiversity. Consistent with the growth of approaches linking biodiversity to cultural diversity and community management in the 1990s, the Karen have come to be associated with environmentally friendly forms of agriculture and sustainable traditions of resource management. This trend has also coincided with the emergence of the community forest campaign in Thailand. Previous chapters have indicated that popular images of Karen livelihood may not be an accurate depiction of contemporary trends in Karen land use, but it is clear that this environmentally benign imagery has emerged in part to counter the hard-line conservationist view that human presence necessarily results in habitat and species loss. This political agenda has certainly shaped the production of knowledge about Karen livelihood and, in particular, knowledge about the specific relationship between cultural and biological diversity. There are several iconic studies of Karen land use and biodiversity that demonstrate how the community-management approach has influenced the generation of environmental knowledge.

Thung Yai Naresuan

Probably the most influential contribution to this subgenre has been Pinkaew's account (1996) of the "local ecological knowledge" of the Karen in the Thung Yai Naresuan forest in western Thailand. Thung Yai Naresuan is probably the most famous conservation area in Thailand, with biodiversity richness said to be nationally and internationally significant. Yet, when this wildlife sanctuary was declared in 1974, it created residential insecurity for the estimated 4,000 Karen living in the area: "the Karen have become citizens who encroach and use the land illegally and need to be moved from this area in order to . . . preserve wild animals according to the law" (Pinkaew 1996:16). In response to this threat, Pinkaew describes a local livelihood system that preserves and enhances biodiversity values and in which cultural values and knowledge systems emphasize an intimate relationship with the encompassing ecological system. "The guarding of the land means guarding of all lives that live on the earth, whether it be animals, plants, or humans. The land is something that has life and diversity" (Pinkaew 1996:125).

Pinkaew illustrates the relationship between Karen culture and the environment in three ways. First, she argues that Karen cultivation is not destructive of forest because the farmers tend to avoid clearing areas of primary forest; rather they prefer to clear bamboo forests about which they have extensive ecological knowledge and complex systems of classification (Pinkaew 1996:71). Forest protection is reinforced by an array of spiritual precepts and taboos that govern the selection of sites for clearing and prohibit the cutting of large trees in which spirits are believed to reside (Pinkaew 1996:78).

The second point, which has been taken up by many other researchers and advocates, is that Karen swidden fields mimic the diversity of the forest itself. Rather than viewing agricultural activity as reducing biodiversity, Pinkaew (1996:88) highlights the incredible diversity of Karen cultivation:

> The interesting thing in the Karen system of planting vegetables in the rice fields is that it is a multiple cropping system, which is another special characteristic of original agriculture. There are no less than 48 types of plants in the field, 14 of those being rice. Plants that are sown and grown in the same field seem simple and unplanned. But really it is a growing system based on organising the timing and position of planting, consistent with the type of the plant and its particular preferences.

The third point is the Karen emphasis on wildlife protection. For example, before burning fields it is a custom to call out loudly "in order to chase out wild animals, big and small, that live in the field, by letting them all know to leave the field before the fire is lit. This is so that their farming will not unnecessarily bother other lives" (Pinkaew 1996:79). There is also said to be strict regulation of hunting. The killing of an elephant is considered to be a "sin equal to killing a monk" (Wirawat 1996:7). Similarly, hunting of hornbills is prohibited because "it is a bird that is honest to its family" (ibid.). And gibbons are protected because their calls "help to announce danger and changes in the weather" (ibid.).[6]

In this account of Karen livelihood, Pinkaew is clearly breaking down the distinction between "production" and "conservation" that is condemned by Shiva. In this and later works, Pinkaew (2000, 2001) is a vigorous critic of Western-inspired conservation practices that seek to demarcate people and nature into different zones. Hers is a holistic vision in which livelihood activities, cultural identity, and political strategy are inseparable from the encompassing ecological system. Her approach is in striking contrast to Dearden's gloomy account of unsustainable resource exploitation and "faunal deserts." But is Pinkaew really challenging Dearden's perspective, or is she just describing a fragile backwater not yet reached by the "probing tentacles of commercialisation"?

Mae Laan Kham

Pinkaew's approach is taken up in another publication, *Rai Mun Wian* (Rotational shifting cultivation), by Waraalak Ithiphonorlan (1998). This is a study of the village of Mae Laan Kham, which is located in a national park in Chiang Mai province. Like Pinkaew, Waraalak suggests that Karen shifting cultivation (referred to as *rai mun wian*) is not a threat to primary forest, given that the soil is most appropriate in areas where bamboo is abundant (Waraalak 1998:38). She also argues that rotational shifting cultivation contributes to the biodiversity value of the area by creating a patchwork of fallow plots of varying ages, "each having value and benefits for people, for animals, and to protect the natural abundance of the upland ecological system" (Waraalak 1998:21). For example, the vigorous regrowth in fallow fields is said to provide "refuges and breeding areas" for numerous types of forest animals (Waraalak 1998:26). According to Waraalak (1998:38–39), fallow plots can provide sources of wildlife refuge that are superior to those found in primary forest. And, as with Pinkaew, particular emphasis is placed on the biodiversity of Karen cultivation. In Waraalak's terms (1998:42), "rotational shifting cultivation is virtually a natural bank that protects original plant varieties." She writes that "there are more than eighty varieties of local vegetables that are eaten by the Pakakeyor [Karen]. They are the plants that maintain their ethnic identity. They use these foods in rituals that maintain the ethnic identity of the group" (Waraalak 1998:11). A later publication by Waraalak (2004: table 3) underlines the relationship between biological and cultural diversity, showing that the Karen in Mae Laan Kham have 13 names for types of cucumber, 10 names for varieties of cowpea, 13 names for yam, and 28 names for rice varieties (figure 8.1 shows a Karen woman collecting vegetables). Reduction in fallow periods caused by forest regulation is said to result in a reduction of this crop diversity, with a direct impact on local biodiversity (Waraalak 1998:39).

Mae Khong Saay

Another commonly discussed village is the "genuinely forest village" of Mae Khong Saay (Pritsana and Montri 1998:48), which is located in Chiang Dao Wildlife Protection Area to the north of Chiang Mai. Accounts of Mae Khong Saay contain the familiar statements about the ecologically benign nature of rotational shifting cultivation, the protec-

FIG. 8.1 *Karen woman collecting vegetables*

tion of local wildlife, and the more general claims about the intimacy of the relationship between local people and the natural environment: "living with respect for nature is still the heart of the community" (Pritsana and Montri 1998:49). The villagers are said to place particular emphasis on the protection of fish species through methods such as releasing small fish that are born in the paddy fields in the wet season into the rivers; stirring up ant nests near the rivers so the ants can be food for the fish; protecting their natural breeding areas with the declaration of no fishing areas; and strictly enforcing a ban on the use of chemicals or explosives for fishing (Pritsana and Montri 1998:91). The account of the village provided by Pritsana and Montri places particular emphasis on the local moral values that underlie biodiversity protection. For example, in their discussion of the hunting taboos that apply to the gibbon and the hornbill, they write, "The gibbon is an animal that likes a calm environment and does not steal from others. And the hornbill is an animal that lives with the one partner for all its life. These give people direction on how to live their own lives—peacefully, simply, and emphasizing the importance of family" (Pritsana and Montri 1998:77–78). Similarly, in relation to forest protection they report that cutting down a tree that contains a nest is regarded as "virtually the same as destroying the house of someone else in order to build your own house" (Pritsana and Montri 1998:79).

Mae Khong Saay is an interesting case because the protection of biodiversity is explicitly linked with the village's relative underdevelopment, a theme that is present, though more implicit, in the accounts discussed above. "Mae Khong Saay is a forest community" one report notes, "that is oriented to the simple life. The powerful and rapid current of development has not yet reached it. The system of production is just for meeting basic needs" (NDF 1999:78, 84). The subsistence economy is said to rely heavily on forest products, and vigorous protection of natural resources reduces dependence on the outside world. A particular feature is that the village had received no support at all from the state whether for education, electricity, or public health. Yet, this state neglect is seen as being favorable in terms of cultural maintenance and biodiversity protection. State education has not yet oriented children in the village to the external economy, and the transmission of ecological knowledge between elders and youngsters remains strong. This situation is contrasted with another Karen village where road access and market integration has, apparently, disrupted the relationship between the farmers and their forest resources. Modernization and the accrual of new technologies or artifacts are associated with a loss of heritage, knowledge, and environmental protection. "Day by day the new generation will be separated from the original local wisdom and knowledge of the community" (Pritsana and Montri 1998:56). The lamentable state of affairs in the "modernized" Karen village is described as follows:

> The passing on of various forms of knowledge has not continued. The dependence on local resources has declined. At the same time the biodiversity of plants and animals has declined too. . . . Several families have pick-ups and almost every family has motorcycles. The majority of the village have electricity and electrical appliances such as televisions and fans. The continuation of the original point of view is a heavy burden on the community . . . who have the duty to create a balance between the increasing desires of the villagers which conflict with the ecological system of the community forest. (Pritsana and Montri 1998:56, 99)

Swiddenning and Secondary Forests

One final study is worth considering because it supports those that argue that shifting cultivation systems are not necessarily ecologically degrading. Unlike the previous three studies, this work was conducted as an orthodox botanical study based on the identification of forest condition and species diversity associated with different land-use systems. Schmidt-Vogt (1999) worked in three upland villages, one Karen, one Lawa, and one Akha. His study challenges many of the popular assumptions about "untouched" or "pristine" nature in the uplands and argues that "the development of vegetation in the Northern highlands is largely the result of human pressures" and that much of the "natural" forest cover in the upland zone between 700 and 1,500 meters is made up of "secondary vegetation formations on fallow swiddens" (Schmidt-Vogt 1999:239). Like the authors considered above, Schmidt-Vogt (1999:240) describes a shifting cultivation environment that is "species-rich" and "complex and dynamic," with the number of useful plants "increased though the variety of environmental conditions" brought about by selective forest clearing and fallow patches at various stages of regrowth. Overall, he found that the regrowth forests that followed shifting cultivation were "structurally complex or even very complex," with considerable variation in relation to height and diameter and some "characterised by a distinct layering" (Schmidt-Vogt 1999:231). He found that weed infestation—though common in the early stages of fallow—was limited, mainly due to shading from tree growth and an increasing shortage of viable seeds. Importantly, he found that "most secondary forests are surprisingly species-rich in comparison to nearby old-growth forests," and in sample stands in the three villages he found between 60 and 81 plant species (Schmidt-Vogt 1999:233).

There was, however, some variation. In the Akha village in Chiang Rai province—made up of recent migrants who settled in the area in about 1981—there were considerably greater resource constraints than in the Lawa and Karen villages. In Chiang Rai he found that "regrowth on swiddens . . . is more irregular" due to more intensified land use that has arisen, in part, from official restrictions on forest clearing. In areas cultivated for relatively short periods, long fallow "can lead to the formation of bamboo groves, interspersed with young trees" (Schmidt-Vogt 1999:241) and, as has been found in a number of Karen villages, this is the preferred area for the establishment of new swiddens. However, on plots subject to more long-term cultivation, degradation was evident: "resprouting plants decline and weeds are capable of forming nearly impenetrable thickets, which persist for many years" (Schmidt-Vogt 1999:241). Interestingly, he also found that "the forests on fields abandoned by the

Hmong [who used to farm in the area] are notably all species-poor, and characterized by the prevalence of one species" (Schmidt-Vogt 1999:234). But Schmidt-Vogt's assessment remains optimistic, suggesting that even in the relatively resource-poor Akha village, "farmers are sufficiently competent and flexible to devise systems which exert less pressure on forests" (Schmidt-Vogt 1999:242). His overall conclusion is that shifting cultivation in secondary forest is environmentally preferable to permanent "monocropping systems" and state-sponsored "reforestation programmes, which are carried out with only a limited number of species" (Schmidt-Vogt 1999:243).

EXPLORING THE BIODIVERSITY DEBATE

The "protectionist" and "community management" approaches to biodiversity in Thailand are frequently set in opposition to each other, and this opposition is voiced through other debates such as the ongoing disagreement about community forestry. But there are important commonalities in underlying beliefs about biodiversity and its threats. The protectionist approach, especially in its more authoritarian modes, takes the view that human presence and biodiversity protection are, by and large, incompatible. Human presence in protected areas is only acceptable where it is based on low-impact livelihoods. Advocates of community management have effectively challenged the ecological necessity of expulsion from protected areas, but their underlying assumptions about the relationship between biodiversity and land use are often very similar. For defenders of local communities, a benign relationship with nature persists only so long as the local economy remains predominantly subsistence oriented. Only a very particular type of human presence in the forest is defended. While few of these advocates would defend the expulsion of commercially oriented farmers in order to protect biodiversity, their persistent valorization of subsistence-oriented lifestyles and their critique of modernization adds legitimacy to the protectionist perspective. In other words, a "discourse coalition" has emerged in which a particular causal link between agricultural transformation and biodiversity decline is assumed. One reason for the persistence of the biodiversity crisis narrative is that it provides a common framework for debating environmental policy in northern Thailand and furnishes potent imagery to both sides of the political argument.

How can a more nuanced approach to the relationship between agricultural transformation and biodiversity be developed? How can debates about biodiversity be pursued in ways that do not reinforce stereotypes about social groups and their appropriate role in the uplands? Is it possible to develop an approach to biodiversity that relies less on simplifying complex social and environmental processes?

Assessing Biodiversity Functions

The first important point to make is that—despite the confidence with which analysts discuss the biodiversity crisis in upland Thailand—there is still much uncertainty about overall biodiversity loss and its relationship with different forms of land use. Various studies, of course, have been undertaken to indicate the extent of biodiversity richness in northern Thailand. But, apart from the study by Schmidt-Vogt (1999), there is relatively little detailed or rigorous analysis of the effects of human activity on biodiversity in the uplands. As Dearden (1995:112) himself wrote in the mid-1990s, "scientific evidence in the formal sense of the collapse of faunal diversity in the North is virtually non-existent. This is because no large-scale baseline studies have been undertaken, and scarcely any monitoring is currently being attempted of wildlife populations." Since then the research situation appears to have changed little.[7]

With such basic research lacking in northern Thailand, the ability to make informed policy judgments about some of the more complex biodiversity issues is heavily compromised. Instead, there is a tendency to rely upon generalized associations of land use and biodiversity change from other locations. And common statements about biodiversity loss often suggest that land use is generally degrading when the observed impacts (such as from hunting or forest product collection) only apply to quite specific forms of biodiversity.

Tomich, Thomas, and van Noordwijk (2004:234) highlight some of the important areas of uncertainty in their discussion of key environmental research issues in upland areas of Southeast Asia. They argue that there is a lack of clarity on what the basic "functions and dysfunctions" of biodiversity are. To what extent are ecosystem functions compromised by biodiversity decline? Is this a simple linear relationship (lower biodiversity means less ecosystem function), or are there key thresholds below which loss of diversity may be catastrophic? What is the level of redundancy in the ecosystem? For example, is there a functional need for all the nitrogen-producing microbes in the soil, or can the system cope reasonably well with a substantial reduction, save for some particular "keystone" species?

It is also important to ask how far debates are driven by selective valuations of biodiversity. In Thailand, much attention to date has focused on the loss of charismatic bird and animal species, with relatively less attention given to the processes and impacts of less visible biodiversity loss. Schmidt-Vogt's study (1999) suggests that a shift in emphasis away from faunal impacts may generate a much more nuanced picture than the biodiversity crisis narrative suggests. Of course there may be ecological, ethical, or aesthetic reasons for the preservation of certain charismatic species, but these specific valuations and functions need to be distinguished from a generalized crisis narrative.

Rethinking Commercialization and Monocropping

A second theme to consider is the role of commercialization—and especially monocropping—as a destroyer of biodiversity. To date it appears that the impact of upland commercialization has been subject to more rhetoric than research. "The market economy," Lohmann (1991:100) writes, "is a corrosive acid bath which dissolves most of the diversity-protecting practices it comes into contact with." Of course, it would be foolhardy to deny the relationship between agricultural transformation and biodiversity loss. International experience does suggest that there are links between large-scale agricultural commercialization and biodiversity decline (Swanson 1995; Wood et al. 2000). For example, in areas of large-scale agricultural production such as the midwestern United States, modern agricultural landscapes have, in some areas, simplified food chains and reduced the habitats of many preexisting woodland birds, mammals, and insects. But there is a need to question the uncritical transfer of these forms of knowledge to the very different context of smallholder agriculture in the diverse landscapes of northern Thailand.

Somewhat surprisingly, an article coauthored by Dearden represents an important example of an alternative perspective on upland biodiversity. Dearden, who previously wrote of the "faunal desert" brought about by commercialization, appears to have adopted a very different perspective, perhaps under the influence of his coauthor. In their study of wildlife use in two Hmong villages, Waranoot and Dearden (2002:2021) challenge the argument that subsistence-oriented upland cultivation "may be the most appropriate and culturally suitable means available for preserving biodiversity in many upland areas of southeast Asia." Their paper makes a number of key points. First, the authors suggest that cash crops such as cabbages and cut flowers are more biodiversity-friendly than the more traditional maize-opium-rice combination because they can support substantially more people per area of land and, as such, help to reduce forest clearing. "Little support was found for the suggestion . . . that cash cropping would necessarily lead to greater deforestation as a result of low crop value" (Waranoot and Dearden 2002:2020). They acknowledge that this benefit has to be balanced against the possible effects of chemical inputs, though they recognize that very little scientific data is available on the environmental impacts of agrochemical use. The second key point is that cash cropping appears to reduce hunting activity, given that the opportunity cost of labor increases (although there are ongoing risks of hunting by outsiders). Interestingly, they note relatively high levels of disapproval among Hmong women of hunting, primarily because it diverts male labor away from agricultural pursuits (Waranoot and Dearden 2002:2016). Third, they suggest that increased cash incomes have resulted in greater access to purchased meat, reducing the demand for "wild meat" (ibid.).

Waranoot and Dearden focus mainly on the issue of hunting, but it is also useful to focus specifically on agriculture itself. Recent discussion of rotational shifting cultivation has demonstrated its ability to maintain, or even enhance, diversity. But what of the arguably much more common situation of commercially oriented upland cultivation? Is the pejorative label "monocropping" an accurate reflection of the impact of such systems on biodiversity? There are some indications that it may be an overly narrow perspective. Even on superficial inspection it is evident that in areas of supposedly monocropped fields there is substantial cultivation of herbs and vegetables along field edges, terrace bunds, tracks, and irrigation canals. There are also often patches and strips of diverse vegetation, especially in gullies, along streamlines, and on ridgetops. Referring to a Hmong village in Chiang Mai province, Kanok (2003:296) suggests that many of the vegetation "edges" that lie "within and between major land uses" are actively managed by farmers "for growing a variety of traditional crops and local vegetables formerly grown in swidden fields for household consumption." He argues that these edges may have an important role in the preservation, at a landscape level, of local biodiversity.

Home gardens, where there is often an abundance of fruit, vegetable, and herb cultivation, may also make a contribution to biodiversity preservation. Several studies in Thailand have documented the high level of diversity in these small managed patches. A recent study among Karen farmers, some of whom had adopted intensive strawberry cultivation, found that home gardens may play an important role in preserving species otherwise in short supply. There seems to be good evidence of a system of "capture and cultivate," whereby valued wild species are brought into home gardens to ensure their ongoing availability: "this practice . . . may hold considerable value as a method of biodiversity preservation" (Johnson and Grivetti 2002a:293).

These studies do not necessarily amount to a critique of the view that biodiversity is in significant decline in some areas, but they highlight the importance of what has been called "agrodiversity." This concept has been proposed as a more accurate way of depicting the complex relationships between local cultivation systems and local ecosystems. According to Brookfield and Padoch (1994:43), agrodiversity can be understood as "the many ways in which farmers use the natural diversity of the environment for production, including not only their choice of crops but also their management of land, water and biota as a whole." Agrodiversity focuses on the multiplicity and complexity of farming systems by examining various dimensions of diversity: biophysical diversity, management diversity, species diversity, and organizational diversity (Brookfield et al. 2003:23). This multidimensional approach may provide a particularly useful framework for analyzing farming systems in areas, such as the northern Thai uplands, where landscapes are highly variable (even over very small scales), where there is substantial cultural complexity, where external (state, NGO, private sector, and farmer-to-farmer) influences on agricultural production are diverse, and where the microcomplexities of household organization and farm management remain poorly understood. Kanok's study (2003)—which was undertaken as part of an international project focusing on agrodiversity—shows potential for this approach to cast doubt on popular stereotypes that too readily associate Hmong agriculture with ecological degradation.

In a reassessment of popular perceptions of monocropping, some further consideration could also be given to the reasons why farmers adopt commercially oriented agricultural systems. A number of writers who lament the loss of local crop varieties suggest that monocropping heightens farmer risk in terms of pest and disease infestation and also in terms of market exposure. In much of the literature on traditional agricultural systems, local plant variety is seen as underlying livelihood security. But this needs to be weighed against the demonstrable livelihood benefits of more intensive systems of production. A number of studies have suggested that the adoption of monocropped cash crops has both raised income and substantially reduced land pressure in areas of population growth. Waranoot's argument (2002) about the "limitations of subsistence in the uplands" is an important contribution. She points out that Hmong farmers recognize that food security, in terms of rice, is more viably met by purchasing rice with the revenue from cash crops than it is from the cultivation of rice itself. "Various studies of Hmong agriculture," she reports, "indicate that the newly adopted cash crops, such as cut-flowers, yield the highest average gross margin per unit area" (Waranoot 2002:107). These high returns mean that per capita land requirements are much lower than they would be under a subsistence rice production system, substantially reducing pressures for land clearing in surrounding forest areas.

Similar observations have been made in relation to upland Karen and Lawa farmers in Mae Hong Son province, where it appears that adoption of relatively intensive cash cropping has taken pressure off shifting cultivation systems that were suffering from increasingly short fallow periods. In fact, there is evidence that the persistence of these rotational fallow systems—much lauded for their biodiversity values—is made possible by the presence of alternative sources of income in the form of cash crops, the sale of forest products, and off-farm wage labor (Kanok et al. 1994:43–47; Waranoot 2002:108). The villagers of Mae Laan Kham, famous for its "traditional" cultivation systems, derive substantial income from wage laboring in lowland garlic farms in nearby villages (A. Walker fieldwork 2004). Similarly, the forest community of Mae Khong Saay has many young people working outside as laborers, petty traders, and even as road construction workers in northeast Thailand (Pritsana and Montri 1998:49).

In brief, the inverse relationship that many observers assume between commercialization and biodiversity warrants some extended field scrutiny. The popular stereotype of monocropping may conceal substantial plant diversity at a landscape scale. Some research has been undertaken on the livelihood and nutritional benefits of diverse "patches" or "edges" in predominantly commercial landscapes, but relatively little work has been done on examining what environmental services these islands of diversity may provide. Also, the negative stereotype of monocropping tends to divert attention away from the ability of commercial agriculture—or the subsistence cultivation of improved rice varieties—to take pressure off plant and animal resources in the surrounding areas. The findings of a number of researchers that relatively affluent communities are often in the best position to effectively manage local forests should raise some doubts about the inevitability of the "corrosive acid bath" of commercialization (see Kessler 1998; Chusak and Dearden 1999; Sopin et al. 1990). There are subtle relations between biodiversity and livelihood diversity—of which commercial agriculture is one component—and these subtleties are too readily erased by a simplifying narrative of biodiversity crisis.

CONCLUSION

Biodiversity loss is a major concern in northern Thailand, as it is in many other parts of the world. There is anxiety—even alarm—about the loss of particular species and, more generally, about the destruction of biologically rich forest ecosystems. As with the other issues examined in this book, discussions of biodiversity loss tend to be informed by the language of environmental crisis: species "collapse," "faunal deserts," and "extinctions" all brought about by population pressures, "overexploitation," and "rampant commercialization." These discussions regularly resort to the specter of "monocropping"—a potent linguistic tool that reduces diverse processes of agricultural transformation to the simplified imagery of vast fields of uniform cultivation, reminiscent of the American Midwest. Once again a simplified narrative of cause and effect (commercialized monocropping brings about biodiversity decline) is evident. This narrative taps into popular anxieties and stereotypes and, at the same time, downplays the social and biophysical diversity of the region.

Of course, highlighting the simplifying force of this narrative is not the same as denying that there are some very real threats to biodiversity. But it is important to introduce some greater uncertainty and local specificity into the discussion. There is a surprising lack of detailed research on the biodiversity impacts of recent upland transformation. This is particularly the case in relation to "uncharismatic" biodiversity such as insects and soil organisms. Put simply, we really do not know what is happening to the region's overall biodiversity.

This lack of research and the tendency for public debate to transform "concerns" into "facts" needs to be understood in its political context. Biodiversity protection (along with watershed protection) is one of the main issues that drives the ongoing debate about the appropriate role for upland people in accessing and managing natural resources. The "protectionist" paradigm cites species and habitat decline as justifying, in some cases, the relocation of upland communities and an expanded role for state regulation. By contrast, the "people-oriented" paradigm points to the relationship between cultural diversity and biological diversity—in traditional, subsistence-oriented production systems—to argue for continued presence and enhanced local management. Both sides share the view that recent transformations in the uplands are a threat to biodiversity. And both sides are also inclined to the view—whether implicitly or explicitly stated—that some ethnic groups (like the Karen) are more biodiversity-friendly than others (such as the Hmong). This view reinforces (and is reinforced by) the various other ethnoenvironmental stereotypes that circulate in northern Thailand. In other words, the persistence of the biodiversity crisis narrative is not so much a product of scientific evidence but of the discursive agreement between seemingly opposed sides in the conservation debate. This agreement resonates with fundamental cultural perceptions about the desirable wild(er)ness of the upland forested zone and productively interacts with popular prejudices against particular minority groups.

In order to open up this "problem closure" there is an urgent need for more locally specific studies about the relationship between livelihood and biodiversity. At present, in Thailand, most discussions of biodiversity in the uplands paint a picture of "either/or," but there is a need to explore possibilities for "both/and." Studies of indigenous ecological knowledge show that various forms of upland livelihood can enhance biodiversity in certain ways, but—in their enthusiasm to reject commercialization—most studies have tended to paint overly romantic images of upland lifestyles that provide a restricted view of livelihood opportunity and deny potential linkages between modern lifestyles and biodiversity preservation. Promise appears to lie in the agrodiversity approach, which has greater potential to analyze the various aspects of diversity in terms of the actual livelihood challenges that people face. As Stocking (2002:39) argues, in relation to the "enigma" of biodiversity, "it is vital that biodiversity be seen in its pragmatic context, not only in ecologists' jargon as a 'life support system' but also in a real practical context in making the environment more secure and people's livelihoods better supported." This could make an important contribution to the ecosystem approach, proposed under the Convention on Biological Diversity, which is "a strategy for the integrated management of land, water and living resources that promotes conservation and sustainable use in an equitable way," but which also "recognizes that humans, with their cultural diversity, are an integral component of ecosystems" (Convention on Biological Diversity 2000). This approach can provide for greater acknowledgement of diversity both in agricultural practices—including the varied approaches people take to the challenges of commercialization—and in perceptions of environmental values and ecosystem functions.

9 *Rethinking Environmental Knowledge*

THIS BOOK HAS SOUGHT TO ILLUSTRATE how environmental politics in one location—one that is extremely well known and widely researched by different disciplines—has become dominated by environmental beliefs that are simplistic, misleading, and highly selective. Since at least the 1960s, a variety of observers have claimed that the upland zones of northern Thailand are in a state of urgent environmental crisis. While environmental problems do exist, and interventions are required, the common belief that upland agriculture is causing immense damage to uplands and lowlands is simply not supported by available evidence. Yet, despite this lack of evidence, the narrative of upland crisis is widely popular and highly persistent. In Thailand, newspapers, television, government statements, and books regularly refer to the belief that population growth, deforestation, and commercialization are causing water shortages, soil erosion, declining biodiversity, and agrochemical contamination. The message is underlined by roadside signs in the north, installed by the government, which report in matter-of-fact terms that deforestation causes drought and undermines agricultural livelihoods. In the streets of Bangkok, colorful murals outside schools repeat this message with stark images of deforested hillsides, desperate farmers, threatened wildlife, and contaminated streams.

This vision of upland crisis is used to support very different approaches to the management of the uplands. On the one hand, conservationists and state regulators have used the language of rigorous science and uncontested certainty to argue that urgent steps are required to protect fragile upland catchments from further degradation. On the other hand, people-oriented proponents of community development have drawn on the language of indigenous knowledge to argue that local residents have the traditional skills to manage this fragile landscape, provided they are shielded from the disruption of both state regulation and commercialization.

This book proposes that this has become an unproductive debate between those who hold that upland residents are "forest destroyers" and those who see them as "forest guardians." What makes this debate unproductive is that, ultimately, it is based on a shared assumption of upland crisis, born of a series of questionable beliefs about environmental processes in the uplands. The conclusions that emerge from the previous chapters are stark:

- Popular explanations of upland degradation in northern Thailand are highly simplistic and contested by research both inside and outside Thailand.
- Land-use policies claiming to address problems such as water shortages, soil erosion, and biodiversity loss may not address their underlying causes, and might even exacerbate problems.
- Local livelihoods in the uplands are restricted because of a range of official land-use controls that are often based on prejudicial views of upland agriculture and questionable assumptions about its environmental impacts.
- Alternative solutions favoring local livelihoods have played an important role in countering official prejudice, but they frequently rely too heavily on simplistic representations of traditional upland lifestyles and too readily assume that commercial agriculture results in ecological degradation.
- Many of the participants in the debate about environmental management in northern Thailand have been aware of research criticizing these positions for years, but have not acknowledged these insights, nor generally changed their approaches accordingly.

Why does this situation occur? In some cases, it may simply result from underlying environmental complexity and a time lag between research findings and the response of government agencies and activists. This book, however, takes a different perspective. A variety of social and political factors influence the explanation of environmental change in northern Thailand. In particular, the concept of "environmental narratives" has been shown to refer to simplified cause-and-effect statements that provide flawed summaries of environmental change, but that persist despite contrasting evidence. Environmental narratives are assertions about complex and uncertain biophysical processes that have become "stabilized," or made to appear "factual" by social and political influences that deny greater underlying complexity and uncertainty. Because of their rush to endorse particular management approaches, advocates on different sides of environmental debates claim greater certainty about the cause and effect of environmental processes than can reasonably be asserted.

The existence of these narratives does not imply that environmental policy is unwarranted, or that research is futile. But a more politicized account of how environmental knowledge is formed is necessary before assuming that it provides an accurate basis for explaining environmental problems or for indicating appropriate regulatory responses. Two questions need to be asked: Where do environmental narratives come from? And what can be done about them?

EXPLAINING NARRATIVES

Many readers might be surprised—if not deeply worried—that so much environmental policy in Thailand is based on beliefs that are unsupported by research and insensitive to local complexity. Perhaps more worryingly, it is increasingly clear that these beliefs may not actually address underlying environmental problems, and may place unnecessary restrictions on rural livelihoods through strict land-use regulation, reforestation of agricultural lands, and, in some cases, forced resettlement.

For many scientists working on environmental change, the correct response to problems of environmental knowledge lies in conducting more research and communicating more effectively with policymakers. Scientific progress, they assert, will lead to more sophisticated environmental policy. Consequently, inadequate environmental policies result from inappropriate communication between scientific research and policy. Yet, while there is clearly a need for more research and discussion, it is also apparent that research (and public debate) challenging simplified environmental narratives has existed for years, but it has failed to change entrenched viewpoints (Tomich, Chomitz et al. 2004). In fact, scientific research is often selectively drawn upon to buttress prevailing views. Instead, understanding and overcoming the problem of narratives requires a more complex and politicized approach than the belief that scientific research is somehow independent of politics and that policymakers will always listen to its findings. It is important to focus on the ways in which simplified narratives arise and persist.

Three factors seem significant in the emergence of environmental narratives.

Environmental Knowledge and Values are Coproduced

A key point of narrative analysis is that environmental knowledge (including scientific knowledge) does not exist in a politically neutral and universally applicable form, but reflects various social and political influences and values. One main aspect of this process is "problem closure," or the manner in which one specific way of viewing environmental change becomes dominant in framing diverse environmental changes and problems. Over time, these values and assumptions about problems become subsumed in popular discussions, literature, and imagery to give the impression that the underlying environmental values and problem definitions are both factual and generally applicable. Many social analysts call this process the emergence of discourse—the shared understandings, assumptions, and judgments that provide the frameworks for discussion, debate, and analysis.

At this basic discursive level, perceptions of the uplands of northern Thailand are shaped by the cultural distinction between the lowland settlements (*muang*) and the upland forests (*pa*). Whereas in the past the *pa* represented an undesirably wild antithesis to the settled and civilized *muang*, in recent decades its wild(er)ness has taken on much more desirable connotations. This transformation is due, in part, to the increased integration of the north into Thailand's overall administration. It is also linked to political activities aimed at pacifying and stabilizing diverse minorities; to increasing recognition of the importance of natural resources; and to an increased appreciation of environmental values by a growing and urbanized middle class. This desire for the wildness of the *pa* underpins many environmental debates. For state regulators, wilderness is best preserved by excluding, or strictly regulating, human presence. For NGOs, and the various other advocates of upland residents, the wildness of the *pa* can best be preserved by supporting forest-oriented lifestyles and by emphasizing traditional forms of social organization and agriculture. Associated with these positions are the stereotypical classifications of ethnic minorities in the uplands as either ecological "guardians" or forest "destroyers." In both cases, value-laden knowledge has been generated or harnessed by different parties to facilitate different visions of, and policies for, the uplands. And both perspectives have helped cement an environmental discourse that suggests the uplands are in crisis and that modernization of upland livelihoods is a key driver of degradation.

The role of underlying values in shaping what is seen as legitimate knowledge is well illustrated by a simple, yet stark, example. The following two quotations offer sharply differing accounts of environmental change in northern Thailand. The first was spoken by a lowland Thai villager and was cited in a people-oriented advocacy magazine:

When I was a boy, our village was surrounded by dense forest. There were tigers and lots of big trees, some two meters in diameter. When I was about 30, I saw the forest beginning to disappear, but then there was still water in the streams. Fifteen years later, the stream had disappeared too. Now we only have artesian wells, which are so inadequate that people fight over them. (Quoted in Anurak 1995).

This statement was used by the magazine to illustrate the outrage and anxiety felt by many people in Thailand because of the apparent catastrophic changes and social conflicts wrought by deforestation. Yet, this statement is seemingly contradicted by a highland Mien farmer from a community that historically practiced shifting cultivation:

It has been a saying in our people for many, many years that in order to get a regular, year-round long-term supply of water you need to cut down the largest trees around the village. I have seen it myself. It is only since we arrived in Thailand that we have heard people claim that this is not the case, and it is the Thai extension workers who tell us this. (Quoted in Forsyth 2004:202)

The two statements are clearly very different. Of course, each may reflect local experiences of hydrological complexity in the uplands. But popular narratives of environmental degradation in northern Thailand would undoubtedly represent the first quotation as accurate because it fits with the dominant discourse of wilderness and ecological fragility, and for many readers it provides a strong sense that scientific knowledge is being supported by the local knowledge of a concerned observer. By contrast, many would consider the second statement to be evidence of dangerous misinformation and representative of the environmentally destructive attitudes of some hilltribe farmers. The assumption that one statement is more accurate than the other indicates that environmental knowledge in northern Thailand is, in very significant ways, a function of wider value judgments about the appropriate state of the uplands, the purpose of environmental management, and the status of different speakers.

As it stands, the first statement reflects many commonly held political concerns about environment and modernization—observed in Thailand and many other parts of the world—that focus on the destruction of wilderness, a loss of equilibrium and harmony in the countryside, and encroaching conflict and strife as a result (Giddens 1994). A number of political concerns coexist: government departments seeking to regulate land use; lowland farmers worried about water shortages; NGOs arguing for the importance of indigenous knowledge; and domestic or international conservationists concerned about the loss of wilderness. They all subscribe to the imagery of deforestation and drought, and hence create a "discourse coalition" based on their shared belief in crisis. Given the framing of environmental discussion in these terms, the statement by the highland Mien farmer is, quite simply, unacceptable.

Environmental Knowledge Is Linked to Statemaking

Narratives perform important functions for the Thai state. Framing environmental management in terms of widely shared and seemingly neutral narratives allows the state to reduce social contestation about the purposes of land-use policies, and helps enforce state control over territory and diverse social groups. The Thai government has sought to consolidate its control over the land, resources, and people of northern Thailand for decades. Environmental narratives play an important part in achieving this objective by attributing specific ideas of blame, responsibility, and appropriate behavior, which can both legitimize government interventions and delegitimize alternative approaches.

One of the important aspects of the linkage between statemaking and environmental knowledge lies in the establishment of who speaks with expertise. This matter has been widely discussed in relation to the establishment of colonial power in new territories. For example, Sivaramakrishnan (1999:6), writing about British control over forests in eastern Bengal, commented,

The contours of power—or the limits of statemaking—are shaped by structures and processes of knowledge acquisition and dissemination. Forest management was not only predicated on requisite scientific knowledge but on techniques of validating or valorizing certain knowledge while discounting others. Thus was expertise constituted. The struggle over what knowledge was designated as expertise, who generated it, how it was certified, where it was located, and by whom it was practiced also became integral to statemaking.

Usually, such state power over the generation of authoritative knowledge was seen in the establishment of formal state agencies to adjudicate questions of forestry and other aspects of resource management in ways that could "depoliticize" complex strategies for control and legitimization by ascribing these decisions to the supposedly neutral "scientific" world. The Royal Forest Department of Thailand in particular has tended to take on the mantle of scientifically neutral expertise to legitimize its statements about the need for urgent protection of fragile watershed zones, strict limitations on land use, and reestablishment of forest cover by means of plantation forestry. This positioning as expert is often combined with the claim that natural-resource regulators are the guardians of national security and loyal implementers of the royal family's vision for forest protection. This makes it very difficult for critics to be seen as legitimate.

The watershed classification scheme, adopted by the Royal Forest Department, is a good example of forest regulators taking on the mantle of scientific neutrality. The classification scheme is communicated as an exercise in neutral science, with watershed classes based on seemingly objective criteria of land cover, slope, and elevation. Formal scientific studies of these data sources enable the classification scheme to be applied in apparently objective and neutral ways to watersheds throughout the entire country. But this exercise in scientific classification is also profoundly political, as it declares lowland agriculture legitimate, while the cultivation of upland slopes is rendered illegal unless, on the more gentle slopes, it accords with the department's vision of appropriate land use (that is, tree planting). This is a "territorializing" vision that cocreates state control, scientific information, and preferred land uses. The likelihood that the resolution of spatial data about the uplands it too crude to enable informed judgments about land use underlines the bureaucratic simplification of this classification system. The classification scheme also provides a seemingly neutral justification for selective state action. In some cases, it implies that urgent action is required to address the destructive actions of hill tribes in fragile watershed zones, while in other cases forestry plantations, mines, and even tourist resorts proceed, seemingly without official comment. The classification of land as protected or nonprotected also clearly overlaps with strategic concerns about land in border regions, or in remote zones where insurgency has been experienced in the past. And watershed classification provides a justification for the establishment of an extensive network of watershed management units and the extension of other elements of state control.

But statemaking does not simply involve the emergence of state bureaucracies apparently autonomous from society. It also involves responses to, and sometimes alliances with, nonstate actors. In Thailand, there are various synergies between formal state policies and the ambitions of conservation groups, or those who may benefit from plantation forestry and the increased state control over land use and economic activities. In northern Thailand, these synergies have been most publicly evident in relation to the Chom Thong dispute where the Royal Forest Department and groups representing both lowland farmers and elite conservationists have combined to demand the resettlement of upland villages. These demands, of course, imply significant challenges to the livelihoods of upland farmers and have been contested by those who allege they are unethical and environmentally unfounded, leading to some alternative statements about environmental processes. Nonetheless, the most vocal environmental groups involved in Chom Thong have generally overlooked these contestations and have used the language of global environmentalism (and occasionally national security) as a justification for resettlement. Moreover, they have cultivated alliances with key state institutions to facilitate their campaign for the relocation of Hmong farmers. Such social divisions in how environmentalism is used as a legitimizing principle—and the particular social bases it may represent—is often overlooked by those who see nonstate activism, or civil society, as necessarily progressive and as representing a coherent and unifying force.

These synergies are also evident in the state's relationship with groups that appear implacably opposed to state approaches. This subtle aspect of statemaking—and the unlikely discourse coalitions it can generate—is well illustrated by the case of community forestry. This campaign seems to have some significant limitations: first, an unrealistic overemphasis on traditional "community" and, second, a lack of attention to the crucial role of agricultural land in upland livelihoods. In this debate, the narrative employed by the state is that urgent protective action is required to maintain forest cover and to prevent the environmental problems that arise from forest clearing. However, rather than questioning the simplified assumptions underlying the state approach, advocates for the rights of upland residents have adopted a very similar narrative of fragility and crisis, the only difference being the argument that upland residents, rather than the state, are the appropriate custodians. Of course, this advocacy is radical in its decentralizing vision, but it is fundamentally constrained by the shared preoccupation with upland environmental crisis.

The engagement of these critical groups with the state's vision of the uplands has important implications for reaffirming particular policy approaches and for enforcing a certain type of environmental citizenship (Agrawal 2005). Rather than merely arguing for the possibility of forest and agricultural coexistence, campaigners for the rights of upland communities have come to argue that upland forest and upland agriculture are intrinsically linked and that this link is underpinned by specific belief systems, cultural practices, and forms of social organization. Agricultural activity is regularly described in terms of its crucial ecological functions and, consequently, upland agriculture has come to be descriptively and normatively framed in terms of its role as a component of the broader forested ecosystem. Despite the constant emphasis on alternative forms of indigenous knowledge, this construction of upland residents as model ecological citizens leaves the predominant environmental management orthodoxies promoted by the Thai state completely unchallenged. Rather than drawing on the growing body of evidence, both in Thailand and internationally, that questions popular environmental narratives, advocates for decentralized forest management have selectively assembled a body of ecological knowledge about the relationships between forest, soil, and water that echoes the official knowledge of the state and conservation groups. The possibility that there may be alternative forms of ecological knowledge (such as the statement quoted above that forest clearing can increase water supply) is simply not entertained. The overall effect is that upland livelihoods are legitimate only in a very limited sense—provided they accord with the dominant preoccupation with the protection of fragile ecosystems.

Narratives exist, then, because they offer convenient opportunities for the state and other actors to achieve political objectives by emphasizing specific knowledge claims above others. They also provide a mutually understood common ground on which environmental debate can take place. But narratives also emerge because of the misapplication of scientific generalizations. Many environmental narratives in northern Thailand are based on common assumptions of environmental cause and effect (often drawing on famous examples of environmental change both inside and outside Thailand) that may not be as generalizable as commonly thought. But often generalizations persist because scientific and policy networks do not consider how local conditions and needs vary between contexts.

For example, the so-called Universal Soil Loss Equation (USLE) was developed to predict soil erosion after the Dust Bowl in the United States. But various critics have argued that the equation is actually not universal, and may be inapplicable to locations in northern Thailand where factors such as slope length, rainfall, and soil management practices are significantly different from the United States. Also, the framing of soil problems through the unifying theme of erosion—important as it is— may not be the most effective way of either understanding the most common local problem of declining soil fertility, the impact of local agriculture on soils, or the contribution of nonanthropogenic processes to lowland problems of sedimentation. Nonetheless, the USLE has been the most commonly adopted approach to studying soil degradation in northern Thailand, and it is regularly used to justify controls on upland agriculture and to support other state-led initiatives such as plantation forestry and the watershed classification scheme.

The generalizing of scientific concepts is also evident in the strategic use of particular terms. For example, in Thailand, the terms "deforestation" and "monocropping" are popularly used in pejorative ways to refer to necessarily degrading forms of resource use. Such words conjure images of "cabbage mountains"—clear-cut landscapes where diverse ecosystems have been reduced to exploitative short-term agriculture. Undoubtedly, such extreme cases of environmental degradation have existed in northern Thailand and appropriate regulatory strategies are clearly needed to address them. But, terms and images are frequently used to reduce diverse kinds of forest disturbance and commercial upland agriculture to the singular category of degradation. Indeed, some observers have argued that "deforestation" is used so ambiguously that it is virtually meaningless as a description of land-use change. And "monocropping" is hardly an adequate description of the spatially and socially diverse livelihood systems of those engaged in upland cash cropping. In their simplification, these terms also intersect and resonate with popular characterizations of particular social groups, especially the Hmong given their longstanding involvement with upland commercial cultivation. (By contrast, the pejorative imagery of monocropping is rarely used to refer to the Royal Forest Department's establishment of single-species tree plantations.) The point of this semantic analysis is that supposedly neutral descriptions of environmental processes and activities always carry a history and context that shape how they are seen in new contexts. In other words, "cabbage" has baggage.

For that matter, the term "watershed" is also controversial. In standard hydrological language, a watershed is the total land area that contributes water to a stream or river (often also called the "catchment"). But in Thailand, and in many other countries, the term has taken on a much more limited meaning, focusing on upland areas, and this narrow focus influences the scientific generalizations used to regulate watershed land use. As Pinkaew (2000) has argued, this is a limited notion and is another example of an apparently neutral biophysical concept that has been shaped by historical political discourse. Government watershed management initiatives focus their attention on the upper reaches of river systems—where preservation of forest cover is considered essential—rather than giving holistic attention to the impacts of land use throughout the catchment area. The lowlands tend to feature only to the extent that they are, supposedly, negatively affected by activities in the upland parts of the watershed. For example, the categorization of land as a "watershed forest" is based on the concerns of water users outside the zone who wish to gain access to the water inside it (Barham 2001). The crucial role of the lowlands in sustainable management of water resources is conveniently avoided. Seemingly neutral watershed classifications may include all parts of the watershed, but in the political contexts of northern Thailand their effect is to focus regulatory attention on upland landscapes and the upland farmers who are resident there.

The driving force behind some of these partial viewpoints has been the transfer of ideas and scientific explanations from abroad and the engagement of organizations and actors in Thailand with foreign discourses. The transfer of cause-and-effect statements developed in different social settings to Thailand may be called "actor networks" (Callon 1986), because they carry entwined environmental explanations and values to locations where different problem closures or physical processes may result in alternative causes and effects. The application of the so-called Universal Soil Loss Equation in Thailand is one example. Another is the famous dispute in Chom Thong. This has attracted international media attention because it conforms to certain images of rural life, Buddhism, and forests that resonate with internationally circulated stereotypes about Thailand (also reinforced by Thailand's successful tourism advertising). Many Western journalists working or publishing in Thailand have also written about the importance of adopting an internationally standard "green" agenda of reforestation and nature conservation.[1] While these viewpoints should certainly be heard, they may also carry beliefs about environmental cause and effect that may not be applicable to different environments and alternative valuations, and the local voices of support that they draw on may not be uniformly representative. Some observers may claim that "the green urge is universal and transcends national and cultural boundaries" (Fahn 2003:324). But assumptions about environmental impacts and values may not be as universal or transferable as they suggest.

PUTTING NARRATIVES IN THEIR PLACE

The narratives arising from such partial viewpoints, then, have come to be seen as "factual," but actually result from a combination of normative values, historic framings, particular networks, and specific experiences rather than innate and generalizable properties of an apolitical "nature" (Latour 1993). These narratives are harnessed by current actors to legitimize further political choices about statemaking and redefining social order, yet result in insisting upon explanations for environmental problems that are ineffective and may even exacerbate problems. What can be done to overcome these influences? Can environmental knowledge be generated more critically, transparently, and inclusively?

These questions, of course, are important for research on environmental narratives in general. Many policymakers and environmental scientists are worried that discussing environmental narratives will reduce concern for the environment by focusing too much on what may be exaggerated.

Similarly, does narrative analysis encourage a relativist approach to environmental explanation by emphasizing the social construction of environmental knowledge rather than pursuing scientific progress? And what are the implications for building effective environmental management and governance?

This book does not suggest that science can be cleansed of social influence, or that practical management of environments can be separated from normative debates about what should be done or who should benefit. However, various steps can be taken to make social influences more transparent and more democratically governed, and that consequently lead to environmental explanations that address underlying environmental and social problems more effectively. This depends on using scientific studies more critically within narrative analysis.

Three steps will assist in this process.

Redefine Problems

One of the most important social and political influences on environmental knowledge is problem closure, or the use of one dominant definition in the collection of data and the generation of explanations. Closing—or defining—problems in such singular ways limits the range and perceived purpose of information to predefined objectives, and hence restricts attention to alternative ways of experiencing or explaining environmental change. Redefining perceived problems by increasing the range of social consultation may therefore diversify the generation of environmental knowledge and the purposes to which it is put. It may also reduce the chance of single-focus, simplistic narratives being used out of context.

Clearly, in northern Thailand, too much environmental discussion is narrowly based on the protection of fragile upland areas for the benefit of those living downstream. Of course, there are important linkages between upland and lowland environmental processes—after all, water does flow down hill. But framing environmental discussion on the basis of a common lowland discourse is fundamentally limiting: it promotes unrealistic claims about biophysical processes; it maintains a selective regulatory focus on upper catchment areas; and it reflects the aspirations and anxieties of only some social groups. Persisting with this approach is unlikely to provide a basis for meaningful engagement with the region's farmers, nor will it provide a basis for the sustainable management of natural resources.

A more inclusive approach to upland management requires a broadening of the basic terms of the debate. First, there is a need for much more attention to the relationship between livelihood and environment in upland areas themselves. Detailed studies of this interaction have typically provided insights into upland environmental processes that are more accurate and nuanced than popular degradation narratives suggest. While there is clearly a role for some generalization and comparison, locally specific experiences of livelihood challenges need to play a much more important role in problem definition. Second, there is a need to look beyond upland agricultural activity for the sources of environmental problems. This broader perspective has identified, for example, that upland agriculture may not be the only source of lowland sedimentation. Roads may be an even more important source. Similarly, substantial increases in lowland water demand may be more responsible for water shortages than supposed damage to upland water supply. And, naturally occurring environmental variation (especially very substantial short- and medium-term variation in rainfall) may often underlie the environmental problems that capture so much public attention. There is no good reason to maintain a simplistic focus on the environmental impacts of upland agriculture.

One specific aspect of problem closure is the predominant focus on forest cover in upper watershed zones. Often, deforestation is seen as the fundamental driver of environmental degradation, a problem assumed to be best addressed by widespread tree planting. At present, it is difficult to discuss options for upland development in this region without adopting a narrative that emphasizes the crucial and necessary role of forests. This book—and much other international research—has, however, suggested that many of these popular assumptions about the environmental functions of trees need to be reviewed. To be clear, there are various reasons for supporting forest conservation, and in some cases tree planting, in the northern Thai uplands. But forest management should not be based on simplified narratives that provide misleading accounts of biophysical processes. Some questioning of assumptions that tree cover is universally and inevitably desirable will enable sober consideration of a more diverse range of land-use options. And a healthy skepticism about the universal desirability of tree planting may also prompt some rethinking of the widespread encouragement of plantation forestry and orchard expansion. The fact that some of the bitterest environmental disputes in northern Thailand have taken place in areas with extensive fruit trees should raise some doubts about the frequent assertion that tree planting in upland areas is environmentally benign.

Use Diverse Knowledge Claims Critically

Diversifying the definition of problems, however, is not sufficient. There must also be an attempt to see each definition of problems in context—according to the perspectives and circumstances of different social actors—and to use these in complementary ways to increase the accuracy of environmental explanations. One means of achieving this is to adopt insights from philosophies of science that seek alternatives to the universalizing assumptions of positivism by acknowledging the social embeddedness of truth claims.[2] These approaches may acknowledge various elements of social embedding, such as who was consulted in the creation of cause-and-effect statements; which problem closures were used; and what social conditions underlie the circumstances in which statements are considered to be true (Morad 2004; Poon 2005).

For example, the observation that upland land-use change results in lowland water shortages may be considered true by some lowland farmers based on their specific experiences. In this case, the problem closure of water shortage and the observation of upland change may be the truth conditions. Yet, considering this kind of knowledge claim side-by-side with others may allow a form of triangulation—based on different social experiences, institutional contexts, and problem closures—in order to indicate greater levels of complexity in hydrological processes. There are a number of cases where, for example, scientific knowledge (such as monitoring rainfall, erosion, or stream discharge) has combined with farmers' statements and other observations to contradict popular narrative explanations of environmental problems. Using these diverse knowledge sources, and looking for synergies or contradictions, reduces the reliance on knowledge generated from one source alone, allowing each to be viewed in its own context. The Mien villager's claim quoted above—that removing trees can increase water supply—is an example of a knowledge claim that can be subject to critical assessment, not just dismissed because of its discordance with the dominant protectionist narrative. (As it happens, the statement is supported by more formal scientific work looking at river discharge and forest clearing elsewhere.) Similarly, hill farmers should not simply be dismissed as ignorant because they claim no experience of "erosion." Rather, efforts should be made to appreciate the ways in which farmers experience, and respond to, the diverse challenges of soil management; and such studies should consequently be used to redefine fixed beliefs about environmental problems, their causes, and the scales at which they operate.[3]

This kind of approach highlights one possible way in which scientific knowledge can be used progressively in critical narrative analysis. Scientific research should not be seen as uniform in its purpose or limitations, but rather should be differentiated according to how far its mode of inference is positivist or nonpositivist. The objective of positivist research is to find universal, generalizable trends and rules. Most recently, this has been applied using a framework that tests universal, propositional hypotheses, in which one hypothesis is considered universally accurate until proven inaccurate. But under more socially embedded approaches, it is possible to link generalizations and social contexts more transparently. This kind of research has been called "not positively positivist" (Poon 2005), and has been inspired by alternative traditions within scientific inference (Morad 2004). These approaches offer important ways of combining empirical investigation with a critical engagement with environmental knowledge and values. They allow for the empirical testing of different truth claims without necessarily forgetting that these claims reflect social and political influences. In upland areas, for example, much can be learnt about soil degradation and how far agriculture contributes to lowland sedimentation by analyzing hill farmers' concerns rather than assuming that all lowland problems result from agriculture. Similarly, water shortages can be explained by considering the growing demand for water in both the uplands and lowlands alongside questions about water supply.

Viewing knowledge claims critically also involves not taking alternative forms of "indigenous" or "local" knowledge at face value. The definition of "local" itself is often achieved via the values and projections of dominant narratives. While some have argued that it is strategically important to promote the conservationist credentials of local knowledge,[4] there is a real risk that such knowledge becomes selectively packaged so as to exclude what are seen to be discordant elements. (Accounts of local knowledge in northern Thailand simply do not express the view that cutting down large trees can increase water supply.) What is needed is a much more open approach to local knowledge. There is a pressing need for accounts of local knowledge that deal with farmers' understandings of seemingly unpalatable issues—hunting, chemical use, cultivating cash crops, and selection of timber for construction. Of course, such accounts will not provide a coherent or unified template for environmental management (that is an unrealistic expectation), but they are likely to highlight alternative perspectives, possible solutions, success stories, and areas where support, or even regulatory intervention, may be appropriate. For example, while it is an unhelpful stereotype to portray all members of some ethnic groups as voracious hunters, alternative accounts that suggest that upland farmers would recoil from cutting down a tree that contains a bird's nest do not provide a realistic basis for addressing the very real challenges of biodiversity management. It is simply unrealistic to expect that "traditional" knowledge systems will be sufficient to allow farmers to deal with the challenges of agricultural transformation in rapidly changing contexts.

Diversify Expertise and Increase Participation

Finally, there is the issue of who claims environmental expertise and how expertise is defined. Environmental policy in Thailand relies heavily on various formal expert institutions such as the Royal Forest Department and the Land Development Department. But, as this book has demonstrated, these agencies do not develop policy—or the discourses policies are based on—in isolation. They are involved in knowledge networks that shape responses to perceived environmental problems: government departments are subject to political pressures; they are lobbied by NGOs; they respond to royal initiative; and they react to international environmental agendas. These are certainly broad networks and they involve diverse discourse coalitions, but there are often important limitations on how environmental expertise is defined. Three issues appear particularly important.

First, despite the regular appeals to science, there is often resistance to accepting that international scientific research is based on legitimate expertise. As members of the World Agroforestry Centre (ICRAF) have noted, a lot of the environmental research undertaken by international institutions has had limited impact on policy making in Southeast Asia (Tomich, Chomitz et al. 2004). They argue that many watershed management regimes in Asia have overlooked long-term nonanthropogenic sources of change; the intense variability of environmental processes between time and space scales; and the multiple causes of watershed degradation. In Thailand there is often a tendency to dismiss research on these issues as inappropriately Western perspectives on the particular situation in Thailand (an ironic dismissal given the extent of foreign influence in the establishment and development of these agencies). One example of this occurred at an international workshop on watershed management at Chiang Mai in 2001, when a senior representative of the Royal Forest Department made a summary speech explaining that part of the department's role was to assist "national security." He went on to list which of the research papers presented were to be made available to the public according to how far he considered them to be "scientific" (Forsyth personal observation 2001). These somewhat nationalistic views about appropriate knowledge also gain support when "foreign" research on issues such as the relationship between forests and water is thought to contradict statements about the environment made by the highly revered king and queen. It should be quite clear by now that this book is certainly not arguing that foreign research should automatically be accepted in Thailand, but there is a need to separate definitions of expertise from simplistic nationalism, and to ensure that labeling something as "foreign" is not used to prevent open policy dialogue.

Second, judgments about expertise in environmental debates are also shaped by ethnicity. In the uplands of northern Thailand, representations of social order have become crystallized into a classification of uplanders that sees the Karen as environmental "guardians" and the Hmong (and others) as environmental "destroyers." But these are highly selective representations that ignore, for example, the extent of Karen involvement in commercial agriculture and that, through often racist imagery, persistently exaggerate the negative impacts of Hmong agricultural activity. This simplistic ethnic imagery also ignores the very substantial presence of "lowland" northern Thai farmers in the uplands. Consequently, policy networks frequently judge environmental expertise on the basis of these simple ethnic distinctions. A key challenge for future environmental management in the uplands is to break what have come to appear as natural and inevitable links between ethnicity, livelihood practices, and environmental outcomes. Moving beyond these restrictive ethnic templates will enable policy discussions to be more inclusive and to draw on a much wider range of environmental expertise.

A third key issue is the persistent marginalization—and vilification—of commercially oriented upland farmers in environmental debates. There is a tendency in many environmental policies—including alternatives proposed by people-oriented NGOs—to reject commercialization as a livelihood option in the uplands. This book has proposed a more pragmatic, open, and inclusive approach to upland commercialization and the farmers who adopt it. Anyone working within the uplands cannot fail to be struck by the degree of interest among a wide spectrum of farmers in engagement with the market, even among groups, such as the Karen, who are widely believed to have a strong subsistence orientation. Trends toward more commercialized agriculture—although uneven—are evident throughout the region, and it is not tenable to suggest that this simply results from the external imposition of the market system. The agency of upland farmers in this transformation must be acknowledged. Part of this acknowledgement should be an acceptance that commercially oriented farmers have legitimate forms of environmental knowledge and that these can contribute to the development of sustainable management strategies that address contemporary challenges in the uplands.

Participatory land-use planning (PLP) is one possible means of achieving a more inclusive approach to environmental management that relies

PARTICIPATORY LAND-USE PLANNING

Participatory land-use planning is an approach to land-use planning that has been proposed in various countries to make environmental policy more locally governed and inclusive. In Thailand, it has been defined as an "approach where farmers and forest authorities are allowed to participate in an interactive dialogue of acquiring knowledge and understanding . . . in order to develop proper land use practices of interest to both" (Suporn and Phrek 1993). Typically, a small upland catchment is selected, often because it has been the site of conflict, either between villages or between local residents and government agencies. The area is then mapped, and facilitated discussions take place between the various stakeholders. Discussions may be supported by participatory activities such as "transect walks," whereby the detailed characteristics of the local area are examined. These activities give farmers the opportunity to contribute their local knowledge about land-management practices, forest regeneration, and plant species. Ultimately, key land-use zones are identified. Importantly, the zones attempt to cater to both local and official systems of land classification and are mapped onto the local landscape, forming a mosaic of land uses that serve both livelihood and conservation objectives. These broad zones have been referred to as "agroforestry landscape mosaics" less on narrow definitions of expertise. The PLP approach starts from the premise that different stakeholders perceive and prioritize the environment in different ways and that sustainable management decisions need to take account of these different perspectives. As such, PLP may help overcome the influence of simplified narratives and allow greater self-governance of localities by allowing for a multiplicity of environmental perspectives and explanations without the imposition of one overriding view or problem closure. In principle, when it is implemented properly, PLP does not place naïve trust in local visions of environmental management alone, nor does it seek to replace official narratives with alternative simplistic views. Rather, PLP seeks to achieve a successful marriage of diverse land-management perspectives in transparent and locally inclusive ways.

But, at the same time, the optimism about PLP must be tempered by an attempt to ensure that these approaches are genuinely participatory. Critics of participatory approaches have suggested that the knowledge

by the World Agroforestry Centre (ICRAF), which argues that landscape-level mosaic planning can provide a mechanism for identifying appropriate trade-offs between local livelihoods and environmental services (Thomas et al. 2002).

In Chiang Mai province, the Sam Mun Highland Development Project has pioneered this participatory methodology, prompting, according to one commentator, "a re-think of the whole approach of the Thai government in managing upland watersheds" (Garrity 1998:10). The project was established in the late 1980s to implement programs of integrated rural development and opium replacement in remote areas of Mae Hong Son and Chiang Mai provinces. Its participatory techniques have been adopted and developed by many other upland development projects (see, for example, Thai-German Highland Development Programme 1998; Promboon 1996; Charal et al. 2002). Diversified mapping techniques have also been widely promoted by, for example, the Northern Farmers' Network to demonstrate alternative claims to land, water, and forest resources that contest the official representations on government maps. This "counter-mapping" approach is said to provide local farmers with "political space and language with which to communicate and negotiate with the state authorities" (Pinkaew 2001:156).

they produce often tends to reflect dominant perspectives on what are appropriate and desirable forms of behavior. In northern Thailand it is hard not to be struck by how often accounts of PLP are shot through with prevailing assumptions about environmental processes—the need to maintain watershed forest cover to ensure water supply; the desirability of consolidating and even relocating upland cultivation; and the importance of tree planting to maintain local environmental values. These concerns may well reflect local priorities, but they often appear to be an attempt to channel local aspirations along predefined paths of responsible environmental management. In other words, simply calling a process "participatory" does not necessarily involve the rejection, revision, or reform of environmental narratives, especially if development practitioners also see these as factual. Reviewers of participatory processes in northern Thailand have commented on their inability to overcome highly uneven power relations between villagers, development workers, and government officials.[5] This is an important point. But what also needs attention is the extent to which there are more subtle, narrative, influences at work that shape the outcomes of participatory processes. Unless participatory land-use planning can provide a forum for the expression of genuinely alternative environmental visions, it serves as just another element of the statemaking process.

Making reform truly participatory is, of course, a challenge not just limited to Thailand, but is a key part of the development challenge throughout the world. Reforming state bureaucracies to overcome decades of organizational heritage is a profound challenge, requiring careful campaigning, engagement with elements within organizations that are self critical, and taking opportunities to create alternative knowledge networks. Yet, until widespread reform of government agencies can be achieved, challenging the underlying narratives that add legitimacy to their policies and regulatory interventions is a crucial first step.

NOTES

1 ENVIRONMENTAL CRISIS AND THE CRISIS OF KNOWLEDGE

1. The English-language daily, *The Nation*.

2. The focus is on the upland areas in the provinces of Chiang Rai, Phayao, Chiang Mai, Lamphun, Mae Hong Son, Lampang, Nan, Phrae, and Uttaradit. The physical characteristics of this region are discussed in detail in chapter 2.

3. Tuenjai Deetes cofounded the Hill Area Development Foundation in 1986.

4. There is insufficient space in this book to summarize all debates about scientific knowledge, but the term "positivism" has various applications. Early positivists such as the physicist Ernst Mach (1838–1916) sought to observe generalizable trends in empirical data. This was then enhanced as "logical positivism" under the so-called Vienna School of philosophers during the 1920s, who reformed the scientific method to focus on verification of such trends. Most famously, Karl Popper then challenged logical positivism in the 1960s by arguing that verification should be replaced by falsification as the means of inferring statements about reality. Under Popper's approach, scientists should consider theories and hypotheses true until empirical evidence contradicted them, thus generating new theories and hypotheses. Popper called this approach "critical rationalism," but it is still popularly called "positivism." See Hess (1997) and Forsyth (2003: chapter 3) for an extended discussion.

5. Haas (1992:3) defined an epistemic community as a "network of professionals with recognized experience and competence in a particular domain and an authoritative claim to policy-relevant knowledge within that domain or issue area. . . . What bonds members of an epistemic community is their shared belief or faith in the verity and the applicability of particular forms of knowledge or specific truths." This definition places much emphasis upon a definition of expertise as located within formal scientific networks. Later work has suggested that epistemic communities may become broader if a more inclusive definition of expertise is adopted (such as activists, journalists, or local resource users). An advo-

cacy coalition is an alliance between different organizations in order to help parties gain expertise or political help towards an objective. They frequently include alliances between international NGOs and grassroots activists.

6. Cultural Theory is largely based on the work of Mary Douglas; the capital C and T indicate its difference from other cultural theories.

7. Desire to follow rules is sometimes known as "grid," and to act communally as "group." Hence, egalitarians prefer to act communally but distrust rules set by the state; individualists dislike both rules and acting communally; hierarchists like to set rules and act in groups; and fatalists feel powerless either to set rules or to act communally.

8. Dryzek (1997:8) defines a discourse as follows: "A discourse is a shared way of apprehending the world. Embedded in language, it enables those who subscribe to it to interpret bits of information and put them together into coherent studies or accounts. Each discourse rests on assumptions, judgments, and contentions that provide the basic terms for analysis, debates, agreements and disagreements."

2   MOUNTAINS, RIVERS, AND REGULATED FORESTS

1. See discussion of discourse coalitions in chapter 1.

2. Some areas of the upper north do not drain into the Chao Phraya river system. In the far north, the Kok and Ing Rivers flow into the Mekong, their catchments areas marking the boundaries of Chiang Rai and Phayao provinces. In recent years, controversial plans for major engineering works have been proposed to divert water from the Kok and Ing Rivers into the Chao Phraya basin. And in Mae Hong Son province the Pai and a number of other tributaries flow into the Salween.

3. When annual streamflow data at a gauge in the Chaem River catchment were compared with rainfall data from the catchment area above the gauge the r^2 correlation was 0.79 (A. Walker 2002:220).

4. Nok Nguak is the pseudonym of a Western environmental columnist in the *Bangkok Post*. The pseudonym is the Thai name for a hornbill.

5. Information in this section is derived from Rundel and Kansri (1995), Pooma and Barfod (2001), and Thawatchai (1988).

6. The Royal Forest Department defines the northern region as including the provinces of Chiang Rai, Chiang Mai, Phayao, Lamphun, Mae Hong Son, Lampang, Nan, Phrae, Uttaradit, Phetchabun, Phitsanulok, Sukothai, Khampheang Phet, Phichit, Nakhon Sawan, Uthai Thani, and Tak.

7. In this book the far northern provinces are defined as Chiang Rai, Phayao, Chiang Mai, Lamphun, Mae Hong Son, Lampang, Nan, Phrae, and Uttaradit.

8. And note that these data say nothing about forest quality.

9. There have been extensive plantings of tree crops in lowland areas, but these are not included in official forest cover data.

10. For more detailed accounts of the development of forest policy in the north,

from which this summary is drawn, see Mingsarn (n.d.), Thomas and Kamon (1990), Sureeratna (2001), Tongroj (1990), Vandergeest (1996a), and Anat et al. (1987).

11. Data provided to A. Walker by Office of Highland Development, Land Development Department.

12. And the officially declared forest reserve (which includes "economic" as well as conservation forest) in the northern region exceeds the area of actual forest cover by 1.4 million hectares (RFD 2004b: tables 1 and 5)!

13. "Meo" is a derogatory term used by lowland Thai to refer to the Hmong.

14. Hearn (1974:8) lists the main locations for conflict in the far north as the provinces of Nan, Chiang Rai (including the current Phayao province, which was divided from Chiang Rai in 1977), and Chiang Mai.

15. In 1992 Forsyth recorded an oral history of one elderly hill farmer who had experienced interference from communist forces based in Laos and who willingly assisted the Thai government's research into communist activity in Chiang Rai and Nan. Vietnamese and Chinese agents were also present at Khao Khor, a long-standing insurgency area in Phetchabun province (Bo Yang 1987:150).

16. Though field observations by Forsyth suggest that some villagers did relocate to join the *nikhom*.

17. During the 1990s, the Thai government adopted the so-called Khor Jor Kor Land Resettlement and Green Northeast Thailand programs in northeastern Thailand. These projects—adopted almost immediately after the short-lived military government of 1991 to 1992—sought to place pine, teak, and eucalyptus plantations on agricultural land formally classified as forest reserve. Many projects developed into protracted standoffs between the government, villagers, and NGOs in locations such as Buri Ram province. Further cases of villagers resisting reforestation occurred in Khon Kaen province in 1999 (Onnucha 1999).

18. Plodprasop Suraswadi, who held this position from 1998 to 2002.

19. Whether or not this more restricted version ever makes its way into legislation remains to be seen.

20. Fermented tea is a popular snack in northern Thailand, typically chewed with salt.

21. Some exceptions are listed, but these relate to the administration of the community forest, collection and harvesting of forest products under local regulation, and tree planting. The legislation does make provision for "zones for use," but the Thai term used here (*kaan chay soy*) usually implies, in discussions of forest management, collection of forest products rather than agricultural activity.

3 UPLAND PEOPLE

1. The English term "hill tribe" remains widely used, despite concerns from anthropologists that the ethnic structures in Thailand are dissimilar to the tribal groups in other parts of the world where the term "tribe" was originally used.

2. Thailand's total population is about sixty-six million. The total population of the nine far northern provinces is over five million.

3. The Chom Thong dispute is discussed in detail in chapter 4.

4. There are two major subgroups of Karen: the Sgaw and the Pwo. Sgaw villages are located mainly within the Ping River catchment area while the Pwo tend to be located farther west, closer to Mae Sariang.

5. The level of international concern is indicated by the Alternatives to Slash-and-Burn initiative of the Consultative Group on International Agricultural Research. See http://www.asb.cgiar.org.

6. In 1966, a Thai government survey declared that "the destruction of forests and watersheds . . . is caused primarily by a system of shifting cultivation called slash and burn farming. Such practice in rotating farming land is primitive and destructive in nature" (Boonserm 1966:13).

7. Indeed, according to the World Agroforestry Centre (ICRAF), "the consequences of [slash-and-burn] are devastating, in terms of climate change, soil erosion and degradation, watershed degradation, and loss of biodiversity" (ICRAF 1999).

8. For example, Bupho (1997), Waraalak Ithiphonorlan (1998), Kannika and Bencha (1999), and Kunlawadi (1993, 1997).

9. This area of Tak province is the region described briefly in chapter 2 as the location of insurgencies in the late 1960s, which had inspired the "road that cost nine men per mile." Later there was enforced resettlement of Hmong villagers to establish a wildlife sanctuary.

10. Where trees are blessed and their trunks wrapped in cloth that resembles the robe of a monk.

4 FORESTS AND WATER

1. The conference was organized by the World Agroforestry Centre to discuss "environmental services and land use change: bridging the gap between policy and research in Southeast Asia."

2. Evapotranspiration is the amount of water that is lost from soil or vegetation from direct evaporation and consumption by plants as part of their metabolic process (transpiration).

3. In a brief study of land use and forests in this area, Savage (1994) documents some of the impacts of the Hmong village of Pa Kluay on nearby pine forests.

4. M.R. stands for Mom Ratchawong, which is an indication of royalty in Thailand.

5. For example, one Australian television documentary about the Chom Thong dispute was titled *The Princess, the Monk, and the Rainforest* (Van Beld 1991), although the forest in Mae Soi is not rainforest.

6. Dhammanaat has attracted substantial national and international recog-

nition. In 1990, for example, Phongsak was named on the United Nations Global 500 Roll of Honour.

7. In 1992 Phra Phongsak was implicated in a scandal in which a photograph—purporting to show him embracing a woman—was sent to newspapers, leading him to step down from the monkhood and become only a peripheral figure in the dispute (see Fahn 2003:143).

8. The director of the Royal Project Foundation, His Serene Highness Prince Bhisatej Rajani, was known to be critical of the Dhammanaat Foundation. And key figures in Dhammanaat have been very critical of Royal Project Foundation activities.

9. Rainfall data used in this chapter were obtained from the Web site of the Royal Irrigation Department (http://www.rid.go.th).

10. Alford (1992:267) also refers to this relatively wetter period: "An important feature of this time-series is the peaks that characterized the decade of the 1970s. There is evidence that much of Asia was experiencing increased precipitation and streamflow during this decade."

11. In Nigeria, Lal (1996) found that five years of fallowing after shifting cultivation increased soil infiltration rates by a factor of ten.

12. However, even taking into consideration the effect of paths, the study concludes that cultivated areas contribute a similar magnitude of stormflow to the stream network as do unpaved roads, despite the fact that roads occupy 95 percent less catchment area (Ziegler et al. 2001; see also I. Douglas 1999:1733–34).

13. The Web site of the Royal Forest Department also provides brief details of a number of studies that warrant comment. Two studies (Thitirojanawat, Pukjaloon, and Poonawarat 2000; Thitirojanawat, Pukjaroon, and Rouysungnern 2000) suggest that the water-holding capacity and porosity of soil under shifting cultivation is only slightly lower than that found in soil under forest cover. Another study (Paramee 2000) found that rates of runoff in "natural dry dipterocarp forest, which has been affected by annual forest fire" were four to seven times higher than agroforestry areas planted with jackfruit, cashew nut, or mango.

14. See, for example, Hamilton (1987:258–60); Bruijnzeel (1997:147–51); Calder (1998:5); Chomitz and Kumari (1998:23); Niskanen (1998); and Harden and Mathews (2000).

15. For example, in a study undertaken in South Africa, Bosch (1979), found that forestation of former grassland with pine resulted in reductions in both annual streamflow (of 440 millimeters) and streamflow during the dry season (of 15 millimeters). This was supported by later research in South Africa by Scott and Smith (1997), who found that the reduction in dry-season flows were proportionally greater than the reduction in annual flow rates. Similarly, links between pine plantations and reduction in streamflow have been found in Kenya (Blackie 1979). See also Sahin and Hall (1996).

1. A detailed resource, production, and marketing household survey was conducted in Mae Uam during December 1998 by A. Walker and colleagues. The survey covered six of the seven villages in the catchment, and a total of 138 samples were collected, representing approximately 20 percent of the households in each village. Detailed information was obtained on all sources of subsistence and cash income including cropping, livestock production, nontimber forest harvesting, and off-farm employment.

2. The land-cover data were derived from Landsat satellite imagery acquired in August 1985, February 1990, and February 1995 (NRCT 1997:43). The National Research Council of Thailand study (NRCT 1997:45–46) classified land cover into five categories: forest, agriculture, urban, bareland/openland, and grass/regrowth. The forest category includes permanent natural forest and reforestation. The agricultural category is said to include "permanent or temporary agricultural area that are mostly occurred [sic] in flat plain or lowland." From analysis of the spatial distribution of this category, and limited ground truthing, it is clear that in the majority of cases this refers to paddy fields and some permanently cultivated fields on the fringes of paddy. Bareland/openland is defined in the study as "the area of new cleared area or prepared highland agricultural area." We refer to this category as "rain-fed hillslope fields."

3. These data are then scaled by two factors: catchment size and average elevation. The source catchment has minimal agricultural activity, so the streamflow (supply) data is not affected by irrigation extractions (demand).

4. Calculations are based on crop-coefficient data provided by the Royal Irrigation Department (1994).

5. The total area of irrigated paddy is estimated on the basis of land-cover data, village mapping, and household surveys.

6. Soybeans are nitrogen fixing.

7. Tanabe (1994:66) estimates per capita consumption of rice in northern Thailand at 300 kilograms.

8. See note 2 in this chapter for details on the land-cover data.

6   EROSION

1. There is some debate about how to define rills and gullies. Turkelboom (1999:158) defines gullies in Chiang Rai province as at least 10 to 15 centimeters deep and as existing on ploughed land, although Forsyth (1996) discusses gullies as larger channels of 1 to 2 meters deep, partly resulting from long-term geomorphological processes.

2. The role of erosion in the decline of historic civilizations is a perennial source of discussion (Whitmore and Turner 2001; Diamond 1998; Goudie 2001).

3. This comment, of course, should not be taken to suggest that erosion is unproblematic.

4. The map of predicted erosion was based on the assumption that erosion would result from two important factors: slope steepness and frequency of historic land use. The map of slope topography was divided into five categories according to degree of slope. The map of cumulative historic frequency of land use was divided into four quartiles to indicate increasingly higher levels of historic land use. The final map of predicted erosion was achieved by multiplying the two indices of slope steepness and historic land use together, and then by dividing this final index into four quartiles. The highest and lowest quartile indicated "most" and "least" eroded land. It was acknowledged that this map included various assumptions and conveniences about how both land-use frequency and slope steepness were identified and classified. Nevertheless, measurements of actual erosion in each category were found to be different to a statistical significance of 95 percent.

5. The disadvantages of the cesium-137 method are the need for sophisticated equipment and multiple measurements, to reduce measurement errors (Ritchie and McHenry 1990). Moreover, the approach does not differentiate between water and tillage erosion. In keeping with most applications of this technique, soil was measured to a depth of 25 centimeters.

6. Nipon (1991) provides a useful summary of erosion research in northern Thailand using experimental plots and the USLE. For example, in Doi Tung, Chiang Rai, ploughing on slopes of between 20 and 50 percent resulted in 120 tonnes per hectare per year. In the same locality, another study measured 89 tonnes on slopes of 54 percent under traditional upland rice. The Royal Project Foundation in Chiang Mai measured 370 tonnes for ploughed land of 40 percent slope. The United Nations measured between 51 and 100 tonnes for various slopes under shifting cultivation in Mae Klang, Chiang Mai. These rates, however, were measured using experimental plots and the USLE rather than the cesium-137 technique.

7. The most common language in the village was Iu Mien, the Mien's own language, but many villagers spoke Thai, and the village school taught the Thai language.

8. Turkelboom's finding was not exceptional, as international research has found that sedimentation can occur on slopes of 78 percent. See Moeyersons (1990).

9. The price of cabbage was especially attractive during the early 1990s, but declined in the late 1990s.

10. This road passed through the Mien study site discussed above, where the existence of gullies was an important component of erosion in the region.

11. Although for the most intense storms, tree canopies of plantations may break up large drops of rainfall and dissipate the kinetic energy. This effect may be seen on most tree species except for those with large leaves, such as teak, which often do not have this ameliorating effect.

12. Interestingly, soil organic matter declined with plantation age. For exam-

ple, the highest organic content measured in the study was 3.65 percent in a diverse, natural teak forest; the lowest was 1.96 percent in a fifty-year old teak plantation (Sutthathorn 1999). In another study, Möller and colleagues (2002) found that soil organic matter under a twenty-year old pine plantation in northern Thailand had no significantly higher levels of organic matter than nonreforested land— a finding they attributed to the rapid growth of the pines and the comparative lack of organic input from pine needles.

7   AGROCHEMICALS

1. That is, planting two or three crops in succession per year.

2. Minimal fallow has meant an average of 1.5 years, but many households practice almost no fallow at all (Samata 2003:155).

3. This section has benefited from survey data collected by Nicolas Becu.

4. The Chom Thong dispute was introduced in chapter 4 as an iconic example of how upland agriculture has been linked to lowland environmental problems.

5. This account draws on fieldwork by Forsyth in 2005 and Jarat (2000).

6. The issue of monocropping is discussed further in chapter 8.

7. Measuring water quality is complicated at the best of times, as there are diverse techniques with different levels of accuracy and reliability. Underlying levels of pollutants such as nitrogen vary widely over different time and spatial scales and may occur from various nonanthropogenic sources as well as from agrochemicals. Accurate measurement and comparison are therefore best achieved through long-term monitoring, using similar equipment and techniques.

8. Of course, it is not just annual cropping that produces this effect. Remember the findings referred to in chapter 6 about the low soil organic matter in some forestry plantations.

8   BIODIVERSITY

1. Various other authors have written stridently about biodiversity in Thailand, such as Thawatchai and colleagues (1985), Graham and Round (1994), Stewart-Cox (1996), Savage (1994), and Hardwick and colleagues (2004), as well as numerous journalists. Dearden is selected as a focus because he makes the clearest connections between different land uses and biodiversity impacts.

2. Johnson and Grivetti (2002a:490) have expressed similar concerns about the impacts on nutrition of plant species being lost due to deforestation.

3. Nectarivorous birds feed on nectar; forest obligates are birds found only in forests; and frugivores feed on fruit.

4. See chapter 2 for a discussion of this system of upland classification.

5. Parks were assessed according to three criteria: the extent of land clearing since park establishment, current condition of the park compared to condition

of surrounding areas, and "factors correlated with effective park protection" (Bruner et al. 2001: 125).

6. Wirawat provides the preface to Pinkaew's book.

7. In personal communication with A. Walker in 2004, Dearden confirmed that "your observation is correct re lack of any detailed biodiversity studies."

9   RETHINKING ENVIRONMENTAL KNOWLEDGE

1. For example Gray (1987) wrote an article titled, "Killing trees is like killing ourselves," and Hillgren (1988) authored the piece, "Third World nations must plant trees."

2. For example, the use of the Duheim-Quine thesis (based on the work of Willard Quine) or the institutional realism of John Searle may allow means of seeing the social context of cause-and-effect statements in ways that demonstrate both generalized observations and social context (Searle 1995; Morad, 2004; Poon, 2005).

3. For more discussion on this approach see Dahlberg and Blaikie (1999) and Forsyth (2003:224–26).

4. This issue is discussed further by A. Walker (2001b; 2001a).

5. As Missingham (2000: 22) has written in relation to the famous Sam Mun Watershed project: "Although project documents refer to 'participation' in many places, [the Sam Mun] project appears to have been strongly 'top down.' Control and decision-making rested with bureaucratic agencies. 'Participation' in project documents refers to the extent to which people in the target villages attended meetings, training workshops and agricultural extension programs, and joined local organized groups initiated and managed by government officials or project development workers."

BIBLIOGRAPHY

Abamo, A. P. 1992. *Credit Utilization and Its Impact on Farm Productivity in Chiang Mai Province*. Chiang Mai: Agricultural Systems, Chiang Mai University.

Adeel, Z., Monthip Tabucanon, Yuwaree In-na, Mattana Thanomphan, Gullaya Wattayakorn, K. Tsukamoto, and Suphat Vongvisessomjai. 2002. *Capacity Development Needs in the Chao Phraya River Basin and the Gulf of Thailand*. Tokyo: United Nations University.

AgHealthNews. 2002. Chemical exposure alarmingly high in Thailand's Hmong farmers. *AgHealthNews*, no. 2002–04. http://agcenter.ucdavis.edu/Newsltr /OLN200204.html#05 (accessed 14 April 2005).

Agrawal, A. 1995. Dismantling the divide between indigenous and scientific knowledge. *Development and Change* 26:413–39.

———. 2005. *Environmentality: Technologies of Government and the Making of Subjects*. Durham, N.C.: Duke University Press.

Agrawal, A., and C. Gibson. 1999. Enchantment and disenchantment: The role of community in natural resource conservation. *World Development* 27 (4): 629–49.

Aguettant, J. L. 1996. Impact of population registration on hilltribe development in Thailand. *Asia-Pacific Population Journal* 11 (4): 47–72.

Alford, D. 1992. Streamflow and sediment transport from mountain watersheds of the Chao Phraya Basin, northern Thailand: A reconnaissance study. *Mountain Research and Development* 12 (3): 237–68.

Ammar Siamwalla, Suthad Setboonsarng, and Direk Patamasiriwat. 1991. *Thai Agriculture: Resources, Institutions and Policies*. Bangkok: Thailand Development Research Institute Foundation.

Anak Pattanavibool and P. Dearden. 2002. Fragmentation and wildlife in montane evergreen forests, northern Thailand. *Biological Conservation* 107 (2): 155–64.

Anan Ganjanapan. 1997. The politics of environment in northern Thailand: Ethnicity and highland development programs. In *Seeing Forests for Trees: Environment and Environmentalism in Thailand*, ed. Philip Hirsch. Chiang Mai: Silkworm Books.

———. 1999. Will the community forest law strengthen management of community forests? In *3 Decades of Community Forestry: In the Midst of Confusion of Thai Society* [in Thai]. Chiang Mai: Northern Development Foundation.

———. 2000. *Local Control of Land and Forest: Cultural Dimensions of Resource Management in Northern Thailand*. Chiang Mai: Regional Center for Social Science and Sustainable Development, Faculty of Social Sciences, Chiang Mai University.

———. 2001. *The Community Dimension: Local Thinking about Rights Power and Resource Management* [in Thai]. Bangkok: Thai Research Fund.

Anat Arbhabhirama, D. Phantumvanit, J. Elkington, and P. Ingkawusan. 1987. *Thailand Natural Resources Profile: Is the Resource Base for Thailand's Development Sustainable?* Bangkok: Thailand Development Research Institute.

Anchalee Kongrut. 2003. Contamination: Soil studies of watershed areas to be made. *Bangkok Post*, 1 June.

Anecksamphant, C., S. Boonchee, P. Inthapan, U. Tejajai, and A. Sajjapongse. 1995. The management of sloping lands for sustainable agriculture in northern Thailand. In *ASIALANDS: The management of sloping lands for sustainable agriculture in Asia (Phase II) 1992–1994, IBSRAM Network Document Number 12*, ed. A. Sajjapongse and C. R. Elliot. Bangkok: International Board for Soil Research and Management.

Anonymous. 2003. Ajahn Phongsak Techadhammo and his forest conservation movement. Manuscript.

Anonymous. N.d. *Draft Community Forest Laws: Differences between the People's Version and the Government Versions* [in Thai].

Anurak Wangpattana. 1995. "Development": Propaganda, promises, lies and profit. *Watershed* 1 (1): 10–29.

Apffel-Marglin, F., and S. A. Marglin. 1990. *Dominating Knowledge: Development, Culture, and Resistance*. Oxford: Clarendon.

Apinyaa Tanthawiwong. 2001. Summary of the important content from the 6 case studies. In *The Cultural Dimension in the Era of the Sufficiency Economy* [in Thai], ed. Princess Maha Chakri Sirindhorn Anthropology Centre. Bangkok: Princess Maha Chakri Sirindhorn Anthropology Centre.

Aranya Siriphon. 2006. Local knowledge, dynamism and the politics of struggle: A case study of the Hmong in northern Thailand. *Journal of Southeast Asian Studies* 37 (1): 65–81.

ASB (Alternatives to Slash-and-Burn). 2004. *Alternatives to Slash and Burn: Policy Brief January 2004*. Edited by T. Tomich. Nairobi: ASB, International Centre for Research in Agroforestry.

Atchara Rakyutithaam. 1998. Chom Thong: When highlanders are "the accused." In *Concealed Murder on the Path to Conservation* [in Thai], ed. Prayong Doklamyai, Suebsagul Kijanugorn, Prisana Pornmama, Waraalak Ithiphonolarn, Decho Chaitap, Nanta Benjasilarak, Atchara Rakyuthithaam, and Jetpa Chotgitpiwaat. Chiang Mai: Northern Development Foundation.

Aylward, B. 2000. Economic analysis of land-use change in a watershed context. Paper read at UNESCO Symposium/Workshop on Forest-Water-People in the Humid Tropics, 31 July–4 August, Kuala Lumpur.

Bandith Tansiri, Thirayut Citjamnong, and Daranee Srisong. 1993. *Land Use Plan for the Highland Areas of Chiang Mai Province* [in Thai]. Bangkok: Land Development Department.

Bangkok Post. 1987. Tribesmen forced back into Burma. *Bangkok Post*, 26 September.

———. 1989a. Editorial: Welcome reprieve for nation's forests. *Bangkok Post*, 12 January.

———. 1989b. Villagers ask Prem to halt logging right. *Bangkok Post*, 22 April.

———. 1991a. Forestry to resettle hilltribe people. *Bangkok Post*, 2 April.

———. 1991b. Hilltribes pushed back into Burma. *Bangkok Post*, 23 September.

———. 1994. Forestry Department—treading the same path. *Bangkok Post*, 9 January.

———. 1995. Hilltribe eviction protest tops 2,000. *Bangkok Post*, 13 May.

Bangkok World. 1973. Suppression of Reds in Chiang Rai improving. *Bangkok World*, 27 March.

Barham, E. 2001. Ecological boundaries as community boundaries: The politics of watersheds. *Society and Natural Resources* 14:181–91.

Bassett, T., and K. B. Zuéli. 2001. Environmental discourses and the Ivorian Savanna. *Annals of the Association of American Geographers* 90 (1): 67–95.

BBC News. 2001. Thailand flood kills 70. BBC News–Asia Pacific, 12 August. http://news.bbc.co.uk/1/hi/world/asia-pacific/1487394.stm (accessed 23 August 2004).

Bernard, A. 1953. L'evapotranspiration annuelle de la fôret equatoriale congolaise et son influence sur la pluviosite. *Comptes Rendus*, Rome: IUFRO Congress: 201–4.

Blackie, J. 1979. The water balance of the Kericho catchments. *East African Agriculture and Forestry Journal* 43:55–84.

Blaikie, P. 1985. *The Political Economy of Soil Erosion in Developing Countries*. New York: Longman.

Blaikie, P., and H. Brookfield. 1987. *Land Degradation and Society*. London: Methuen.

Bocco, G. 1991. Gully erosion: Processes and models. *Progress in Physical Geography* 15 (4): 392–406.

Bonell, M., and L. A. Bruijnzeel. 2004. *Forests, Water, and People in the Humid Tropics: Past, Present, and Future Hydrological Research for Integrated Land and Water Management*. New York: Cambridge University Press.

Boonchuey Srisavasdi. 1963. *The Hill Tribes of Siam*. Bangkok: Khun Aroon.

Boonserm Weesakul. 1966. Preliminary socio-economic survey of the hill tribes in Thailand: 1965–66. In *Preliminary Socio-Economic Survey of the Hill Tribes in Thailand: 1965–66*, ed. Central Bureau of Narcotics. Bangkok: Ramin Press.

Bosch, J. M. 1979. Treatment effects on annual and dry period streamflow at Cathedral Peak. *South African Forestry Journal* 108:29–38.

Bo Yang. 1987. *Golden Triangle: Frontier and Wilderness*. Hong Kong: Joint Publishing Company.

Brechin, S. R., P. R. Wilshusen, C. L. Fortwangler, and P. C. West. 2002. Beyond the square wheel: Towards a more comprehensive understanding of biodiversity conservation as social and political process. *Society and Natural Resources* 15:41–64.

Brenner, V., R. Buergin, C. Kessler, O. Pye, R. Schwarzmeier, and R.-D. Sprung. 1999. *Thailand's Community Forest Bill: U-Turn or Roundabout in Forest Policy*. Socio-Economics of Forest Use in the Tropics and Subtropics (SEFUT) Working Paper No. 3. Freiburg: Albert-Ludwigs University.

Brookfield, H., and C. Padoch. 1994. Appreciating agrodiversity: A look at the dynamism and diversity of indigenous farming practices. *Environment* 36 (5): 6–11, 37–45.

Brookfield, H., H. Parsons, and M. Brookfield. 2003. How PLEC worked towards its objectives. In *Agrodiversity: Learning from Farmers across the World*, ed. H. Brookfield, H. Parsons, and M. Brookfield. Tokyo: United Nations University Press.

Brown, L. 2001. *Eco-economy: Building an Economy for the Earth*. London and Washington, D.C.: Earthscan and Earth Policy Institute.

Bruijnzeel, L. A. 1989. (De)forestation and dry season flow in the tropics: A closer look. *Journal of Tropical Forest Science* 1 (3): 229–43.

———. 1990. *Hydrology of Moist Tropical Forests and Effects of Conservation: A State of Knowledge Review*. Amsterdam and Paris: UNESCO.

———. 1997. Hydrology of forest plantations in the tropics. In *Management of Soil, Nutrients and Water in Tropical Plantation Forests*, ed. E. K. Sadanandan Nambiar and A. G. Brown. Canberra: Australian Centre for International Agricultural Research.

———. 2004. Hydrological functions of tropical forests: Not seeing the soil for the trees? *Agriculture, Ecosystems and Environment* 104 (1): 185–228.

Bruner, A. G., R. E. Gullison, R. E. Rice, and G. A. B. da Fonseca. 2001. Effectiveness of parks in protecting tropical biodiversity. *Science* 291:125–28.

Bryant, R., and S. Bailey. 1997. *Third-World Political Ecology*. London: Routledge.

Bunge, M. 1991. What is science? Does it matter to distinguish from pseudoscience? A reply to my commentators. *New Ideas in Psychology* 9 (2): 245–83.

Bupho. 1997. *My Pakakoeyo Life* [in Thai]. Bangkok: Samnakphim Sarakhadi.

Calder, I. 1998. *Water-Resource and Land-Use Issues.* Colombo: International Water Management Institute.

———. 1999. *The Blue Revolution: Land Use and Integrated Resource Management.* London: Earthscan.

Calder, I., and B. Aylward. 2002. *Forests and Floods: Perspectives on Watershed Management and Integrated Flood Management.* Rome and Newcastle: Food and Agriculture Organization of the United Nations and University of Newcastle.

Calder, I., and D. Kaimowitz. 2004. A flood of evidence (letter to the editor). *The Economist,* 8 October.

Callon, M. 1986. Some elements of a sociology of translation: Domestication of the scallops and the fishermen of Saint Brieuc Bay. In *Power, Action and Belief: A New Sociology of Knowledge?* ed. J Law. London: Routledge and Kegan Paul.

Carupa Congmu. 1997. Mae Chaem. In *Chiang Mai* [in Thai], ed. Sudara Sutchaya. Bangkok: Sarakadee Press.

Chaipattana Foundation. 2005. Highland Agricultural Development Station. http://www.chaipat.or.th/chaipat/journal/aug03/hill_e.html (accessed 18 April 2005).

Chakrit Ridmontri. 1998. New forestry chief rules out man and nature coexistence. *Bangkok Post,* 15 April.

Chamnonk Pransutjarit. 1983. Impacts of land use evolution on streamflow and suspended sediment in Mae Taeng Watershed, Chiang Mai. MSc. thesis, Kasetsart University, Bangkok.

Chanpaga, U., and T. Watchirajutipong. 2000. Interception, throughfall, and stemflow of mixed deciduous with teak forest. Royal Forest Department, Bangkok. http://www.forest.go.th/Research/English/Research_Project/environment.htm (accessed 18 August 2000).

Chanphen Chutimataewin. 1998. The impact of a Karen upland-rice cultivation on soil erosion: A case study of Ban Mae-Rid, Mae-Sarieng, Mae Hong Son province. MSc. thesis, Mahidol University, Bangkok.

Chapman, E. C. 1978. Shifting cultivation and economic development in the lowlands of northern Thailand. In *Farmers in the Forest: Economic Development and Marginal Agriculture in Northern Thailand,* ed. P. Kunstadter, E. C. Chapman, and Sanga Sabhasri. Honolulu: University Press of Hawai'i.

Charal Thong-Ngam, Thamanoon Arretham, Prasong Kaewpha, Songsak Thepsarn, Narit Yimyam, Chavalit Korsamphan, and Kanok Rerkasem. 2002. Scaling up a PLEC demonstration site for the national pilot programme: A case example of a Hmong Njua village in northern Thailand. *PLEC News and Views* 19:7–16.

Charley, J. 1983. Tropical highland agricultural development in a monsoonal climate: The utilization of *Imperata* grassland in northern Thailand. *Mountain Research and Development* 3 (4): 389–96.

Charoensuk, S., W. Jirasuktaveekul, and S. Onarsa. 2000. Rainfall intercepted by teak plantation. Royal Forest Department, Bangkok. http://www.forest.go.th /Research/English/Research_Project/environment.htm (accessed 18 August 2000).

Chayan Vaddhanaphuti and K. Aquino. 2000. Citizenship and forest policy: Community forestry in Thailand. *Asia-Pacific Community Forestry Newsletter* 13 (1).

Chomitz, K. M., and K. Kumari. 1998. The domestic benefits of tropical forests: A critical review. *The World Bank Research Observer* 13 (1): 13–35.

Chupinit Kesmanee. 1989. The poisoning effect of a lovers triangle: Highlanders, opium and extension crops, a policy due for review. In *Hill Tribes Today: Problems in Change*, ed. J. McKinnon and B. Vienne. Bangkok: White Lotus–Orstom.

Chusak Wittayapak and P. Dearden. 1999. Decision-making arrangements in community-based watershed management in northern Thailand. *Society and Natural Resources* 12:673–91.

Chusit Chuchart. 1989. From peasant to rural trader: The ox-train traders of northern Thailand, 1855–1955. *Thai-Yunnan Project Newsletter* 7:2–8.

Cohen, E. 1989. "Primitive and remote": Hill tribe trekking in Thailand. *Annals of Tourism Research* 16 (1): 30–61.

Cohen, P. 1984a. Opium and the Karen: A study of indebtedness in northern Thailand. *Journal of Southeast Asian Studies* 15 (1): 150–65.

———. 1984b. The sovereignty of Dhamma and economic development: Buddhist social ethics in rural Thailand. *Journal of the Siam Society* 72:197–212.

Collingridge, D., and C. Reeve. 1986. *Science Speaks to Power: The Role of Experts in Policy Making*. London: Pinter.

Conklin, Harold C. 1954. An ethnoecological approach to shifting agriculture. *Transactions of the New York Academy of Sciences* 77:133–42.

———. 1957. *Hanunoo Agriculture: A Report on an Integral System of Shifting Cultivation in the Philippines*. Rome: Food and Agriculture Organization of the United Nations.

Conservation International. 2004. Biodiversity hotspots: Indo-Burma. http://www .biodiversityhotspots.org/xp/Hotspots/indo_burma/ (accessed 23 August 2004).

Convention on Biological Diversity. 2000. Ecosytem approach introduction. United Nations Environment Programme. http://www.biodiv.org/programmes/ cross-cutting/ecosystem/default.asp (accessed 11 May 2005).

Cooper, R. 1984. *Resource Scarcity and the Hmong Response: Patterns of Settlement and Economy in Transition*. Singapore: Singapore University Press.

Corbridge, S. 1986. *Capitalist World Development: A Critique of Radical Development Geography*. Basingstoke, U. K.: Macmillan.

Costa, M. H., A. Botta, and J. A. Cardille. 2003. Effects of large-scale changes in land cover on the discharge of the Tocantins River, Amazonia. *Journal of Hydrology* 283:206–17.

Cutrim, E., D. Martin, and R. Rabin. 1995. Enhancements of cumulus clouds over deforested lands in Amazonia. *Bulletin of the American Meteorological Society* 76:1801–5.

Dahlberg, A., and P. Blaikie. 1999. Changes in landscape or in interpretation? Reflections based on the environmental and socio-economic history of a village in northeast Botswana. *Environment and History* 5 (5): 127–74.

Damri Janapirakanit, Yuphin Bunjanawiroj, and Naanapat Jittar. 1999. *A Book for Learning to Read* [in Thai]. Bangkok: Department of External Education, Ministry of Education.

DANIDA. 2004. Strengthening farmers' IPM in pesticide-intensive areas. http://www .ipmthailand.org/en/IPMDANIDA/ipmdanida.htm (accessed 15 January 2004).

Dartmouth Flood Observatory. 2003. 1988 Global register of extreme flood events. www.dartmouth.edu/~floods/Archives/1988sum.xls (accessed 20 April 2005).

Davis, R. B. 1984. *Muang Metaphysics: A Study of Northern Thai Myth and Ritual.* Bangkok: Pandora.

Dearden, P. 1995. Development, the environment and social differentiation in northern Thailand. In *Counting the Costs: Economic Growth and Environmental Change in Thailand*, ed. J. Rigg. Singapore: Institute of South East Asian Studies.

———. 1999. "Dern sai klang," walking the middle path: Civil society and biodiversity conservation in Thailand. Paper read at Seventh International Conference on Thai Studies, 4–8 July, Amsterdam.

Dearden, P., Surachet Chettamart, and Dachanee Emphandu. 1998. Comment. Protected areas and property rights in Thailand. *Environmental Conservation* 25 (3): 195–97.

Dearden, P., Surachet Chettamart, Dachanee Emphandu, and Noppawan Tanakanjana. 1996. National parks and hill tribes in northern Thailand: A case study of Doi Inthanon. *Society and Natural Resources* 9:125–41.

Delang, C. O. 2002. Deforestation in Northern Thailand: The result of Hmong farming practices or Thai development strategies? *Society and Natural Resources* 15:483–501.

———. 2003. *Living at the Edge of Thai Society: The Karen in the Highlands of Northern Thailand.* London: RoutledgeCurzon.

Del Castillo, D. R. C. 1990. Analysis on the sustainability of a forest-tea production system: A case study of Ban Kui Tuai, Tambon Pa Pae, Amphoe Mae Taeng, Changwat Chiang Mai. MSc. thesis, Chiang Mai University.

Department of Agricultural Extension. 2004. Food safety. http://ndoae.doae.go.th /foodsafety/index.htm (accessed 13 January 2004).

Diamond, J. 1998. *Guns, Germs, and Steel: The Fates of Human Societies.* New York: Norton.

Donner, W. 1978. *The Five Faces of Thailand: An Economic Geography.* St. Lucia, Aus.: University of Queensland Press.

Douglas, I. 1999. Hydrological investigations of forest disturbance and land cover impacts in South-East Asia: A review. *Philosophical Transactions of the Royal Society of London. Series B: Biological Sciences* 354 (1391): 1725–38.

Douglas, I., T. Greer, K. Bidin, and M. Spilsbury. 1992. Impacts of rainforest logging on river systems and communities in Malaysia and Kalimantan. In *Proceedings of the Conference on the Political Ecology of South East Asia's Forests, 23–24 March 1992*. London: School of Oriental and African Studies.

Douglas, M. 1966. *Purity and Danger: An Analysis of Concepts of Pollution and Taboo*. London: Routledge & Kegan Paul.

Draft Community Forest Bill. N.d. *Draft Community Forest Bill: People's Version* [in Thai]. Project of Community Development for the Protection and Revival of Natural Forests in the Wang Watershed, Chiang Mai.

Dryzek, J. 1997. *The Politics of the Earth*. Oxford: Oxford University Press.

Dunne, T., and W. Dietrich. 1982. *Sediment Sources in Tropical Drainage Basins*. Madison, Wisc.: American Society of Agronomy, Soil Science Society of America.

Eckersley, R. 1992. *Environmentalism and Political Theory: Towards an Ecocentric Approach*. London: University College London Press.

Eckholm, E. 1976. *Losing Ground: Environmental Stress and World Food Prospects*. New York: Norton.

Edwards, K.A. 1979. The water balance of the Mbeya experimental catchments. *East African Agricultural and Forestry Journal* 43:231–47.

Ekawit na Thalaang. 2001. *Lanna Local Wisdom* [in Thai]. Bangkok: Aamrin.

Elliott, S., K. Hardwick, and D. Blakesley, eds. 2000. *Forest Restoration for Wildlife Conservation*. Chiang Mai: Chiang Mai University.

Elliott, S., P. Navakitbumrung, C. Kuarak, S. Zangkum, V. Anusarnsunthorn, and D. Blakesley. 2003. Selecting framework tree species for restoring seasonally dry tropical forests in northern Thailand based on field performance. *Forest Ecology and Management* 184 (1/3): 177–91.

Enters, T. 1992. Land degradation of resource conservation in the highland of Northern Thailand: The limits to economic evaluations. Ph.D. diss., CRES, The Australian National University.

———. 1995. The economics of land degradation and resource conservation in northern Thailand: Challenging the assumptions. In *Counting the Costs: Economic Growth and Environmental Change in Thailand*, ed. J. Rigg. Singapore: Institute of South East Asian Studies.

———. 2000. *Methods for the Economic Assessment of the On- and Off-Site Impacts of Soil Erosion*. Bangkok: International Board for Soil Research and Management.

Enzensberger, H. 1974. A critique of political ecology. *New Left Review* 84:3–31.

Ewers, K. 2003. Governance framework for local land use strategies. Paper read at Local Land Use Strategies in a Globalizing World: Shaping Sustainable Social and Natural Environments, 21–23 August, Institute of Geography, Geocenter, University of Copenhagen, Denmark.

Fahn, J. 2003. *A Land on Fire: The Environmental Consequences of the Southeast Asian Boom*. Boulder, Colo.: Westview Press.

Fairhead, J., and M. Leach. 1996. *Misreading the African Landscape: Society and Ecology in a Forest-Savanna Mosaic*. Cambridge: Cambridge University Press.

———. 1998. *Reframing Deforestation: Global Analyses and Local Realities. Studies in West Africa*. London: Routledge.

FAO (Food and Agriculture Organization of the United Nations). 1978. *Forestry for Local Development*. Rome: FAO.

Ferguson, J. 1994. *The Anti-Politics Machine: "Development," Depoliticization, and Bureaucratic Power in Lesotho*. Minneapolis: University of Minnesota Press.

Forsyth, T. 1992. Environmental degradation and tourism in a Yao village of north Thailand. Ph.D. diss., University of London.

———. 1994. The use of cesium-137 measurements of soil erosion and farmers' perceptions to indicate land degradation amongst shifting cultivators in northern Thailand. *Mountain Research and Development* 14 (3): 229–44.

———. 1995. The *mu'ang* and the mountain: Perceptions of environmental degradation in upland Thailand. *South East Asia Research* 3 (2): 169–92.

———. 1996. Science, myth and knowledge: Testing Himalayan environmental degradation in northern Thailand. *Geoforum* 27 (3): 375–92.

———. 2003. *Critical Political Ecology: The Politics of Environmental Science*. New York: Routledge.

———. 2004. Social movements and environmental democratization in Thailand. In *Earthly Politics: Local and Global in Environmental Politics*, ed. S. Jasanoff and M. Long. Cambridge, Mass.: MIT Press.

———. 2005. The political ecology of the ecosystem approach for forests. In *The Ecosystem Approach for International Conservation*, ed. J. Sayer. Gland, Switz.: World Wildlife Fund and World Conservation Union.

Fox, J., Dao Minh Truong, A. Rambo, Nghiem Phuong Tuyen, Le Trong Cuc, and S. Leisz. 2000. Shifting cultivation: A new old paradigm for managing tropical forests. *BioScience* 50 (6): 521–28.

Freeman, M. 2001. *A Guide to Northern Thailand and the Ancient Kingdom of Lanna*. Bangkok: River Books.

Fritsch, J. M. 1992. *Les Effets du Défrichement de la Fôret Amazonienne et de la Mise en Culture sur l'hydrologie de Petite Bassins Versants: Opération Ecerex en Guyane Française*. Paris: ORSTOM.

Funtowicz, S., and J. Ravetz. 1993. Science for the post-normal age. *Futures* 25 (7): 739–56.

Garrity, D. P. 1998. Participatory approaches to catchment management: Some experiences to build upon. Paper read at Managing Soil Erosion Consortium Assembly, 8–12 June, Hanoi.

Gearing, J. 1999. The struggle for the highlands. *Asia Week*, 29 October.

Geddes, W. R. 1976. *Migrants of the Mountains: The Cultural Ecology of the Blue Miao (Hmong Njua) of Thailand*. Oxford: Clarendon.

Geertz, C. 1963. *Agricultural Involution: The Processes of Ecological Change in Indonesia*. Berkeley: University of California Press.

———. 1985. *Local Knowledge: Further Essays in Interpretative Anthropology*. New York: Basic.

Giambelluca, T. W., and A. D. Ziegler. 1996. Influence of long-term land cover change on river flow in northern Thailand. Paper read at FORTROP '96: Tropical Forestry in the 21st Century, 25–28 November, Kasetsart University, Bangkok.

Gibson, C., M. McKean, and E. Ostrom. 2000. *People and Forests: Communities, Institutions and Governance*. Cambridge, Mass.: MIT Press.

Gibson, T. 1983. Toward a stable low-input highland agricultural system: Ley farming in *Imperata* cylindrical grasslands of northern Thailand. *Mountain Research and Development* 3 (4): 378–85.

Giddens, A. 1994. *Beyond Left and Right: The Future of Radical Politics*. Cambridge: Polity.

Girard, D. 1997. In the tangerine grove. International Development Research Centre. http://archive.idrc.ca/books/reports/V222/grove.html (accessed 17 June 2004).

Goodman, J. 1997. *Akha: Guardians of the Forest*. Chicago: Art Media Resources.

Goudie, A. 2001. *The Human Impact on the Natural Environment*. Oxford: Blackwell.

Government of Thailand. 1997. Constitution of the Kingdom of Thailand. http://www.ect.go.th/english/laws/constitutioneng.html (accessed 24 February 2005).

———. 1998. Solving the problems of land in forest areas, following the resolution of National Forest Committee [in Thai]. Cabinet meeting 3/1998, 10 June, Bangkok.

Grandstaff, S., and Waraporn Srisupan. 2004. Agropesticide contract sprayers in Central Thailand: Health risks and awareness. *Southeast Asian Studies* 42 (2): 111–31.

Grandstaff, T. 1980. *Shifting Cultivation in Northern Thailand: Possibilities for Development*. Tokyo: United Nations University.

Gray, D. 1987. Killing trees is like killing ourselves. *Bangkok Post*, 11 November.

Graham, M., and P. Round. 1994. *Thailand's Vanishing Flora and Fauna*. Bangkok: Finance One.

Gua, B. 1975. Opium, bombs and trees: The future of Hmong tribesmen in northern Thailand. *Journal of Contemporary Asia* 5 (1): 70–81.

Haas, P. 1992. Introduction: Epistemic communities and international policy coordination. *International Organization* 46 (1): 1–35.

Hafner, J. A., and Yaowalak Apichatvullop. 1990. Farming the forest: Managing people and trees in reserved forests in Thailand. *Geoforum* 2 (3): 331–46.

Hajer, M. 1995. *The Politics of Environmental Discourse.* Oxford: Clarendon.

Hallsworth, E. G. 1987. *Anatomy, Physiology, and Psychology of Erosion.* New
York: Wiley.

Hamilton, L. 1985. Overcoming myths about soil and water impacts of tropical
forest land uses. In *Soil Erosion and Conservation,* ed. S. El-Swaify, W. Moldenhauer, and A. Lo. Ankeny, Iowa: Soil Conservation Society of America.

———. 1987. What are the impacts of deforestation in the Himalayas on the
Ganges-Brahmaputra lowlands and delta? Relations between assumptions and
facts. *Mountain Research and Development* 7:256–63.

Hamilton, L., and A. Pearce. 1988. Soil and water impacts of deforestation. In
Deforestation: Social Dynamics in Watershed and Mountain Ecosystems, ed.
J. Ives and D. Pitt. London: Routledge.

Hanks, J., and L. Hanks. 2001. *Tribes of the North Thailand Frontier.* New Haven:
Yale University Press.

Harden, C. P. 1992. Incorporating roads and footpaths in watershed-scale hydrologic and soil erosion models. *Physical Geography* 13:368–85.

Harden, C. P., and L. Mathews. 2000. Rainfall response of degraded soil following reforestation in the Copper Basin, Tennessee, USA. *Environmental Management* 26 (2): 163–74.

Hardwick, K., J. R. Healey, S. Elliott, and D. Blakesley. 2004. Research needs
for restoring tropical forests in Southeast Asia for wildlife conservation: Accelerated natural regeneration. *New Forests* 27:285–302.

Harper, D. E. 1988. Improving the accuracy of the Universal Soil Loss Equation
in Thailand. Paper read at Land Conservation for Future Generations: Proceedings of the 5th International Soil Conservation Conference, 18–29 January, Bangkok.

Harper, D. E., and S. A. El-Swaify. 1988. Sustainable agricultural development in
north Thailand: Conservation as a component of success in assistance projects. In *Conservation Farming on Steep Slopes,* ed. W. C. Moldenhauer and
N. W. Hudson. Ankeny, Iowa: Soil and Water Conservation Society of America.

Hatch, T. 1983. Shifting cultivation in Sarawak. In *Proceedings of the Workshop on
Hydrological Impacts of Forestry Practices and Reafforestation,* ed. K. Awang,
Lai Fodd See, Lee Su See, and Abd. Md. Derus. Serdang: Faculty of Forestry,
University Pertanian Malaysia.

Hearn, R. 1974. *Thai Government Programs in Refugee Relocation and Resettlement in Northern Thailand.* Auburn, N.Y.: Thailand Books.

Henderson-Sellers, A. 1993. Continental vegetation as a dynamic component of
a global climate model: A preliminary assessment. *Climatic Change* 23: 337–77.

Hess, D. 1997. *Science Studies: An Advanced Introduction.* New York and London: New York University Press.

Hillgren, S. 1988. Third World nations must plant trees. *Bangkok Post*, 29 April.

Hinton, P. 1978. Declining production among sedentary swidden cultivators: The case of the Pwo Karen. In *Farmers in the Forest: Economic Development and Marginal Agriculture in Northern Thailand*, ed. P. Kunstadter, E. C. Chapman, and Sanga Sabhasri. Honolulu: University Press of Hawai'i.

——. 2002. The "Thailand controversy" revisited—anthropologists as spies. *The Australian Journal of Anthropology* 13 (2): 155–77.

Hirsch, P. 1990. *Development Dilemmas in Rural Thailand*. Singapore: Oxford University Press.

——1993. *Political Economy of Environment in Thailand*. Manila: Journal of Contemporary Asia Publishers.

——. 1997a. *Seeing Forests for Trees: Environment and Environmentalism in Thailand*. Chiang Mai: Silkworm Books.

——. 1997b. Community forestry revisited: Messages from the periphery. Paper read at Community Forestry at a Crossroads: Reflections and Future Directions in the Development of Community Forestry (RECOFTC Report No. 16), 17–19 July, Regional Community Forestry Training Center, Bangkok.

Hoare, P. 1984. The declining productivity of traditional highland farming systems in northern Thailand. *Thai Journal of Agricultural Science* (17 July): 189–219.

Holbrook, N. M., J. L. Whitbeck, and H. A. Mooney. 1995. Drought responses of neotropical dry forest trees. In *Seasonally Dry Tropical Forests*, ed. S. H. Bullock, H. A. Mooney, and E. Medina. Cambridge: Cambridge University Press.

Houghton, R. 1990. The global effects of tropical deforestation. *Environmental Science and Technology* 24 (4): 414–21.

Hulme, M. 2001. Climatic Perspectives on Sahelian Desiccation: 1973–1998. *Global Environmental Change* 11 (1): 19–29.

Hurni, H., and Sompote Nuntapong. 1983. Agro-forestry improvements for shifting cultivation systems: Soil conservation research in northern Thailand. *Mountain Research and Development* 3 (4): 338–45.

IBSRAM (International Board for Soil Research and Management). 1997. *Model Catchment Selection for the Management of Soil Erosion Consortium (MSEC) of IBSRAM: Report on the Mission to Thailand and Indonesia (1–23 August 1996) and the Philippines (19–27 January 1997)*. Bangkok: IBSRAM.

ICEM (International Center for Environmental Management). 2003. *Lessons Learned from Global Experience. Review of Protected Areas and Development in the Lower Mekong Region*. Indooroopilly, Queensland, Aus.: ICEM.

ICRAF (International Centre for Research in Agroforestry). 1999. *ICRAF in Southeast Asia*. Publicity brochure. Bogor, Indo.: ICRAF.

Ives, J. D. 1980. Northern Thailand: The problem. In *Conservation and Development in Northern Thailand: Proceedings of a Programmatic Workshop in Agroforestry and Highland-Lowland Interactive Systems*, ed. J. D. Ives, Sanga Sabhasri, and Pisit Vorauri. Chiang Mai: United Nations University.

————. 2004. *Himalayan Perceptions: Environmental Change and the Well-Being of Mountain Peoples*. London: Routledge.

Ives, J. D., and B. Messerli. 1989. *The Himalayan Dilemma: Reconciling Development and Conservation*. London: Routledge.

Jantawat, S., ed. 1987. *Proceedings of the International Workshop on Soil Erosion and its Counter Measures, November 11–19 1984, Chiang Mai*. Bangkok: Chuan Press.

Jarat Kheereesantikul. 2000. Human rights violations being committed against Hmong in Nan, Thailand. Unpublished report circulated by e-mail September 2000.

Jasanoff, S., ed. 2004. *States of Knowledge: The Co-Production of Science and Social Order*. London and New York: Routledge.

Jasanoff, S., and M. Long-Martello. 2004. *Earthly Politics: Local and Global in Environmental Governance*. Cambridge, Mass.: MIT Press.

Jasanoff, S., C. Markle, J. Petersen, and T. Pinch, eds. 1995. *Handbook of Science and Technology Studies*. Thousand Oaks, Calif.: Sage.

Jintana Amornsanguansin and J. K. Routray. 1998. Planning and development strategy for effective management of community forestry: Lessons from the Thai experience. *Natural Resources Forum* 22 (4): 279–92.

Jipp, P., D. Nepstad, K. Cassel, and C. R. de Carvalho. 1998. Deep soil moisture storage and transpiration in forests and pastures of seasonally dry Amazônia. *Climatic Change* 39:395–412.

Johnson, N., and L. E. Grivetti. 2002a. Environmental change in northern Thailand: Impact on wild edible plant availability. *Ecology of Food and Nutrition* 41:373–99.

————. 2002b. Gathering practices of Karen women: Questionable contribution to beta-carotene intake. *International Journal of Food Sciences and Nutrition* 53:489–501.

Jones, S. 1997. An actor-level analysis of the constraints on sustainable land management in northern Thailand: A study from Chiang Dao district. *South East Asia Research* 5 (3): 243–67.

Jonsson, H. 2005. *Mien Relations: Mountain People and State Control in Thailand*. Ithaca, N.Y.: Cornell University Press.

Judd, L. C. 1977. *Chao Rai Thai: Dry Rice Farmers in Northern Thailand: A Study of Ten Hamlets Practicing Swidden Agriculture and a Restudy Twenty Years Later*. Bangkok: Suriyaban Publishers.

Julian, M. 2003. Water flow renewed in northern Thai valley. Canadian Friends Service Committee. http://cfsc.quaker.ca/qconcern/archives/234mae_soi.html (accessed 12 December 2003).

Jungbluth, F. 1996. *Crop Protection Policy in Thailand: Economic and Political Factors Influencing Pesticide Use*. Hannover, Ger.: Pesticide Policy Project.

Kamol Sukin. 2000. Forest dwellers reject "neutral" forum's findings. *The Nation*, 1 May.

Kannika Phromsao and Bencha Silarak. 1999. *The Seven Layer Forest: From the Words of Headman Joni Odochao* [in Thai]. Bangkok: Local Wisdom Foundation.

Kanok Rerkasem. 2003. Thailand. In *Agrodiversity: Learning from Farmers Across the World*, ed. H. Brookfield, H. Parsons and M. Brookfield. Tokyo: United Nations University Press.

Kanok Rerkasem, Benjavan Rerkasem, Mingsarn Kaosa-ard, Chaiwat Roongruang-see, Sitanon Jesdapipat, Benchaphun Shinawatra, and Pornpen Wijukprasert. 1994. *Assessment of Sustainable Highland Agricultural Systems*. Bangkok: Thailand Development Research Institute Foundation.

Karnjariya Sukrung. 1997. The fight for the forests. *Bangkok Post*, 19 June.

Kaysfeld International. 2004. Chiang Mai geographyhttp://www.kaysfeld.dk /Thailand/ChiangMai/Geography_%20for_Northern_Thailand.htm (accessed 27 June 2004).

Kessler, Christl. 1998. Community forestry in Thailand. The World Bank/WBI. http://srdis.ciesin.org/cases/thailand-002.html (accessed 24 October 2002).

Keyes, C. F. 1979. The Karen in Thai history and the history of the Karen in Thailand. In *Ethnic Adaption and Identity: The Karen on the Thai Frontier with Burma*, ed. Charles F. Keyes. Philadelphia: Institute for the Study of Human Issues.

Khomnet Chetthaphatthawanit, Buntha Siphimchai, and Silao Ketphrom. 1996. *Khut: Taboos in Lanna* [in Thai]. Chiang Mai: Social Research Institute, Chiang Mai University.

Kienholz, H., G . Schneider, M. Bichsel, M. Grunder, and K. Mool. 1984. Mapping of mountain hazards and slope stability. *Mountain Research and Development* 4 (3): 247–66.

Klinge, R., J. Schmidt, and H. Folster. 2001. Simulation of water drainage of a rain forest and forest conversion plots using a soil water model. *Journal of Hydrology* 246:82–95.

Kultida Samabuddhi. 2001. Farmers blamed for deforestation, floods. *Bangkok Post*, 10 August.

———. 2002. Academic slams senators over ban. *Bangkok Post*, 29 March.

———. 2004a. Rainmaking planes, pumps on wish list. *Bangkok Post*, 4 March.

———. 2004b. Weather agency rejects link to El Niño. *Bangkok Post*, 28 March.

———. 2005. Community forestry bill scrutiny panel votes for restriction. *Bangkok Post*, 16 September.

Kunlawadi Bunphinon. 1993. Karen lifestyle: A lifestyle in harmony with nature [in Thai]. *Niwet* 20 (3): 43–56.

———. 1997. Collective resource management: Mechanisms for forest protection in the Karen village of Sanephong [in Thai]. *Niwet* 24 (3): 19–31.

Kunstadter, P. 1978. Subsistence agricultural economies of Lua' and Karen hill farmers, Mae Sariang district, northwestern Thailand. In *Farmers in the Forest: Economic Development and Marginal Agriculture in Northern Thailand*, ed. P. Kunstadter, E. C. Chapman, and Sanga Sabhasri. Honolulu: University Press of Hawai'i.

Kunstadter, P., E. C. Chapman, and Sanga Sabhasri. 1978. *Farmers in the Forest: Economic Development and Marginal Agriculture in Northern Thailand*. Honolulu: University Press of Hawai'i.

Kunstadter, P., T. Prapamontol, B. Sirirojn, A. Sontirat, A. Tansuhaj, and C. Khamboonruang. 2001. Pesticide exposures among Hmong farmers in Thailand. *International Journal of Occupational Environmental Health* 7 (4): 313–25.

Kunstadter, P., Tippawan Prapamontol, Umnat Mevatee, Rasamee Thawsirichuchai, and Wirachon Yangyernkun. 2003. Seasonal and annual changes in pesticide exposure among highland Hmong villagers in Northern Thailand. Paper read at International Symposium on Uses and Effects of Pesticides in Southeast Asia, 11–13 December, Queen Sirikit Botanic Garden, Chiang Mai.

Lal, R. 1983. Soil erosion in the humid tropics with particular reference to agricultural land development and soil management. *International Association of Hydrological Science Publications* 140:221–39.

———. 1996. Deforestation and land use effects on soil degradation and rehabilitation in western Nigeria. I. Soil physical and hydrological properties. *Land Degradation and Development* 7:19–45.

Land Development Department. 1989. *Soil Erosion in Thailand*. Bangkok: Land Development Department.

———. 2004. Home page of Land Development Department. http://www.ldd.go .th/gisweb (accessed 27 August 2004).

Lang, C., and O. Pye. 2001. Blinded by science: The invention of scientific forestry and its influence in the Mekong region. *Watershed* 6 (2): 25–34.

Latour, B. 1993. *We Have Never Been Modern*. Hemel Hempstead, U. K.: Harvester Wheatsheaf.

Leach, M., and R. Mearns. 1996. *The Lie of the Land: Challenging Received Wisdom on the African Environment*. Portsmouth, N.H.: Heinemann.

Learn Online. 2002. *Biodiversity in Thailand: E Learning*. Bangkok: E Learning.

Lindert, P. H. 2000. *Shifting Ground: The Changing Agricultural Soils of China and Indonesia*. Cambridge, Mass.: MIT Press.

Lohmann, L. 1991. Who defends biological diversity: conservation strategies and the case of Thailand. In *Biodiversity: Social and Ecological Perspectives*, ed. V. Shiva, P. Anderson, H. Shucking, A. Gray, L. Lohmann, and D. Cooper. Penang, Malay.: World Rainforest Movement.

———. 1999. *Forest Cleansing: Racial Oppression in Scientific Nature Conservation*. Corner House Briefing 13. Dorset, U. K.: Corner House.

Long, N., and A. Long, eds. 1992. *Battlefields of Knowledge: The Interlocking of Theory and Practice in Social Research and Development*. London: Routledge.

MAMAS (Managing Agrochemicals in Multi-use Aquatic Systems). 2004. New method to assess risk of pesticide applications in Central region of Thailand: Case study in Pathumthani and Nakhonpahom Provinces. http://www.mamasproject.org (accessed 26 March 2004).

Manu Srikhajon and Ard Somrang. 1980. *Soil Erosion in Thailand*. Bangkok: Land Development Department.

Marghescu, T. 2001. Restoration of degraded forest land in Thailand: The case of Khao Kho. *Unasylva* 52 (207): 52–55.

Marston, R., J. Kleinman, and M. Miller. 1996. Geomorphic and forest cover controls on monsoon flooding, central Nepal Himalaya. *Mountain Research and Development* 16 (3): 257–64.

Matsumoto, J. 2003. Monsoon system study in GAME-T Project University of Tokyo. http://hydro.iis.u-tokyo.ac.jp/GAME-T/ doc/20030325_TMD /TMD030325_Matsumoto.ppt (accessed 13 March 2004).

McCoy, A. W. 1972. *The Politics of Heroin in Southeast Asia*. Singapore: Harper and Row.

McDaniel, M. 2005. Land divestiture: Thai Forestry Department creates human rights disaster at Hooh Yoh village. Akha Heritage Foundation. http://www.akha.org/upload/hoohyoh/hoohyoh.htm (accessed 18 April 2005).

McKinnon, J. M. 1986. Resettlement and the three ugly step-sisters, security, opium, and land degradation: A question of survival for the highlanders of Thailand. Chiang Mai: Tribal Research Centre.

Mecir, A. 2003. A love of the land. *Sawasdee* (January): 36–43.

Meher-Homji, V. 1980. Repercussions of deforestation on precipitation in Western Karnataka, India. *AECH Met. Geogph Biokl Series B* 28:385–400.

Mingsarn Kaosa-ard. 2004. Natural resources and the environment. In *Thailand Beyond the Crisis*, ed. P. Warr. London: RoutledgeCurzon.

———. N.d. *Ecosystem Management in Northern Thailand*. Chiang Mai: Resources Policy Support Initiative.

Mingtipol, O., P. Oksen, T. Treue, P. Ittihirunwong, K. Sripun, K. Srigernyoung, S. Aumtong, A. Tancho, S. Dontree, P. Jongkroy, R. Maneekul, P. Ittihirunkul, J. Wichawutipong, S. Bonphitak, S. Phaputnitisarn, P. Kantangkul, N. Waramit, W. Siripoonwiwat, A. Wattanapinyo, P. Pengthemkeerati, and P. Waratanapong. 2002. Information: SLUSE field course January 2003 Mae Tor watershed, Tambol Chiang Dao, Chiang Dao District, Chiang Mai Province, Mae Jo University.

Ministry of Agriculture and Cooperatives. 1984. *Mae Chaem Watershed Development Project: Annual Report 1984*. Bangkok: Ministry of Agriculture and Cooperatives.

Missingham, B. 2000. *Participatory Development in Thailand: A Review of Some*

Relevant Literature. Canberra: Integrated Catchment Assessment and Management Centre, The Australian National University.

Moerman, M. 1968. *Agricultural Change and Peasant Choice in a Thai Village.* Berkeley: University of California Press.

———. 1975. Chiangkham's trade in the "old days." In *Change and Persistence in Thai society: Essays in Honor of Lauriston Sharp*, ed. G. W. Skinner and A. T. Kirsch. Ithaca, N.Y.: Cornell University Press.

Moeyersons, J. 1990. Soil loss by rainwash: A case study from Rwanda. *Zeitschrist fur Geomorphologie N.F* 34 (4): 385–408.

Molle, F., Chatchom Chompadit, and Jesda Kaewkulaya. 2000. Dry season water allocation in the Chao Phraya basin: What is at stake and how to gain in efficiency and equity. Paper read at Chao Phraya Delta: Historical Development, Dynamics and Challenges of Thailand's Rice Bowl, 12–15 December, Kasetsart University, Bangkok.

Möller, A., K. Kaiser, and W. Zech. 2002. Lignin, carbohydrate, and amino sugar distribution and transformation in the tropical highland soils of northern Thailand under cabbage cultivation, *Pinus* reforestation, secondary forest, and primary forest. *Australian Journal of Soil Research* 40:977–98.

Montree Chantawong, Bunthida Katesombun, Orawan Koohacharoen, Pinkaew Leungaramsri, Petchmala Malapetch, Darunee Paisarnpanichkul, Kitti Thungsuro, and N. Rajesh. 1992. People and forests of Thailand. In *The Future of People and Forests in Thailand after the Logging Ban*, ed. Pinkaew Leungaramsri and N. Rajesh. Bangkok: Project for Ecological Recovery.

Morad, M. 2004. Talking hypothetically: The Duhem-Quine thesis, multiple hypotheses and the demise of hypothetico-deductivism. *Geoforum* 35:661–68.

Moran, E. F. 2000. *Human Adaptability: An Introduction to Ecological Anthropology.* Boulder, Colo.: Westview Press.

Morgan, R. 1986. *Soil Erosion and Conservation.* London: Harlow.

Mottin, J. 1980. *History of the Hmong.* Bangkok: Odeon Store.

Murdoch, J., and J. Clark. 1994. Sustainable knowledge. *Geoforum* 25 (2): 115–32.

Murty, D., M. Kirschbaum, R. McMurtrie, and H. McGilvray. 2002. Does conversion of forest to agricultural land change soil carbon and nitrogen? A review of the literature. *Global Change Biology* 8 (2): 105–23.

Nantaa Benjasilarak and Supamaat Silaarak, eds. 1999. *Violations of the Rights of Forest Villagers: People at the Edge of Thailand* [in Thai]. Chiang Mai: Northern Development Foundation.

Nantiya Tangwisutthijit. 1990. A question of resettlement: Are the hilltribes under a crop substitution programme destroying a forest watershed area? *The Nation*, 27 February.

NDF (Northern Development Foundation). 1996. *People and Watershed Forests* [in Thai]. Chiang Mai: NDF.

———. 1999. Study of biodiversity and ecology in community forests in the upper-northern region [in Thai]. In *Local Wisdom and the Management of Natural Resources*, ed. Department of Environmental Quality Extension. Bangkok: Department of Environmental Quality Extension.

———. 2000a. *Lines of Thinking and Directions: Participatory Management of Watershed Resources* [in Thai]. Chiang Mai: NDF.

———. 2000b. *Villager's Networks: Participatory Management of Watershed Resources* [in Thai]. Chiang Mai: NDF.

Nelson, R. G. 1990. The Dhammanaat Foundation. *Social Forestry Network: From the Field*, Network Paper 10e (Summer): 8–10.

Nipon Poapongsakorn, M. Ruhs, and Sumana Tangjitwisuth. 1998. Problems and outlook of agriculture in Thailand. *TDRI Quarterly Review* 13 (2): 3–14.

Nipon Tangtham. 1972. *Research Note: Kog-Ma Watershed Research Station.* Bangkok: Faculty of Forestry, Kasetsart University.

———. 1991. Erosion study and control in Thailand. Paper read at workshop on soil erosion and debris flow control organized by the Indonesian Institute of Science under UNEP-UNESCO-IRTICES-LIPI regional training programme on erosion, October, Jakarta.

———. 1994. The hydrological roles of forests in Thailand. *TDRI Quarterly Review* 9 (3): 27–32.

Niskanen, A. 1998. Value of external environmental impacts of reforestation in Thailand. *Ecological Economics* 26:287–97.

Nok Nguak. 1998. Can Thai forests survive? *Bangkok Post*, 24 March 1998.

Normita Thongtham. 1989. An aristocrat helps villagers to protect their forest. *Bangkok Post*, 2 March.

Northern Meteorological Centre. 2004. Climatological data for the period 30 years (1971–2000). http://www.cmmet.com/forecast/climate.xls (accessed 11 March 2004).

NRCT (National Research Council of Thailand). 1997. *Thailand Land Use and Land Cover Change Case Study.* Bangkok: National Research Council of Thailand.

Nye, P., and D. Greenland. 1960. *The Soil under Shifting Cultivation.* Harpenden, U. K.: Commonwealth Bureau of Soils.

———. 1964. Changes in the soil after clearing tropical forest. *Plant Soil* (21): 101–12.

Oates, J. F. 1999. *Myth and Reality in the Rain Forest: How Conservation Strategies Are Failing in West Africa.* Berkeley: University of California Press.

Oberhauser, U. 1997. Secondary forest regeneration beneath pine (*Pinus kesiya*) plantations in the northern Thai highlands: A chronosequence study. *Forest Ecology and Management* 99:171–83.

Office of Natural Resources and Environmental Policy and Planning. 2004. Biodiversity. http://www.oepp.go.th/bdm/eng_bd_sta.html (accessed 11 July 2004).

Onnucha Hutasing. 1999. Farmers threaten uprising: Evicted villagers want a piece of land. *Bangkok Post*, 15 March.

———. 2000. Plodprasop claims 5% tree boost. *Bangkok Post*, 1 August.

O'Riordan, T., and A. Jordan. 1999. Institutions, climate change and cultural theory: Towards a common analytical framework. *Global Environmental Change—Human and Policy Dimensions* 9 (2): 81–94.

Paanee Towakulphanich. 1996. Organic vegetables . . . for a healthy life [in Thai]. In *Local Agricultural Wisdom: Experience from Lanna*, ed. Alternative Agriculture Network. Chiang Mai: Alternative Agriculture Network.

Pahlman, C. 1990. Farmers' perceptions of the sustainability of upland farming systems of northern Thailand. MSc. thesis, Department of Resource Management, University of Canberra.

Paiboon Hengsuwan. 2003. Contradictions on the struggles over resources and contesting terrain of ethnic groups on the hill in protected area, Chom Thong, Chiang Mai. Paper read at Politics of the Commons: Articulating Development and Strengthening Local Practices, 11–14 July, Chiang Mai.

Palm, C., P. Swift, and P. Woomer. 1996. Soil biological dynamics in slash-and-burn agriculture. *Agriculture, Ecosystems and Environment* 58 (1): 61–74.

Pandee, P., and B. H. P. Maathuis. 1990. Using GIS-technology to come to potential landuse planning strategies. Unpublished paper from the Geo-Ecological Mapping Team, Department of Geography, Chiang Mai University.

Panida Suvapiromchote. 1989. Hillside farming threatens livelihoods. *Bangkok Post*, 6 September.

Panomsak Promburom. 1997. An integrated approach for assessing rice sufficiency level in highland communities of northern Thailand. MSc. thesis, Multiple Cropping Centre, Chiang Mai University.

Paramee, S. 2000. Comparative study of soil loss and surface runoff under agroforestry and natural dry Dipterocarp forest at Huay Hong Kai watershed. Royal Forest Department, Bangkok. http://www.forest.go.th/Research/English/Research_Project/environment.htm (accessed 13 March 2002).

Peluso, N. 1993. Coercing conservation?: The politics of state resource control. *Global Environmental Change-Human and Policy Dimensions* 3 (2): 199–218.

Pendleton, R. 1939. Some interrelations between agriculture and forestry, particularly in Thailand. *Journal of Thailand Research Society (Siam Society), Natural History Supplement* 12 (1): 33–52.

Pennapa Hongthong. 1999. Plantations spark RFD conflict with villagers. *The Nation*, 7 June.

———. 2002. Forest dwellers to remain in limbo. *The Nation*, 27 March.

———. 2004. Gov't moves to end 2nd rice harvest. *The Nation*, 6 April.

Perez, P., N. Ardlie, P. Kuneepong, C. Dietrich, and W. S. Merritt. 2002. CATCHCROP: Modelling crop yield and water demand for integrated catchment assessment in northern Thailand. *Environmental Modelling and Software* 17:251–59.

Pinkaew Laungaramsri. 1996. *Local Ecological Wisdom: Case Study of The Karen in Thung Yai Naresuan Forest* [in Thai]. Bangkok: Project for Ecological Recovery.

———. 1999. Rai, rai lu'an loy, rai mun wian and the politics of "shifting cultivation." *Watershed* 5 (1): 39–46.

———. 2000. The ambiguity of "watershed": The politics of people and conservation in northern Thailand. *Sojourn* 15 (1): 52–75.

———. 2001. *Redefining Nature: Karen Ecological Knowledge and the Challenge to the Modern Conservation Paradigm*. Chiang Mai: Regional Center for Social Science and Sustainable Development, Faculty of Social Science, Chiang Mai University.

Pitipong Peungboon Na Ayuthaya. 1997. Keynote address: Directions of pesticide policy in Thailand. In *Approaches to Pesticide Policy Reform — Building Consensus for Future Action. A Policy Workshop in Hua Hin, Thailand, July 3–5, 1997*, ed. Nipon Poapongsakorn, Lakchai Meenakanit, H. Waibel, and F. Jungbluth.

Ploenpote Atthakor. 2000. Thousands under threat of eviction. *Bangkok Post*, 20 August.

Poffenberger, M., and B. McGean. 1993. *Community Allies: Forest Co-management in Thailand*. Berkeley: Center for Southeast Asia Studies, University of California, Berkeley.

Polcher, J., and K. Laval. 1993. A statistical study of the impact of deforestation on climate using the LMD-GCM. *Macroscale Modelling of the Hydrosphere*, IAHS Publication 214:113–18.

Pongboun, K., P. Thitirojanawat, and P. Witthawatchutikul. 2000. Soil properties under natural forest at Huay Rai subwatershed. Royal Forest Department, Bangkok. http://www.forest.go.th/Research/English/Research_Project/environment.htm (accessed 27 August 2003).

Pongpet Mekloy. 1990. Monks stand up for the forests. *Bangkok Post*, 7 November.

Pooma, R., and A. Barfod. 2001. Vegetation types of northern Thailand. In *Forest in Culture — Culture in Forest: Perspectives from Northern Thailand*, ed. E. Poulsen, F. Skov, Sureeratna Lakanavichian, Sornprach Thanisawanyangkura, H. Borgtoft, and O. Hoiris. Tjele, Den.: Research Centres on Forest and People in Thailand, Danish Institute of Agricultural Sciences.

Poon, J. 2005. Quantitative methods: not positively positivist. *Progress in Human Geography* 29 (6): 766–72.

Pornchai Preechapanya. N.d. *Indigenous Highland Agroforestry Systems of Northern Thailand*. Chiang Mai: Chiang Dao Watershed Research Station.

Pottier, J., A. Bicker, and P. Sillitoe, eds. 2003. *Negotiating Local Knowledge: Power and Identity an Development*. London: Pluto.

Prasong Jantakad and D. Gilmour. 1999. Forest rehabilitation policy and practice in Thailand. MekongInfo. http://www.mekonginfo.org/mrc_en/doclib.nsf/o/543CoD5AFE2A816F472568FEoo2BB3F8/$FILE/ANNEX.html (accessed 3 December 2003).

Pratya Sawetrimon. 1987. 5000 tribespeople to be moved from forest reserve. *The Nation*, 9 March.

Prawase Wasi. 1997. Community forestry: The great integrative force. Paper read at Community Forestry at a Crossroads: Reflections and Future Directions in the Development of Community Forestry (RECOFTC Report No. 16.), 17–19 July, Regional Community Forestry Training Center, Bangkok.

Preeyagrysorn, Ob. 1992. Taungya in Thailand: Perspective of the Royal Forestry Department. In *Taungya. Forest Plantations with Agriculture in Southeast Asia*, ed. C. F. Jordan, Gajaseni Jiragorn, and H. Watanabe. Wallingford, Oxon, U. K.: C.A.B. International.

Pritsana Phromma and Montri Chanthawong. 1998. *Local Communities and Management of Biodiversity* [in Thai]. Chiang Mai: Project for the Development of Northern Watersheds by Community Organisations.

Promboon Panitchapakdi. 1996. Integrated natural resources conservation project 1994–1999. In *Montane Mainland Southeast Asia in Transition*, ed. Benjavan Rerkasem. Chiang Mai: Chiang Mai University.

Protected Areas and Development. 2005. Mekong protected areas: Thailand. http://www.mekong-protected-areas.org/thailand/pa-map.htm (accessed 24 June 2005).

Puginier, O. 2001. Can participatory land use planning at community level in the highlands of northern Thailand use GIS as a communication tool? Paper read at Participatory Technology Development and Local Knowledge for Sustainable Land Use in Southeast Asia, 6–7 June, Chiang Mai.

Rajah, A. 1986. Remaining Karen: A study of cultural reproduction and the maintenance of identity. Ph.D. diss., Anthropology, Research School of Pacific and Asian Studies, The Australian National University.

Rao, M. S. R. M., R. N. Adhikari, S. Chittaranjan, and M. Chandrappa. 1996. Influence of conservation measures on groundwater regime in a semi arid tract of South India. *Agricultural Water Management* 30:301–12.

Renard, R. D. 1979. *Kariang: History of Karen-Tai Relations from the Beginning to 1923*. London: University Microfilms International.

———. 1994. The monk, the Hmong, the forest, the cabbage, fire and water: Incongruities in northern Thailand opium replacement. *Law and Society Review* 28 (3): 657–64.

———. 2001. *Opium Reduction in Thailand 1970–2000: A Thirty-Year Journey*. Chiang Mai: United Nations Drug Control Programme and Silkworm Books.

RFD (Royal Forest Department). 1998. *Community Forestry* [in Thai]. Bangkok: Community Forestry Section, Office of Plantation Forestry.

———. 2004a. Definitions of watershed classes and standards used in watershed classification. http://www.forest.go.th/watershed/English/Concept/define.html (accessed 20 June 2004).

———. 2004b. *Forestry Statistics of Thailand, 2001.* Bangkok: Data Centre Information Office, Royal Forest Department.

———. 2004c. National Park Division. http://www.forest.go.th/nrco/english /npd.htm (accessed 20 May 2004).

———. 2004d. Royal initiative. http://www.forest.go.th/watershed/English/ Concept/command.html (accessed 14 April 2004).

———. 2004e. Watershed Management Division. http://www.forest.go.th /nrco/english/wshmd.htm (accessed 26 June 2004).

———. 2004f. Wildlife Conservation Division. http://www.forest.go.th/nrco /english/wcd.htm (accessed 7 April 2004).

———. 2005. Watershed Management Unit locations. http://www.forest.go.th /watershed/Thai/Workarea/25basin.html (accessed 14 April 2005).

Rijsdijk, A., and L. A. Bruijnzeel. 1991. *Erosion, Sediment Yield and Land-Use Patterns in the Upper Konto Watershed, East Java, Indonesia, Part III: Results of the 1989–1990 Measuring Campaign.* Project Communication No 18. The Hague: Konto River Project, Kingdom of the Netherlands, Ministry of Foreign Affairs, Director General of International Cooperation.

Ritchie, J. A., and J. R. McHenry. 1990. Application of radioactive 137Cs for measuring soil erosion and sediment accumulation rates and patterns: a review. *Journal of Environmental Quality* 19 (2): 215–33.

Roe, E. 1991. "Development narratives" or making the best of blueprint development. *World Development* 19 (4): 287–300.

Roth, R. 2004. On the colonial margins and in the global hotspot: Park-people conflicts in highland Thailand. *Asia Pacific Viewpoint* 45 (2): 13–32.

Rowntree, P. 1988. Review of general circulation models as a basis for predicting the effects of vegetation change on climate. In *Forests, Climate and Hydrology: Regional Impacts*, ed. E. Reynolds and F. Thompson. Tokyo: United Nations University.

Royal Forest Department. See RFD.

Royal Irrigation Department. 1994. *Crop Coefficient and Pan Coefficient* [in Thai]. Bangkok: Royal Irrigation Department.

Ruhs, M., Nat Rattanadilok, and Nipon Poapongsakorn. 1997. Pesticide use in Thai agriculture: Problems and policies. In *Approaches to Pesticide Policy Reform: Building Consensus for Future Action. A Policy Workshop in Hua Hin, Thailand, July 3–5, 1997*, ed. Nipon Poapongsakorn, Lakchai Meenakanit, H. Waibel, and F. Jungbluth. Hannover, Ger.: Pesticide Policy Project.

Rundel, P. W., and Kansri Boonpragop. 1995. Dry forest ecosystems of Thailand. In *Seasonally Dry Tropical Forests*, ed. S. H. Bullock, H. A. Mooney, and E. Medina. Cambridge: Cambridge University Press.

Saberwal, V. 1997. Science and the desiccationist discourse of the 20th century. *Environment and History* 3:309–43.

Sadoff, C. 1991. The value of Thailand's forests. *TDRI Quarterly Review* 6 (4): 19–24.

Saengdaaw Srattaman, Mala Khamjan, and Paithun Phromvijit, eds. 2000. *Journey to the Water Source* [in Thai]. Chiang Mai: Source of Water–Source of Life Project.

Saengkoovong, P., S. Rungrojwanich, and S. Rouysungnern. 2000. Rainfall interception by bamboo. Royal Forest Department, Bangkok. http://www.forest .go.th/Research/English/Research_Project/environment.htm (accessed 18 August 2004).

Sahin, V., and M. J. Hall. 1996. The effects of afforestation and deforestation on water yields. *Journal of Hydrology* 178:293–309.

Saiyud Kerdphol. 1986. *The Struggle for Thailand: Counter-Insurgency 1965– 1985*. Bangkok: Social Research Centre Co.

Salzer, W. 1987. *The TG-HDP Approach Towards Sustainable Agriculture and Soil and Water Conservation in the Hills of Northern Thailand*. Chiang Mai: Thai-German Highland Development Programme.

Samata, R. 2003. Agricultural transformation and highlander choice: A case study of a Pwo Karen community in northwestern Thailand. M.A. thesis in sustainable development, Chiang Mai University.

Sanga Sabhasri. 1978. Effects of forest fallow cultivation on forest production and soil. In *Farmers in the Forest: Economic Development and Marginal Agriculture in Northern Thailand*, ed. P. Kunstadter, E. C. Chapman, and Sanga Sabhasri. Honolulu: University Press of Hawai'i.

Sanitsuda Ekachai. 1990. *Behind the Smile: Voices of Thailand*. Bangkok: Bangkok Post Publishing.

———. 1993. Grasping hands on tree trunks. *Bangkok Post*, 7 May.

———. 1994. *Seeds of Hope: Local Initiatives in Thailand*. Bangkok: Post Publishing Public Co.

———. 1999. An unholy alliance lays siege to Karens. *Bangkok Post*, 14 May.

Sato, J. 2000. People in between: Conversion and conservation of forest lands in Thailand. *Development and Change* 31:155–77.

Savage, M. 1994. Structural dynamics of a montane pine forest: Effects of land use change in northern Thailand. *Mountain Research and Development* 14:245–250.

Sawang Sae Yang, Wachiraporn Patkaeo, Wonpong Wongkayangkun, Sanchai Sae Yang, Tongchart Sae Yang, Prasert Sae Nyararun, Tang Sae Lee, and Kriangkrai Tonomrungreoang. 2002. *Hmong Local Knowledge* [in Thai]. Chiang Mai: Hmong Environmental Network.

Schmidt-Vogt, D. 1999. *Swidden Farming and Fallow Vegetation in Northern Thailand*. Stuttgart, Ger.: Steiner.

Schoenleber, N. 2002. *Economical and Ecological Analysis for Farming Systems in the Mountainous Area of Northern Thailand.* Stuttgart, Ger.: Institute for Farm Management, Department of Analysis, Planning and Organisation of Agricultural Production, University of Hohenheim.

Scholten, J., and Wichai Boonyawat. 1973. *Detailed Reconnaissance Soil Survey of Chiang Rai Province.* Bangkok: Ministry of Agriculture and Cooperatives, Department of Land Development, and Food and Agriculture Organization of the United Nations.

Scott, D. F., and R. E. Smith. 1997. Preliminary empirical models to predict reductions in total and low flows resulting from afforestation. *Water South Africa* 23:135–40.

Scott, J. C. 1998. *Seeing Like a State: How Certain Schemes to Improve the Human Condition Have Failed.* New Haven, Conn.: Yale University Press.

Searle, J. 1995. *The Construction of Social Reality.* New York: Free Press.

Sheng, T. 1988. Some current issues in soil conservation. Paper presented at the 5th International Soil Conservation Conference, 18–29 January, Department of Land Development, Bangkok.

Shiratori, Y., I. Yawata, N. Egami, T. Takemura, J. Tumeni, and H. Hakari. 1973. *Ethnography of the Hill Tribes of South East Asia* [abridged English appendix]. Tokyo: Sophia University.

Shiva, V. 1991a. Biodiversity, biotechnology and profits. In *Biodiversity: Social and Ecological Perspectives,* ed. V. Shiva, P. Anderson, H. Shucking, A. Gray, L. Lohmann, and D. Cooper. Penang, Malay.: World Rainforest Movement.

———. 1991b. Introduction. In *Biodiversity: Social and Ecological Perspectives,* ed. V. Shiva, P. Anderson, H. Shucking, A. Gray, L. Lohmann, and D. Cooper. Penang, Malay.: World Rainforest Movement.

Sillitoe, P. 1983. Losing ground? Soil loss and erosion in the highlands of Papua New Guinea. *Land Degradation and Rehabilitation* 5 (3): 179–90.

———. 1998. It's all in the mound: Fertility management under stationary shifting cultivation in the Papua New Guinea highlands. *Mountain Research and Development* 18 (2): 123–34.

Simpson, B. 2004. Use EM™ to jump start healthy microbial processes in the soil-plant ecosystem. EM Trading. http://www.emtrading.com/indexa.html (accessed 5 March 2004).

Sivaramakrishnan, K. 1999. *Modern Forests: Statemaking and Environmental Change in Colonial Eastern India.* Oxford: Oxford University Press.

Slade, H. 1896. Report submitted to the Thai Government on August 10, 1896. Royal Forest Department, Bangkok. http://www.forest.go.th/rfd/history/history_e.htm (accessed 10 May 2005).

Smadja, J. 1992. Studies of climatic and human impacts and their relationship on a mountain slope above Salme in the Himalayan Middle Mountains, Nepal. *Mountain Research and Development* 12 (1): 1–28.

Smyth, H. 1895. *Notes of a Journey on the Upper Mekong, Siam*. London: John Murray.

———. 1898. *Five Years in Siam: From 1891–1896, Volume 1*. Bangkok: White Lotus.

Social Welfare Department. 1995. *Residence of Highland Communities in Thailand, 1995* [in Thai]. Bangkok: Hill Tribe Welfare Division, Social Welfare Department, Ministry of Labour and Welfare.

Sopin Tongpan, T. Panayotou, Songpol Jetanavanich, Ketty Faichampa, and C. Mehl. 1990. *Deforestation and Poverty: Can Commercial and Social Forestry Break the Vicious Circle?* Bangkok: Thailand Development Research Institute Foundation.

Spate, O. H. K. 1945. The Burmese Village. *Geographical Review* 35 (4): 523–43.

Stewart-Cox, B. 1996. *Wild Thailand*. London: New Holland.

Stocking, M. 2002. Agrodiversity, environmental protection and sustaining rural livelihoods: The global view. In *Cultivating Biodiversity: Understanding, Analysing and Using Agricultural Diversity*, ed. H. Brookfield, C. Padoch, H. Parsons, and M. Stocking. London: Intermediate Technology Development Group.

Stott, P. 1991. *Mu'ang* and *pa*: Elite views of nature in a changing Thailand. In *Thai Constructions of Knowledge*, ed. Chitakasem Manas and A. Turton. London: School of Oriental and African Studies.

Stuetz, W., T. Prapamontol, J. G. Erhardt, and H. G. Classen. 2001. Organochlorine pesticide residues in human milk of a Hmong hill tribe living in northern Thailand. *The Science of the Total Environment* 273:53–60.

Sturgeon, J. C. 2005. *Border Landscapes: The Politics of Akha Land Use in China and Thailand*. Seattle: University of Washington Press.

Suan Pa Sirikit. 1999. *People Living with Forests: Depending on Each Other* [in Thai]. Brochure distributed in Chiang Mai.

Subin Khernkaew. 1999. Hilltribe protesters will disperse today. *Bangkok Post*, 20 May.

Sulak Sivaraksa. 2004. The perils of consumerism. http://www.sulak-sivaraksa .org/about3.php (accessed 4 June 2004).

Sununtar Setboonsarng and J. Gilman. 2004. Alternative agricultures in Thailand and Japan. Horizons Solutions Site. http://www.solutions-site.org/artman /publish/article_15.shtml (accessed 5 March 2004).

Supamart Kasem. 2001. Hmong not doing what they should; Queen had warned of forest destruction. *Bangkok Post*, 2 August.

———. 2003. Dangerous levels of toxins found in veggies from Tak. *Bangkok Post*, 2 April.

Supara Janchitfah. 2002a. Falling trees have long shadows. *Bangkok Post*, 24 March.

———. 2002b. Senators scoff at people power. *Bangkok Post*, 24 March.

Suporn Amaruekachoke and Phrek Gypmantasiri. 1993. *Participatory Land Use Planning and Management for Sustainable Agricultural Production in a Small Watershed of Chiang Mai Province*. Chiang Mai: Multiple Cropping Centre, Faculty of Agriculture, Chiang Mai University.

Supradit Kanwanich. 1997a. Agricultural war: The case of the drying rivers. *Bangkok Post*, 20 July.

——. 1997b. Allegations: The source of life is poisoned. *Bangkok Post*, 27 July.

Suradej Yangsaeng. 2000. This is like dying while still alive. *Watershed* 6 (2): 43–47.

Sureeratna Lakanavichian. 2001. *Forest Policy and History in Thailand*. Chiang Mai: Research Centre on Forest and People in Thailand.

Sutthathorn Suwannaratana. 1999. Comparison of teak and pine plantations in northern Thailand. Ph.D. diss., University of Saarbrucken.

Svasti, M. R. Smansnid. 1998. A Response from Thailand to the World Rain-forest Movement article, "Thailand: The struggle of forest people to remain in the forest." World Rainforest Movement Special Bulletin. http://www.wrm.org.uy/bulletin/Special.html (accessed 12 April 2005).

Swanson, T. M. 1995. *The Economics and Ecology of Biodiversity Decline: The Forces Driving Global Change*. Cambridge: Cambridge University Press.

Takahashi, T., K. Nagahori, Charat Mongkolsawat, and Manas Losirikul. 1983. Run-off and soil loss. In *Shifting Cultivation: An Experiment at Nam Phrom, Northeast Thailand, and Its Impliations for Upland Farming in the Monsoon Tropics*, ed. K. Kyuma and Chaitat Pairintra. Bangkok: Ministry of Science, Technology and Energy.

Tanabe, S. 1994. *Ecology and Practical Technology: Peasant Farming Systems in Thailand*. Bangkok: White Lotus.

Tapp, N. 1989. *Sovereignty and Rebellion: The White Hmong of Northern Thailand*. Singapore: Oxford University Press.

Teerparp Lohitagul. 1996. *Notebook of a Visitor* [in Thai]. Bangkok: Phraw Printers.

Terralingua. 2004. A global map of the correlation between linguistic and biological diversity. http://www.terralingua.org/thisone1.pdf (accessed 4 June 2004).

Thai-Australia World Bank Land Development Project. 1985. *Northern Thailand Upland Agriculture*. Bangkok: Department of Land Development, Ministry of Agriculture and Cooperatives.

Thai-German Highland Development Programme. 1998. *From Ideas . . . to Action*. Chiang Mai: TGHDP.

Thailand Development Research Institute. 1987. *Thailand Natural Resource Profile*. Bangkok: TDRI.

Thammasak Thinnsawat and D. Hardy. 1999. There's no doubt—it's a drought! *Good Morning Chiang Mai* 4 (3): 12–23.

Thawatchai Santisuk. 1988. *An Account of the Vegetation of Northern Thailand*. Stuttgart, Ger.: Franz Steiner Verlag Wiesbaden Gmb.

Thawatchai Santisuk, Tem Smitinand, and W. Y. Brockelman. 1985. *Nature Con-*

servation in Thailand in Relation to Social and Economic Development. Bangkok: Siam Society.

The Nation. 1973. The road that cost nine men per mile. *The Nation,* 1 December.

———. 2001. River valley at risk. *The Nation,* 21 August.

Thiem Komkris. 1978. Forestry aspects of land use in areas of swidden cultivation. In *Farmers in the Forest: Economic Development and Marginal Agriculture in Northern Thailand,* ed. P. Kunstadter, E. C. Chapman, and Sanga Sabhasri. Honolulu: University Press of Hawaiʻi.

Thirayut Senakham and Phonphana Kuaicharoen. 1996. *Rice Varieties: The Role of Communities in Protection and Development* [in Thai]. Bangkok: Alternative Agriculture Network.

Thitirojanawat, P., and S. Chareonsuk. 2000. Verification of the Universal Soil Loss Equation application (USLE) on forest area. Royal Forest Department, Bangkok. http://www.forest.go.th/Research/English/abstracts_water/wse64 .html (accessed 12 June 2004).

Thitirojanawat, P., V. Pukjaloon, and V. Poonawarat. 2000. Water holding capacity and porosity of soils at Su watershed. Royal Forest Department, Bangkok. http://www.forest.go.th/Research/English/abstracts_water/wse62.html (accessed 12 March 2002).

Thitirojanawat, P., V. Pukjaroon, and S. Rouysungnern. 2000. Water holding capacity of soil under different tree plantations. Royal Forest Department, Bangkok. http://www.forest.go.th/Research/English/abstracts_water/wse60 .html (accessed 12 March 2002).

Thomas, D., and N. Middleton. 1994. *Desertification: Exploding the Myth.* Chichester, U. K.: Wiley.

Thomas, D. E., and Kamon Pragtong. 1990. Evolving management systems in Thailand. In *Keepers of the Forest: Land Management Alternatives in Southeast Asia,* ed. M. Poffenberger. West Hartford, Conn.: Kumarian Press.

Thomas, D. E., H. Weyerhaeuser, and Pornwilai Saipothong. 2002. Negotiated land use patterns to meet local and societal needs in northern Thailand. Paper read at Sustaining Food Security and Managing Natural Resources in Southeast Asia, 8–11 January, Chiang Mai.

Thompson, M., R. Ellis, and A. Wildavsky. 1990. *Cultural Theory.* Boulder, Colo.: Westview Press.

Thompson, M., M. Warburton, and T. Hatley. 1986. *Uncertainty on a Himalayan Scale: An Institutional Theory of Environmental Perception and a Strategic Framework for the Sustainable Development of the Himalayas.* London: Ethnographica, Milton Ash Publications.

Tinker, P. B., J. S. I. Ingram, and S. Struew. 1996. Effects of slash-and-burn agriculture and deforestation on climatic change. *Agriculture, Ecosystems and Environment* 58:13–22.

Tomich, T. P., K. Chomitz, H. Francisco, A.-M. N. Izac, D. Murdiyarso, B. D.

Ratner, D. E. Thomas, and M. van Noordwijk. 2004. Policy analysis and environmental problems at different scales: Asking the right questions. *Agriculture, Ecosystems and Environment* 104 (1): 5–18.

Tomich, T. P., D. E. Thomas, and M. van Noordwijk. 2004. Environmental services and land use change in Southeast Asia: From recognition to regulation or reward? *Agriculture, Ecosystems and Environment* 104 (1): 229–44.

Tongroj Onchan. 1990. *A Land Policy Study*. Bangkok: Thailand Development Research Institute Foundation.

Tonmanee, N., and N. Kanchanakool. 1999. Agricultural diffuse pollution in Thailand. *Water Science and Techology* 39 (3): 61–66.

Tribal Research Institute. 1989. Appendix 1: Hill tribe population of Thailand. In *Hill Tribes Today*, ed. J. M. McKinnon and B. Vienne. Bangkok: White Lotus–Orstom.

Trimble, S. 1983. A sediment budget for Coon Creek basin in the Driftless area, Wisconsin 1853–1977. *American Journal of Science* (283): 454–74.

Tuenjai Deetes. 2000. A bridge to the hill tribes. UNESCO Courier. http://www.unesco.org/courier/2000_10/uk/dires.htm (accessed 23 March 2005).

Turkelboom, F. 1999. On-farm diagnosis of steepland erosion in northern Thailand: Integrating spatial scales with household strategies. Ph.D. diss., Katholieke Universiteit Leuven, Belgium.

Turkelboom, F., Poesen J., I. Ohler, and S. Ongprasert. 1999. Reassessment of tillage erosion rates by manual tillage on steep slopes in northern Thailand. *Soil and Tillage Research* 51:245–59.

Turton, A. 2000. *Civility and Savagery: Social Identity in Tai States*. Richmond, Surrey, U. K.: Curzon.

Twidale, C. 1982. *Granite Landforms*. Oxford: Elsevier.

Uamdao Noikorn. 1999. Tough and in the thick of things. *Bangkok Post*, 7 June.

Ukrit Aparasit. 2001. *A Case Study of Doi Inthanon National Park Area: Socio-Economic Characteristics of the Case Study Villages*. Aarhus, Den.: University of Aarhus, Research Centre on Forest and People in Thailand.

Ukrit Aparasit and Lotte Isager. 2001. *Survey Report of Mae Chaem/Doi Inthanon, Including a Presentation of Selected Villages for Further Studies*. Aarhus, Den.: University of Aarhus, Research Centre on Forest and People in Thailand.

UN (United Nations). 1967. *Report of the United Nations Survey Team on the Economic and Social Needs of the Opium-Producing Areas in Thailand, January/February 1967*. Bangkok: UN.

UNEP (United Nations Environment Programme). 1988. *Sustainable Development of Natural Resources: A Study of the Concepts and Applications of His Majesty the King of Thailand*. Bangkok: UNEP.

United Nations Department of Humanitarian Affairs. 1988. South Thailand floods/mudslides. ReliefWeb. http://www.reliefweb.int/rw/rwb.nsf/AllDocsByUNID/818e22daoda39981c1256564004d8a3d (accessed 23 August 2004).

Uraivan Tan-Kim-Yong. 1995. *Muang-Fai Communites Are for People: Institutional Strength and Potentials.* Bangkok: Social Research Institute, Chulalongkorn University.

Uraivan Tan-Kim-Yong, Anan Ganjanapan, Shalardchai Ramitanondh, and Sanay Yanasarn. 1988. *Natural Resource Utilization and Management in Mae Khan Basin: Intermediate Zone Crisis.* Chiang Mai: Faculty of Social Sciences, Chiang Mai University.

USDA (U.S. Department of Agriculture). 1961. *A Universal Equation for Predicting Rainfall-Erosion Losses.* USDA-ARS special report. N.p.: USDA Research Service.

Van Beek, S. 1995. *The Chao Phya: River in Transition.* Kuala Lumpur: Oxford University Press.

Van Beld, J. 1991. *The Princess, the Monk, and the Rainforest.* Video for television.

Vandergeest, P. 1996a. Mapping nature: Territorialization of forest rights in Thailand. *Society and Natural Resources* 9:159–75.

———. 1996b. Property rights in protected areas: Obstacles to community involvement as a solution in Thailand. *Environmental Conservation* 23 (3): 259–68.

———. 1999. Reply: Protected areas and property rights in Thailand. *Environmental Conservation* 26 (1): 7–9.

———. 2003. Racialization and citizenship in Thai forest politics. *Society and Natural Resources* 16:19–37.

Van der Weert, R. 1994. *Hydrological Conditions in Indonesia.* Jakarta: Delft Hydraulics.

Van Keer, K., J. D. Comtois, F. Turkelboom, and Somchai Ongprasert. 1998. *Options for Soil and Farmer Friendly Agriculture in the Highlands of Northern Thailand.* Eschborn, Ger.: Tropical Ecology Support Program.

Van Keer, K., and F. Turkelboom. 1995. Soil conservation and weed control: Friends or foes? *ILEIA Newsletter* 11 (3): 14.

Van Roy, Edward. 1971. *Economic Systems of Northern Thailand: Structure and Change.* Ithaca, N.Y.: Cornell University Press.

Vayda, A. P. 1998. Anthropological perspectives on tropical deforestation? A review article. *Anthropos* 93:573–79.

Vetiver Network. 2005. The vetiver network. http://www.vetiver.com/TVN _FRONTPAGE_ENGLISH.htm (accessed 25 August 2005).

Vincent, J. R., Mingsarn Khaosa-ard, Laxmi Worachai, E. Y. Azumi, Nipon Tangtham, and A. B. Rala. 1995. *The Economics of Watershed Management: A Case Study of Mae Taeng.* Bangkok: Natural Resources and Environmental Program, Thailand Development Research Institute, and Harvard Institute for International Development.

Wakin, E. 1992. *Anthropology Goes to War: Professional Ethics and Counterinsurgency in Thailand.* Madison: University of Wisconsin, Center for Southeast Asian Studies.

Walker, A. 2001a. Introduction: Simplification and the ambivalence of community. *The Asia Pacific Journal of Anthropology* 22 (2): 1–20.

———. 2001b. The "Karen consensus," ethnic politics and resource-use legitimacy in northern Thailand. *Asian Ethnicity* 2 (2): 145–62.

———. 2002. Forests and water in northern Thailand. *Chiang Mai University
Journal* 1 (3): 215–44.

———. 2003. Agricultural transformation and the politics of hydrology in northern Thailand. *Development and Change* 34 (5): 941–64.

Walker, A. R. 1992. North Thailand as geo-ethnic mosaic: An introductory essay.
In *The Highland Heritage: Collected Essays on Upland North Thailand*, ed.
A. R. Walker. Singapore: Suvarnabhumi Books.

Wanat Bhruksasri. 1989. Government policy: Highland ethnic minorities. In *Hill
Tribes Today*, ed. J. McKinnon and B. Vienne. Bangkok: White Lotus–Orstom.

Waraalak Chaitap. 2004. The biodiveristy on rotation land farming in an indigenous Karen community at Ban Mae Lankhum, Chiangmai. Northern Farmers' Network (accessed 12 June 2004)www.grain.org/gd/en/case-studies/cases
/fulltext/doc-pdf/as-full-thailand-karen-en.pdf.

Waraalak Ithiphonorlan. 1998. *Rotational Shifting Cultivation: Mother of Plant
Varieties* [in Thai]. Chiang Mai: Project for the Development of Northern Watersheds by Community Organisations.

Waranoot Tungittiplakorn. 2002. Limitations of subsistence agriculture in the
highlands. In *Environmental Protection and Rural Development in Thailand:
Challenges and Opportunities*, ed. P. Dearden. Bangkok: White Lotus.

Waranoot Tungittiplakorn and P. Dearden. 2002. Biodiversity conservation and
cash crop development in northern Thailand. *Biodiversity and Conservation*
11:2007–25.

Ward, C. 2002. Amid planting season, Thailand faces severe drought. Disaster-
Relief. http://www.disasterrelief.org/Disasters/020225thailanddrought/ (accessed
15 December 2003).

Watts, M. 1983. *Silent Violence: Food, Famine and Peasantry in Northern Nigeria*. Berkeley: University of California Press.

Whitmore, T., and B. L. Turner II. 2001. *Cultivated Landscapes of Native Middle America on the Eve of Conquest*. Oxford: Oxford University Press.

Wilk, J., L. Andersson, and V. Plermkamon. 2001. Hydrological impacts of forest
conversion to agriculture in a large river basin in northeast Thailand. *Hydrological Processes* 15 (14): 2729–48.

Wilshusen, P. R., S. R. Brechin, C. L. Fortwangler, and P. C West. 2002. Rein-
venting a square wheel: Critique of a resurgent "protection paradigm" in international biodiversity conservation. *Society and Natural Resources* 15:17–40.

Wirawat Thiraprasat. 1996. Preface. In *Local Ecological Wisdom: Case Study
of the Karen in Thung Yai Naraesuan Forest* [in Thai], ed. Pinkaew Laungaramsri. Bangkok: Project for Ecological Recovery.

Witoon Lianjumroon. 1997. Agricultural extension and pesticide usage. In *Approaches to Pesticide Policy Reform: Building Consensus for Future Action. A Policy Workshop in Hua Hin, Thailand, July 3–5, 1997*, ed. Nipon Poapongsakorn, Lakchai Meenakanit, H. Waibel, and F. Jungbluth. Hannover, Ger.: Pesticide Policy Project.

Witthawatchutikul, P., and W. Jirasuktaveekul. 2000. Soil water and Et/Ep ratio of forest land, cassava field, and some fruit tree plantations at Tapong Nai, Rayong Province. Royal Forest Department, Bangkok. http://www.forest.go.th/Research/English/Research_Project/environment.htm (accessed 17 August 2004).

Witthawatchutikul, P., and S. Suksawang. 2000. Rainfall intercepted in logged-over dry evergreen forest at Huay Ma Fuang, Rayong Province. Royal Forest Department, Bangkok. http://www.forest.go.th/Research/English/Research_Project/environment.htm (accessed 17 August 2004).

Wolf, E., and J. Jorgensen. 1970. Anthropology on the warpath in Thailand. *New York Review of Books*, 19 November, 26–35.

Wood, A., P. Stedman-Edwards, and J. Mang. 2000. *The Root Causes of Biodiversity Loss.* London: Earthscan.

Wynne, B. 1996. May the sheep safely graze? A reflexive view of the expert-lay knowledge divide. In *Risk, Environment and Modernity*, ed. S. Lash, B. Szersynski, and B. Wynne. London: Sage.

Yanuar Sumarlan. 2004. How participatory is Thailand's forest policy? In *Policy Trend Report 2004*, ed. K. Harada and M. Nanang. Kanagawa, Jap.: Institute for Global Environmental Strategies. '

Ziegler, A., and T. W. Giambelluca. 1997. Hydrologic change and accelerated erosion in northern Thailand: Simulating the impacts of rural roads and agriculture. *Explorations in Southeast Asian Studies* 1 (1). http://www2.hawaii.edu/~seassa/explorations/v1n1/art3/v1n1–frame3.html (accessed 23 June 2003).

Ziegler, A., T. W. Giambelluca, D. Plondke, T. Vana, T., J. Fox, Tran Duc Vien, M. A. Nullet, and S. Evett. 2000. Near-surface hydrologic response in a fragmented mountainous landscape: Tat Hamlet, Da River watershed, northern Vietnam. http://webdata.soc.hawaii.edu/hydrology/projects/vietnam/papers/jhooadz.pdf (accessed 5 July 2003).

Ziegler, A., T. W. Giambelluca, and R. A. Sutherland. 2000. Estimation of basin sediment flux in the Pang Khum Experimental Watershed in Northern Thailand: The contributions of roads and agricultural lands. Case Study No. 28 presented as part of Land-Water Linkages in Rural Watersheds Electronic Workshop, 18 September to 27 October 2000. Food and Agricultural Organization of the United Nations. http://www.fao.org/ag/agl/watershed/watershed/papers/papercas/paperen/case28en.pdf (accessed 19 November 2004).

Ziegler, A., R. A. Sutherland, and T. W. Giambelluca. 2001. Acceleration of Horton overland flow and erosion by footpaths in an upland agricultural watershed in northern Thailand. *Geomorphology* 41 (4): 249–62.

Zimmerer, K. 2004. Environmental discourses on soil degradation in Bolivia: Sustainability and the search for socioenvironmental "middle ground." In *Liberation Ecologies: Environment, Development, Social Movements*, ed. R. Peet and M. Watts. London: Routledge.

Zinke, P. J., Sabhasri Sanga, and P. Kunstadter. 1978. Soil fertility aspects of the Lua' forest fallow system of shifting cultivation. In *Farmers in the Forest: Economic Development and Marginal Agriculture in Northern Thailand*, ed. P. Kunstadter, E. C. Chapman, and Sanga Sabhasri. Honolulu: University Press of Hawai'i.

biodiversity: agrodiversity as, 221; assessing functions of, 218–19; case for protection of, 204–9; commercialization and, 219–23; and community management, 209–17; environmental narratives of, 202–3, 223–24; environmental significance of, 7; debate on, 217–18; forest fragmentation and, 206; and land use, 25; level of, in Thailand, 201; monocropping and, 219–23; reduction in, 3; uncertainty in assessment of, 202–3, 218–19, 223

Blaikie, P., 149

Borneo, 150

Brazil, 155

Brookfield, H., 149

Bruijnzeel, L. A., 105–6, 110, 112, 115, 147, 162

Bruner, A. G., 208–9

Buak Jan, 179–81

Buddhism, 65

buffer zones, 207

bureaucratic reform, 246

Buri Ram province, 249n17

Burma: conquest of northern Thailand, 65; and erosion, 142; ethnic conflict in, 6; opium production, 78; refugees from, 199–200

cabbage: Chom Thong dispute role of, 96; in wildlife sanctuaries, 207; crop substitution with, 134, 143; dry-season cultivation of, 133, 176; growing schedule, 176–77; grown by Karen in Mae Hong Son province, 175–79; soil quality and, 158–59, 193; as "worse than opium," 144

cabbage mountains, 81, 235

Cambodia, 141

cash crops, 79, 81

catchments. See watersheds

cattle trading, 122–23

Central Intelligence Agency (CIA), 6

cerrado, 104

cesium-137 technique, 153–54, 253n5

Chaem River, 35–36, 118, 131

Chaiwat Roongruangsee, 178, 190

Chamnonk Pransutjarit, 163

chao khao, 59. See also upland people

Chao Phraya: catchment of, 31, 248n2; deforestation's effect on flows of, 94, 108; North as headwaters of, 7

Chapman, E. C., 62

Charat Mongkolsawat, 109, 112–13

Chareonsuk, S., 146

Chavalit Yongchaiyudh, Gen., 16

chemical pollution, 25

Chiang Dao district, 160–61

Chiang Dao Wildlife Protection Area, 213

Chiang Kham district, 172–73

Chiang Mai city, 31, 35fig

Chiang Mai province: biodiversity, 204–5, 220; Chom Thong dispute, 67, 96–99; crop diversification by Hmong in, 179–81; erosion, 160–61; farmers' rights rally in, 50; forest cover, 39, 94, 105; hill tribe population, 61; Hmong population, 76; illegal encroachment, 50; Karen agriculture, 213; Karen attacks on Hmong in, 184–85; participatory land-use planning, 245; pesticide use, 170; rainfall interception rates, 106; resettlement actions, 47, 49; roads and erosion, 163; streamflow, 105; villages in forest reserves, 45; watershed classification, 42. See also Mae Chaem district

Chiang Mai University, 51

Chiang Rai province: biodiversity, 216; Chinese Nationalist forces in, 5; deportation of villagers, 48; erosion, 152–60; forest cover, 39, 94; hill tribe population, 61; Hmong population, 76; road building, 162; soil quality, 194

China, 189, 193

Chinese Nationalists, 5

cholinesterase inhibition, 196

Chom Thong Conservation Group, 82

Chom Thong dispute: commercial agriculture, 138; Hmong negative portrayal in, 208; international views of, 237; *khon muang* seen as victim in, 67; organizing against Hmong, 96–98; pesticide use, 182–83; popular narratives used in, 114; rainfall levels, 100; Thai nationalism and, 99; water demand as factor in, 134, 148

Chomitz, K. M., 165

Chulalongkorn, King, 40

Chusak Wittayapak, 95

Classen, H. G., 195–96

climate: elevation's effect on, 24; seasonal rainfall, 32, 34; streamflow as seasonal, 34–35, 108–13; volatility in, 35–37; wet and dry cycles, 101, 102*fig*, 103*fig*

cloud forests, 38, 105

cloud formation, 104

commercial agriculture: and biodiversity, 204, 219–23; as Chom Thong dispute issue, 96, 98; dry-season, 137–38; erosion and, 143–44; marginalization of uplanders engaged in, 243–44; and pesticide overuse, 3

commercialization, 15

communism, 5, 76

communist grass, 6

communist insurgency, 46–47, 249*n15*

community forestry: agricultural land within reserves, 55–56; definition, 51; disagreements on, 217; Forestry

Department legislation, 52; and Karen, 211; legislation for, 52–56, 206; narratives of, 233–34; for water conservation, 95

compost, 193

Comtois, J. D., 167, 193–94

Congo basin, central, 104

Conklin, Harold C., 71–72, 150

conservation forests, 41–42, 46, 61

Conservation International, 201

conservationists, 9–10, 115

Constitution of 1997, 51

controlled burning, 165

Convention on Biological Diversity, 224–25

Costa Rica, 165

countermapping, 245

crisis narratives, 23

crops, 65; diseases of, 161; nitrogen-fixing, 166

crop substitution: criticism of initiative for, 8, 96, 98; crop diversification and, 179; and erosion, 153; and fertilizer use, 174; impact of programs for, 80–81; and water use, 134. *See also* opium

cultural diversity, 209–17

Cultural Theory, 19, 22, 248*n6*

cut-flower production, 179–81, 200

Dachanee Emphandu, 205

dams, 121

DANIDA, 186

Dartmouth Flood Observatory, 93

DDT, 191, 196

Dearden, Philip, 95, 202, 204–7, 212, 218–20, 254*n1*

Deer: brow-antlered, 202; hog, 202

Deetes, Tuenjai. *See* Tuenjai Deetes

deforestation: in Africa, 19–21; as ambiguous term, 11–12, 235–36; drought caused by, 92–95; flooding

90, 195, 197; biodiversity and, 202–3, 223–24; characteristics of, 18; community forestry, 57–58; definitions, 17; and erosion, 139; explaining, 228–29; forests as rainfall sources, 88–91; forests as sponges for water, 88, 91, 114; lowland settlements representing civilization, 27–28; persistence of, 228; political functions of, 18; previous approaches to analysis of, 19, 22–23; selectively representative, 235–37; simplistic framing of, 19, 137; streamflow and forest cover, 104–5, 108; in support of political goals, 22, 114, 134–38; upland culture stereotypes, 59–60, 84–86, 138, 171, 218, 224, 230, 243; water supply vs. demand, 127, 136–38; weaknesses of, 227

environmental science, 11–13, 203

epistemic communities, 247n5

Erhardt, J. G., 195–96

erosion: in an Akha village, 157–60; controlled burning and, 165; farmers' perception of, 168–69; and fertility, 157; grass strips and, 166–67; in a Mien village, 152–56; narratives about, 139; natural causes of, 154–55; need for education about, 144; opium growing and, 143; overpopulation and, 142–43; plantation forestry and, 164–66; popular conceptions of, 140–44; prediction of, 253n4; problem areas, 168; and reforestation, 140; road-building and, 162–64; shifting cultivation and, 150–51; site-specific, 167–68; types of, 140–41; UN report on, 139; Universal Soil Loss Equation (USLE), 145–50

estuarine crocodile, 202

ethnic conflict, 8–9

ethnic minorities: elevation and, 64; local knowledge among, 15; stereotypes of, 59–60, 138, 218, 224, 230, 243; and water demand, 129–30

evapotranspiration, 104

evergreen forests, 37–38

Evett, S., 109, 116, 163

expertise, 231–32, 242–46

extinction, 202, 222

Fahn, James, 3, 16, 96, 202

false gharial, 202

Fang, 187–88

farmers: agrochemicals' threat to health of, 195–97; as conservationists, 115; disputes with Royal Forestry Department, 51; organizing for rights of, 50. See also agriculture

Farmers in the Forest (Kunstadter et al.), 64, 104

faunal desert, 204, 212, 219, 223

fermented tea, 55, 249n20

fertilizer: excessive use of, 82, 181; image of, among villagers, 172–73; increasing applications of, 177; organic, 189; as remedy for soil exhaustion, 157; rice yields affected by, 175–76, 178–79, 199; for strawberries, 189. See also agrochemicals

filter strips, 115–16, 140, 146, 166–67

filter zones, 115

Finland, 41

Finnaid, 41

firebreaks, 97

floodplains, 148

floods, 70, 92–94, 110–12

flowers, 179–81, 200

Fonseca, G. A. B. da, 208–9

Food and Agriculture Organization (FAO), 165

food safety, 185

Forest Act (1941), 41

forest destroyers, 19, 25, 60, 134, 227, 230, 243

forest guardians, 19, 25, 84, 134, 138, 227, 230, 243

Forest Reserve Act (1964), 41

forest reserves, 41–42, 46, 61

forests: fragmentation of, 206; mixed deciduous, 38; patrols of, 97; protection of, 7

forest sponge: drought, 92–95; as environmental narrative, 88, 91–92, 114; flooding, 92–94; seasonal distribution of streamflow, 108–13. See also soil; upland forest

forestry, 164–66

Forest Village Program, 47

Forsyth, T., 152, 165, 194

Fox, T. J., 109, 116, 163

Ganges River, 111

gardens, 220–21

garlic, 189, 222

Geddes, W. R., 77

Geertz, C., 72

geographical information system (GIS), 153

Gerbera jamesonii, 179–81

Germany, 196

Giambelluca, T. W., 90, 109, 113, 116, 162–63

glutinous rice, 65

Golden Triangle, 5–6

governmentality, 22, 24

grader grass, 6

grasses, 6

grass strips. See filter strips

Green Northeast Thailand program, 249n17

greenwash, 23

ground cover, 165

guards, 208–9

Guinea, 21

gullies, 155, 157, 252n1; erosion of, 141, 146, 164–65

Gullison, R. E., 208–9

Haiti, 111

Hajer, M., 17–18, 135

Hamilton, L, 11–12, 167

Hanks, Jane, 162

Hanks, Lucien, 162

Hanunoo (people), 71

Harper, D. E., 144

health, 195–97

Hearn, R., 46

herbicides, 181

heroin, 5

Highland Development Stations, 48

Hill Area Development Foundation, 247n3

hill tribes. See upland people

Hinton, P., 175, 178–79

Hirsch, P., 90

Hmong (people): attacks on, 183–85; cash crops, 222; Chom Thong dispute, 67, 96–99; crop diversification by, 179–81; elevation range of, settlements, 64; as exotic, 59; and forest protection traditions, 83–84; negative images of, 60, 77, 99, 243; as opium growers, 77–78, 80–82; pesticide use by, 181–85, 195–97; images of, in environmental narratives, 60, 63, 77–83, 207; population estimates, 61, 76; as rebels, 77; resettlement of, 48, 233; rituals, 83; as shifting cultivators, 78–79, 217; Thai army conflicts with, 46; as wildlife sanctuary residents, 206

home gardens, 220–21

Huay Kok Ma watershed, 35fig; 105–7

hunting, 204–5, 220
hydrology, 88–92

illegal encroachment, 50
Imperata cylindrica, 142, 165, 174
India: annual rainfall, 104; British control over Bengali forests, 231; decentralized forest management in, 51; erosion and monoculture forests, 165; Ganges streamflow, 111; shifting cultivation in, 70, 104
Indo-Burma biodiversity hotspot, 201
Indonesia, 162, 193
infrastructure, 120
Ing River, 248n2
integrated swidden, 71–72
intercropping, 189, 212
International Board for Soil Research and Management (IBSRAM), 91, 152
international epistemic communities, 13
irrigation: of cabbages, 134; and dry-season cropping, 127–28; for forest conservation, 97; of fruit orchards, 133; in Mae Uam catchment, 120; reduction of water for, 89; of rice, 65, 67–68; technical limits to systems of, 126
Isager, Lotte, 133
Iu Mien, 253n7
Ives, J. D., 143

Jaakko Pöyry Oyj, 41
jhum, 70
Jintana Amornsanguansin, 95, 132
Jones, S., 160–61
Judd, L. C., 62
Jungbluth, F., 174–75

Kanok Rerkasem, 133, 178, 190, 220–21
Karen (people): cabbage cultivation by, 175–79; as commercial farmers, 129–30, 175–79, 244; conflict with *khon muang*, 68–69; cultivation techniques, 72; dam construction proposals, 121–23; elevation range of, settlements, 64, 70; erosion prevention among, 151; as exotic, 59; government intervention with, 75; Hmong attacked by, 184–85; as hunters, 205; Karen consensus, 72–76; land tenure, 130; market penetration into villages of, 74–75; as ox traders, 123; images in environmental narratives of, 63, 69–135 passim, 207, 210–11; population estimates, 61, 69; refugees from Burma, 199; as resident in Mae Uam watershed, 118; seen as ecologically sound, 60, 73–76, 135, 210–43; as soybean growers, 129–30; subgroups of, 250n4; as wildlife sanctuary residents, 206
Kasetsart University, 41
Kenya, 251n15
Khamboonruang, C., 196
Khon Kaen province, 249n17
khon muang, 28; Chom Thong dispute, 67, 96–99; as environmental despoilers, 68–69; images in environmental narratives, 63, 65–69; land tenure, 130; as resident in Mae Uam watershed, 118; as soybean growers, 129–30; as upland people, 60–62, 66; as victims of environmental degradation, 66–68, 99; violence against Hmong by, 183–84
Khor Jor Kor Land Resettlement program, 249n17
King of Thailand Vetiver Awards, 166
knowledge networks, 242

nongovernmental organizations
(NGOs): changing Hmong agricultural techniques, 79; government
synergies with, 233; local knowledge, 231; pesticide-use narratives,
195; and upland preservation, 229;
view of Karen, 74, 135
nonhunting areas, 202
nonpositivist science, 241
Noppawan Tanakanjana, 205
Northern Development Foundation,
91, 184
Northern Farmers' Network, 245
Northern Thailand: biodiversity in,
203; defined, 248n6; environmental
significance of, 7–9; erosion in,
143, 162, 166–69; land shortages
and erosion, 143; political significance of, 4–7; politics of environmental knowledge in, 9, 114;
popular images of, 4
ntoo xeeb ritual, 83
Nullet, M. A., 109, 116, 163

Oates, J. F., 208
opium, 5–6, 77–78, 82, 143. *See also*
crop substitution
orchards: encouraged by Forest
Department, 180; as environmental
problem, 239–40; excessive pesticide use in, 175; irrigation of, 133;
of the *khon muang*, 66; razing of,
184; spraying by refugees, 200
organic farming, 171, 185–86, 188–
90, 198
organic matter, 193
organochlorine pesticides (OCP), 196
overpopulation, 142–43
ox trading, 122–23

pa, 57, 85, 87, 229; defined, 28
pahiros, 147, 155

Pahlman, C., 144
Pai River, 248n2
Pakakeyor. *See* Karen (people)
Pakha, 157–60
Pa Kluay, 96, 98, 134, 182, 208
Papua New Guinea, 150–51
participatory land-use planning (PLP),
244–46
participatory monitoring, 191
paths, 109–10, 113, 116
Pearce, A., 11–12
Pendleton, Robert, 149–50
pesticides: excessive use of, 3, 82;
government study of, 170–71;
health threat of, 195–97; increase
in use of, 181; inexpensive, 174;
levels in water of, 183, 191. *See
also* agrochemicals
pests, integrated management of, 186

Pha Dua, 152–56
Phayao province, 94–95, 132
Phetchabun province, 93–94, 165
Philippines, 71, 150
Phongsak Techadhammo, Phra, 96,
98–99, 183, 251n7
Phop Phra, 82
phumpanyaa tongtin. See local
knowledge
phyllite, 157
pigeon peas, 160
pines: destruction by Hmong of, 208;
in dry dipterocarp forests, 38; erosion and, 165; and streamflows,
115, 251n15
Ping River: analysis of water in,
191; growth of lowland cultivation
along, 132; location of, 31; sediment load, 148; Sgaw group of
Karen in, 250n4; waterflow, 113
Pinkaew Laungaramsri, 82, 97–98,
211–13, 236, 245

pioneer shifting cultivation, 78–79, 82, 152–53

pjengcha, 158

plantation forestry, 164–66, 253*n*12

Plodprasop Suraswadi, 9, 249*n*18

Plondke, D., 109, 116, 163

policy networks, 25

political ecology, 16–17

Popper, Karl, 247*n*4

Pornpen Wijukprasert, 178, 190

positivist science, 11–13, 16, 241, 247*n*4

potatoes, 179

precautionary principle, 203

Pritsana Phromma, 213–15

problem closure, 12, 15, 136, 169, 224, 229, 238–39

prostitution, 49

Pua district, 183–84

pump effect, 112

Pwo. *See* Karen (people)

Quine, Willard, 255*n*1

racism, 99

rai mun wian, 72–73, 82

Rai Mun Wian (Waraalak), 213

rainfall: canopy interception rates, 106–7, 253*n*11; forest loss and, 100–101, 103–4; as function of altitude, 103–4; international research on forests and, 104; on monoculture forests, 165; patterns of, 32, 34, 102*fig*, 103*fig*

Rasamee Thawsirichuchai, 196

Rayong province, 107

reforestation: for erosion reduction, 140; of fallow fields, 75; international standards for, 237; in watershed management units, 45

refugees, 199–200

relativism, 22

resettlement, 46–50

resurgent protectionism, 208

Rhynchelytrum repens, 6

Rice, R. E., 208–9

rice cultivation: irrigation in, 121–22; on land used for cabbages, 175–76, 178–79; low-intensive, for pesticide use, 174–75; as main *khon muang* subsistence crop, 65–66; soil conservation and, 159–60; subsistence growing of, 118–19

Rijsdijk, A., 162

rhinoceros, Javan, 202

rituals of the Hmong, 83

river catchment, 30*map*

river discharge, 148

roads: as development projects, 120; as source of erosion, 151, 162–64; water runoff and, 113, 116; in wildlife sanctuaries, 207

Routray, J. K., 95, 132

Royal Forest Department: attacks on Hmong orchards, 184; biodiversity protection role of, 202; British influence in, 41; and Chom Thong dispute, 98; coexistence in the forest, 9; and community forestry, 52; establishment of, 7, 39; farmers' disputes with, 51; forests as water source, 87–89; fruit orchards encouraged by, 180; history of, 40; pesticide levels in water, 183; plantation forestry, 164–66, 236; redefining expertise for, 242; resettlement of villagers, 46, 48–50; and scientific neutrality, 232; and shifting cultivation, 71; upland forest categories, 37

Royal Irrigation Department, 94, 100, 102*fig*, 133

Royal Project Foundation, 79, 99, 179, 186, 251*n*8, 253*n*6

runoff efficiency, 108

subsistence agriculture, 73, 128–29, 222

Suchira Pryoonpitack, 92

suicide, 197

Sulak Sivaraksa, 201–2

Surachet Chettamart, 205

surface runoff, 92

sustainable agriculture, 185, 208

swidden agriculture. *See* shifting cultivation

Takahashi, T., 109, 112–13

Tak province: backlash against agro-chemical use, 82, 181; biodiversity, 206; forest cover in, 94; resettle-ment efforts, 48, 98

Tansuhaj, A., 196

Tanzania, 107

teak forests, 165

ten hao de ceremony, 83

territorialization, 39

Thai-Australia World Bank Land Development Project, 143

Thai-Belgian Soil Fertility Conserva-tion project, 166

Thai-German Highland Development Programme, 245

Thai-Norwegian Church Aid, 96

Thailand Development Research Institute, 142

Thaksin Shinawatra, 82

thamachat, 28

Thitirojanawat, P., 146

Thomas, D. E., 218

Thung Yai Naresuan forest, 211–12

Tippawan Prapamontol, 195–96

Tomich, T. P., 218

tradition, and traditionalist advocates, 9–10

tragedy of the commons, 204

Tran Duc Vien, 109, 116, 163

transect walks, 244

trees: as crops, 158; ordination of, 83; planting of, 97, 164

Tribal Research Institute, 6, 61

triple cropping, 174. *See also* dry-season cropping

Tuenjai Deetes, 10, 144, 247n3

Turkelboom, F., 156–60, 166–67, 193–94

typhoons, 34

Ukrit Aparasit, 133

Umnat Mevatee, 196

Umphang, 82

Uncertainty on a Himalayan Scale (Thompson), 22

United Nations (UN), 79, 92, 151

United States: Agency for International Development, 120; biodiversity loss in, 219; drug enforcement, 78; Dust Bowl, 141, 145; Navy road-building projects, 162

Universal Soil Loss Equation (USLE), 145–50, 168–69, 235, 237

upland forests: categories of, 37–38; and deforestation, 100–104; food harvested from, 119; state inter-vention in, 39–40; rainfall in, 88–91, 100–104; streamflow and, 104–7, 108–13; as source of natu-ral resources, 87; statemaking in, 37. *See also* forest sponge

upland people: agrochemicals' effect on health of, 195–97; commercial-ism's effects, 204; diversity within villages of, 55; elevation and eth-nicity, 64; as exotic, 59; images in environmental narratives of, 59–60, 84–86, 138, 171, 218, 224, 230, 243; lowland Thai as, 60–66; population estimates for, 60–63; power imbalance between govern-ment officials and, 246. *See also individual ethnic groups*